AF538857

First Published-2010

ISBN 978-81-8356-527-1

Published by:

DISCOVERY PUBLISHING HOUSE PVT. LTD.

4831/24, Ansari Road, Prahlad Street
Darya Ganj, New Delhi-110002 (India)
Phone: 23279245 • Fax: 91-11-23253475
E-mail: parul.wasan@gmail.com
info@discoverypublishinggroup.com
Website: www.discoverypublishinggroup.com

Printed at:
Sachin Printers
Delhi

Preface

The present title "Understanding Wildlife" has been written for those students interested in careers in diverse fields of biological sciences. It provides a structured approach to learning by covering all the important topics in a uniform, systematic format. The book has been comprehensively designed incorporating recent advances in this fast moving field. It also provides accessible information on wildlife in compact form for undergraduate students in biology and related life sciences. It is intelligible to the educated layman, though it deals with some complex ideas. It is an adequate text for all the requirements of students in this area. In addition, busy lecturers who require a quick reference compendium will find it useful, particularly for tutional planning. Simple, yet hopefully clear figures and tables are provided throughout the book.

The over-riding goal of this book, and indeed of the whole *Understanding series*, is to present the essential information concering wildlife in a compact, readily accessible form which leads itself to student learning and revision. The convergence of various approaches has generated a rich panorama of detail, the significance of which we are still attempting to unraval. The present text has been written as an introduction to this rapidly growing field.

To make the work more comprehensive and informative, the author has consulted many authoritative books, research journals, abstracts, monographs etc., so there can be no claim to originality except in the manner of treatment.

The author expresses his thanks to his friends and colleagues whose continue inspirations have initiated him to bring out this book.

The author expresses his gratitude to Mr. Wasan and staff of M/s Discovery Publishing House Pvt. Ltd. for their whole hearted co-operation in the publication of this book.

In the mean time, the author will remain sincerely responsible for any shortcomings of the book and be grateful to the readers for their suggestions and constructive criticism for the continuous betterment of the book. He takes this opportunity to appeal to the readers to send their suggestions straightaway to his Publisher.

Author

Contents

1

INTRODUCTION

Among the more spectacular members of the rich mammalian fauna that occupy the African continent are two large ungulates, the roan antelope (*Hippotragus equinus*) and the sable antelope (*H. niger*). The roan antelope inhabits open or lightly wooded land, whereas the sable antelope travels among the acacias (*Acacia spp.*) of the savanna. In recent decades, sable and roan antelopes have been declining in the southern portions of their range.

In South Africa, attempts are being made to preserve and assist in the recovery of these two species by designating large tracts as nature reserves. Because sable and roan antelopes were locally extirpated, animals were live-trapped in the wild, transported, and released on the nature reserves.

Growth of their populations in many of the 2800-13,000-ha reserves has been slow. In recent years, some herds have declined drastically. When wildlife biologists David Wilson and Stanley Hirst (1977) were asked to determine why numbers of these two antelopes declined on the South African reserves over the past few decades, they were presented with a basic problem in population ecology.

Their task was to identify specific causes for the decline of roan and sable antelopes and to make practical recommendations for their preservation and management. Observers had speculated that such factors as habitat deterioration, encroachment by agriculture, illegal or uncontrolled hunting, and (among roan antelope) the disease called anthrax were responsible for the decline. But no one really knew.

The methods used by Wilson and Hirst as they began to unravel the mysteries of the disappearing antelopes were not unique to studies of African mammals. Similar methods are employed by biologists who work with various animals, whether scarce or abundant, whether they are caribou (*Rangifer tarandus*) in Alaska, cottontail (*Sylvilagus spp.*) in Virginia, or bobwhite (*Colinus virginianus*) in Illinois.

These are problems of population management that encompass basic concepts of population ecology. An extensive body of literature exists on the theory of population ecology, much of which is still evolving. Ecologists attempt to explain such phenomena as population cycles and general causes for the regulation of numbers of animals.

Most of the theoretical population literature is beyond the scope of this book. The purpose of this chapter is to present basic concepts of population ecology and to describe approaches that are useful to biologists who must solve practical problems involving the management of wildlife populations.

SOME DEFINITIONS

A *population* is defined as a group of organisms, usually of the same species, occupying a defined area during a specific time. Populations have characteristics not possessed by individual animals. For example, a population has *density*, meaning a certain number of individuals per unit area: 20 blue grouse (*Dendragapus obscurus*) per 100 ha, or 144 sugar maples (*Acer saccharum*) per ha.

A population has a *birth rate*, or *natality*, defined as the number of births per thousand, per hundred, or per individual per year, and a *death rate*, or *mortality*, defined as the number of deaths per number of individuals per year. A population also has an *age structure*—that is, a distribution of numbers of individuals of various ages.

Naturally, the proportion of individuals of breeding age in a population affects the birth rate and strongly influences growth. Likewise, the proportion of old animals affects the death rate. Populations also have *sex ratios* that influence the reproductive potential.

Fecundity refers to the number of eggs produced per female, or to the number of sperm produced per male. Because sperm numbers rarely influence the birth rate, fecundity nearly always pertains to the number of eggs produced. *Fertility* is the percentage of eggs that are fertile.

Production is the actual number of offspring produced, whether born or hatched, by a population during a specific period of time. Some authorities, however, are more conservative and measure production only as the number of new individuals reaching breeding age (the process is also called *recruitment* when it includes immigration); animals dying between birth and sexual maturity are not counted as recruits.

Changes in such parameters as sex ratio and age distribution greatly influence production.

That is, the number of offspring can vary a great deal depending on the proportion of females and animals of breeding age in a population at a given time.

THE LOGISTIC EQUATION

It has been recognized for some time that animals tend to give birth to many more individuals than will survive to breeding age. If deaths did not offset births, the result would be an infinitely growing population. Under ideal conditions, a population for a time can show a rate of growth that is exponential—that is, it grows at an ever-increasing rate. Such conditions may occur when a small population is introduced into a new and favourable environment.

No shortage of food, cover, or space exists, and no disease, parasites, or predators affect any individuals. The birth rate is maximum, limited only by the reproductive physiology of the species; and the death rate is minimum, with deaths occurring only from old age.

Such conditions have been created in the laboratory for yeast cultures and mouse populations that were provided with room to grow and plenty of food. The equation for such growth is conventionally expressed as:

$$\frac{\Delta N}{\Delta t} = rN$$

where

ΔN = change in number

Δt = change in time

r = the "per head" maximum potential growth rate

N = number of individuals in a population

As an example, suppose we have a population of 50 individuals (N) and each individual has the average capability of contributing one fourth (0.25) of an individual to the population in a given unit of time (r). The change in number per unit time ($\Delta N/\Delta t$) would be expressed as:

$$\frac{\Delta N}{\Delta t} = rN \qquad (1)$$

$$\frac{\Delta N}{\Delta t} = 0.25(50) = 12.5$$

The answer, 12.5, is the number of individuals that is added to the population in the time interval (t). This number then must be added to the original population (N_t) to obtain the number in the new population (N_{t+1}), so that our new population is

$$N_{t+1} = N_t + \frac{\Delta N}{\Delta t}$$

$$N_{t+1} = 50 + 12.5 = 62.5 \tag{2}$$

For the next time step, we simply repeat the process using the same *r* value (0.25) but a new *N* (62.5), to calculate the number added to the population:

$$\frac{\Delta N_{t+1}}{\Delta t} = 0.25(62.5) - 15.5$$

$$N_{t+2} = N_{t+1} + \frac{\Delta N_{t+1}}{\Delta t} \tag{3}$$

$$N_{t+2} = 78$$

As one can see by continuing this process, the population will grow at an ever-increasing rate. The integrated form of the equation is: $N_t = N_o^{e^{rt}}$, where N_t represents the population at *t* time intervals, N_0 is the original population, *r* is the per head potential growth rate, *e is* the base of natural logarithms, and *t* is the time interval by which *r* is expressed.

Such an equation is most useful for populations of organisms such as bacteria, yeast, some insects, and possibly some small mammals in which breeding and growth are continuous. For most wildlife populations, which have a distinct breeding season, growth takes place in steps,

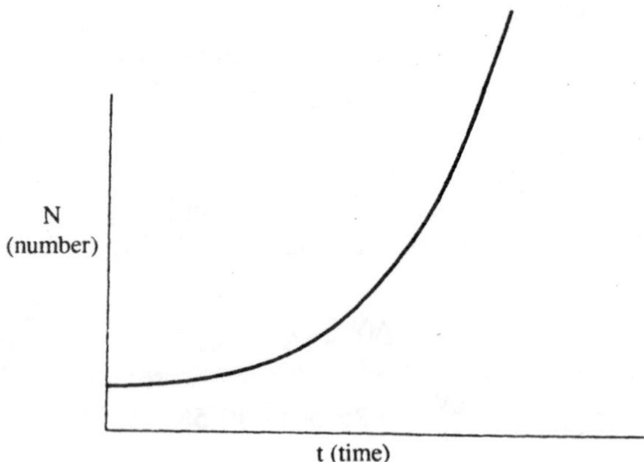

Figure 1.1: Growth of a population with unlimited food and space, $\Delta N/\Delta t = rN$.

and equations (1) and (2) are more appropriately used. Under what conditions might we expect a wild population to express exponential growth? The happy circumstances of practically unlimited food and no biological enemies of whatever size occur very rarely in nature.

But there have been a few instances that have come close to such conditions. These circumstances invariably occur when a population is introduced into a new and favourable environment that has been unoccupied previously by its species. Of the several cases reviewed by Dasmann, only one population, that of white-tailed deer (*Odocoileus virginianus*) introduced to the George Reserve in Michigan, expressed truly exponential growth.

In 1928, 2 bucks and 4 does were introduced into the 480-ha deer-proof fenced enclosure. By 1934 there were 164 deer. During the 6-year period, growth of the deer population was unrestrained by a change in birth or death rates acting under the influence of population size. In this case, the constant, r, was the only factor determining the rate of change in the deer population.

Thus, for those few years, a population of increasing size grew at an increasing rate. Other rapid growth rates have occurred among ring-necked pheasants (*Phasianus colchicus*) introduced to Protection Island, Washington, and European reindeer (*Rangifer tarandus*) introduced to St. Paul Island off the Alaska coast, but these populations showed less than the maximum growth that might be expected under totally favourable circumstances.

Almost any population may approach an unrestricted rate of growth if reduced to a low level, but obviously no population can increase exponentially for very long. The supply of food may not meet the demand of the ever-increasing population; space or cover availability may be limiting; predators may respond to the large numbers of prey; or disease may spread.

Either birth rates decline, death rates increase, or both, so that eventually the population must stop growing. The greater the size of the population, the greater its dampening effect on the growth of the population. This effect has been mathematically defined and applied to the growth equation as follows:

$$\frac{\Delta N}{\Delta t} = rN\frac{(K-N)}{K} \tag{4}$$

where K *is* defined as the maximum number of individuals the environment can sustain. As the population (N) approaches K, $K - N$ approaches zero so that when a population gets very large relative to the number the environment can sustain, its growth rate becomes nearly zero. That is, its potential growth rate (rN) is multiplied by the factor $(K - N)/K$.

For example, suppose the same population we considered earlier with an r of 0.25 has 990 individuals and the maximum number supportable by the environment is 1000:

$$\begin{aligned}\frac{\Delta N}{\Delta t} &= 0.25(990)\left(\frac{1000-990}{1000}\right)\\ &= 247.5(0.01)\\ &= 2.5\end{aligned}$$

$$N_{t+1} = N_t + \frac{\Delta N}{\Delta t} = 990 + 2.5 = 992.5$$

Instead of the population growing by 247 individuals as it would without any limitations, it grows only by 2.5 individuals, owing to limitations placed upon it by the finite environment. Equation (4) is known as the logistic equation. The curve it produces *is sigmoid* (S-shaped) and is illustrated in Figure elsewhere in this chapter.

Populations may sometimes exceed the maximum number that can be sustained by their habitat. In such an occurrence the term $(K - N)$ is negative. Therefore, $\Delta N/\Delta t$ is negative, resulting in a decrease in numbers.

The term K often is referred to as the *carrying capacity*. One must keep in mind that carrying capacity for animals can change from time to time as food production, cover availability, water availability, and other environmental factors vary with the seasons and successive years.

Factors such as territorial behaviour and response to crowding may interact with these external factors, so that the growth of a population may slow down before food, water, or cover shortages are measurable in the habitat. A factor that causes higher mortality or reduced birth rates as a population becomes more dense is referred to as *a density-dependent* factor.

That is, if the probability of an individual being born or surviving is lower as the numbers of animals in the population become higher, a density-dependent factor is acting to restrict population growth. Such factors include food supply, predation, disease, and territorial behaviour. There are few density-independent factors, and they are mainly related to weather, such as cold, rain, and floods.

Usually, populations in the central portions of the geographic range

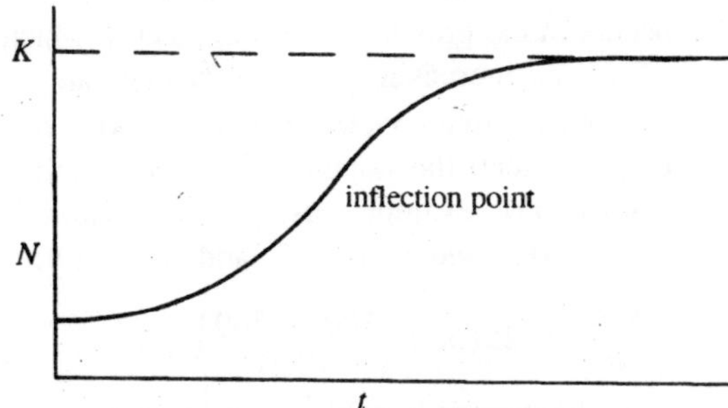

Figure 1.2: Growth of a population with a maximum number of individuals that can be sustained by the environment, $\Delta N/\Delta t = rN(K - N)\ K$.

of their species are limited by density-dependent agencies. Near the periphery of the range, however, where habitat may be marginal and where random weather fluctuations may exceed the tolerance of nearly all animals in the population, density-independent factors may control population numbers.

Such is the case with bobwhite in the northern parts of their range, where severe winters almost invariably result in a drastic reduction in quail numbers. Lack documented a similar effect on herons wintering in England.

The logistic equation is based purely on the operation of density-dependent factors. If a fatal flood or snowstorm strikes at some point, the irregularity in population growth will not be explained by the logistic equation.

The logistic equation, for the wildlife biologist, is useful in illustrating general principles of population growth as well as the theoretical effect of carrying capacity on reducing or stopping population expansion. The early portion of the sigmoid curve can serve as a theoretical model with which the manager can compare the growth rate of the population being managed.

A value for r can sometimes be obtained from knowledge of natality and mortality of the species under ideal captive conditions or from potential birth rates and longevity information in the field. If population growth is close to the growth rate predicted by the early phases of the logistic equation, there is little the manager can do to increase growth of the populations.

There is a further practical application of the logistic equation. If a student runs through the equation, setting N at various levels, it will be discovered that the largest value of $\Delta N/\Delta t$ is obtained when N

is half of the carrying capacity. At half the carrying capacity, an inflection point occurs in the growth curve, the point at which population growth changes from an increasing to a decreasing rate.

In managing for maximum yield of a population, it is therefore desirable to attempt to keep the population at about half the level of the carrying capacity. For example, using the previous hypothetical population with K of 1000 and r of 0.25, and $N = \frac{1}{2}K$:

$$\frac{\Delta N}{\Delta t} = 0.25(500)\left(\frac{1000 - 500}{1000}\right) = 62.5$$

The maximum number of individuals that can be produced in a unit of time is about 62. At any other N, the number produced is fewer.

The factor, $(K - N)/K$, in the logistic equation, has no biological meaning or influence by itself. It must, in a real population of animals, represent some modification of birth rates or death rates. Therefore, the field biologist usually seeks an explanation for increasing or decreasing numbers of animals by examining the ratio of birth rates to death rates and the reasons for irregularities in either or both.

Most animals dealt with by wildlife managers reproduce seasonally, producing an annual spurt of offspring. Only if we stand back and view such a population over 50 or 100 years would these spurts become less visible.

In such a long period of time, comparisons with the logistic equation could be made by wildlife biologists; but management results frequently are required in a much shorter time and the wildlife manager must use other methods to assess the health of a population and evaluate its growth.

Field Studies

Returning to the African antelopes, Wilson and Hirst (1977) noted that population limitation could be effected th ough poor reproductive performance brought about by physiological factors or by increased mortality among juveniles or adults.

They set about to identify the main factors that were impeding the growth of the antelope populations on the Transvaal Nature Reserves first by reviewing available literature on their food and cover. The animals were found to be specific in their feeding and habitat requirements.

Because the soil on several of the nature reserves was poor, the researchers decided to concentrate on feeding habits, food and nutrient availability, habitat selection and availability, and seasonal body conditions, especially of breeding females.

With these factors in mind, they moved into the field, particularly the Percy Fyfe Nature Reserve, a primary study area that contained both sable and roan antelopes, and three other reserves in Transvaal. A reserve in Rhodesia (now Zimbabwe), where these two species thrived, served as a basis for comparison.

Every day for 7 months, with binoculars and a tough vehicle, they made detailed observations of two herds of antelope, one of each species. For 3 years beyond that, antelope on two reserves were watched intensively. When a calf would disappear, a team of 16-20 searchers would comb the area to find it, dead or alive.

Blood samples were taken from captured living animals; and, with recently dead animals, digestive tract contents were collected, and smears and sections were taken from the spleen, liver, kidney, lung, heart, adrenals, lymph glands, and brain. Such organs and tissues were examined for lesions and for parasites.

Healthy live animals were immobilized with a tranquilizer gun; they were then examined and fitted with coloured collars for individual identification. Species and densities of vegetation were recorded and soil fertility was assessed in the search for specific factors that caused the antelope populations to decline.

Among sable antelope studied intensively on two reserves, pregnancy rates were 100 percent when a bull was present during the May-July mating season. In a herd in which females were divided and a bull was not in full-time attendance, only 50 to 70 percent of the potentially breeding females were pregnant.

Even where pregnancy rates were high, however, antelope less than two years old suffered high mortality. Wilson and Hirst found that these young animals carried heavy infections of four different protozoan parasites. Although these parasites appeared to be important in causing the death of the young antelopes, further study revealed that parasites were fatal only if the young antelopes were in poor nutritional condition.

The researchers then compared body condition, as indicated by body weight, blood plasma proteins, packed cell volume of blood, and albumen content of the blood, between the antelopes from the Transvaal, where populations were doing poorly, and those of Rhodesia (Zimbabwe), where populations were thriving. The Transvaal animals were in very poor conditon.

This led Wilson and Hirst to examine the Transvaal range, analyzing nutrient availability in soil, water, and vegetation collected from preferred feeding areas. They also analyzed animal tissues (liver, blood, and milk). Deficiencies in phosphorus, selenium, and protein were found in food plants during the critical dry season.

On one reserve, Wilson and Hirst found, by examining digestive tract contents and observing the feeding behaviour of large herbivores, that competition from zebra (*Equus spp.*), waterbuck (*Kobus ellipsiprymnus*) f, and impala (*Aepyceros melampus*) limited the amount of food available to sable antelopes.

Roan antelope bred throughout the year, with a gestation period of about 275 days and estrus occurring 2-3 weeks after parturition (giving birth). Thus, female roan antelopes could give birth to a calf every 10-10.5 months. Sable antelope, on the other hand, had a shorter gestation period (240-248 days) but bred only once a year. Bulls were capable of producing viable sperm at 16-18 months.

In smaller reserves, the dominant herd bull of roan antelope sometimes killed young maturing bulls, thus disrupting breeding and reducing the population. The breeding success of sable antelope was satisfactory.

Wilson and Hirst found that although numbers of sable antelope on the relatively small Transvaal reserves were not high (less than 100 animals), the densities there (up to 9/km^2) were as high as, or higher than, those of good populations in Rhodesia (Zimbabwe).

Given the competition for food and the lower quality of range, the biologists concluded that a decline in antelope numbers in the Transvaal would be expected. They recommended that two Transvaal reserves be abandoned for conservation of sable antelope, on the basis of nutritional and space inadequacy.

In other reserves they recommended the use of salt licks to provide lacking minerals, and they suggested fertilizing and burning the range to enhance protein availability in forage. They also advised maintaining lower densities of antelope to reduce strain on the limited food resources.

BIRTHS AND DEATHS

The antelope study of Wilson and Hirst (1977) illustrates the elements of an excellent study of a population. To achieve its management objectives, such study involves investigation of adequacy of habitat, specifically nutrition in this case, and its effects upon birth and death rates.

A population grows according to the simple equation:

$$r = b - d$$

where

r = actual growth rate of the population
b = birth rate
d = death rate

In some populations, animals moving in or dispersing from a population may also play a role in its growth rate. The equation then becomes:

$$r = (b - d) + (i - e)$$

where

i = immigration
e = emigration

A rate represents a change per unit time. Growth rate is the number of individuals added per individual in the population per week, per month, or per year. For example, suppose 3000 young are born each year in a population of 1000 cottontails.

This represents a per-head birth rate of 3.0. During the same period, to have a stationary population, there must be a per-head death rate of 3.0, which means that for every individual present in the spring population three must die over the course of the year.

This would offset the per-head birth rate of 3.0. The population growth would then be zero ($r = 3.0 - 3.0 = 0$). Birth rates and death rates differ with age structure and sex ratios of populations.

If there are relatively many females of prime reproductive age, a population naturally will reproduce faster than one that has few females at such an age.

Therefore, the wildlife biologist, to understand population growth, should consider the following seven characteristics pertaining to birth rates:

1. Age of sexual maturity of both males and females.
2. Length of the gestation period.
3. Sex ratios.
4. Whether the species is monogamous or polygamous.
5. Number of females that breed at each age.
6. Number of young per female of various ages.
7. Influence of nutritional condition on reproduction.

Sex Ratios and Mating Systems

Sex ratios express the relative abundance of each sex in wildlife populations. The ratios usually are expressed in one of two ways. The first tells the number of males per 100 females.

The second expresses the percentage of males and females per 100 individuals in the population, with the percentage of males appearing first (e.g., in the ratio 60:40, the population consists of 60 percent males). We shall adopt the latter expression.

Sex ratios may change within populations either because of unbalanced sex ratios at birth, or, more frequently, because of sex-specific mortality associated with age. Causes may be external forces such as hunting or the vulnerability of incubating females to predators.

Johnson and Sargeant (1977) presented strong evidence that red foxes (*Vulpes vulpes*) killed enough hens during the nesting season to distort the sex ratio in a large population of mallards (*Anas platyrhynchos*).

Some inherent mechanisms apparently cause differential mortality during embryonic development in some species, under conditions that are not always clear. Bellrose et al. (1961) recognized these age-related differences and adopted the following categories:

Primary Sex Ratio

The sex ratio at fertilization; normally 50:50 based on simple statistical probability.

Secondary Sex Ratio

The sex ratio at birth or hatching; usually approximates 50:50, but may show the first indication of sex-specific mortality (e.g., 49:51). At birth, the fawns of white-tailed deer suffering from nutritional stress may exhibit a ratio favouring males by as much as 72:28.

Tertiary Sex Ratio

The sex ratio of juveniles; important because it indicates the proportion of each sex later entering the breeding population; for game species, hunting becomes an external influence for the first time; some inherent species-specific differences also may be present.

Quaternary Sex Ratio

The sex ratio of the adult population; often clearly skewed in favour of one sex; some species of diving ducks (e.g., redheads, *Aythya americana*) are heavily unbalanced in favour of males; in most populations of large ungulates, such as deer or bighorn sheep (*Ovis canadensis*), females predominate because hunting pressure normally selects males with antlers or horns.

Waterfowl and other wildlife follow one of three types of mating systems. These systems interact with population sex ratios in ways that profoundly affect annual production. Mating systems include the following:

Monogamy

a. Seasonal. Pair-bonds established only for the current breeding season (e.g., pintails, *Anas acuta*, and other dabbling ducks)

b. Life-time. Pair-bonds established for as long as both mates remain alive (e.g., coyotes, *Canis latrans*, and several other canids; Canada geese, *Branta canadensis*, and allied species)

Polygamy

a. Polyandry. Several males per female; extremely rare in most groups of vertebrates but occurs in a few birds (e.g., Wilson's phalarope, *Steganopus tricolour*)

b. Polygyny. Several females per male (e.g., ring-necked pheasants; elk, *Cervus elaphus canadensis*)

Promiscuity

Indiscriminate mating (e.g., cottontails, *Sylvilagus floridanus;* bobcats, *Felis rufus* and many other felids)

The effect of quaternary sex ratios on production in monogamous species is shown in the following example; the maximum number of nests serves as an arbitrary measure of production:

Sex Ratio	*Maximum Number of Nests per 100 Birds*
50:50	50 (100% production)
60:40	40 (80% production)
40:60	40 (80% production)

The example illustrates the fact that monogamous species require a balanced sex ratio for the maximum production of offspring. Any deviation favouring either sex reduces prpduction. Thus, in normal situations, hunting regulations for such species probably should not set sex-specific bag limits.

However, when a sex ratio is highly imbalanced, hunting regulations can focus the harvest on the more abundant sex. For example, the harvest of ducks in many states is governed by a point system. That is, the bag limit is based on the accumulation of100 points instead of on a set number of birds.

Because the proportion of females is low in some species or populations, the point system places high values on hens and low values on drakes as a means of shifting the shooting pressure from one sex to the other.

In polygynous species, the situation is quite different. Females represent a premium for increased production. Males, within reason, become expendable, as follows:

Sex Ratio	***Maximum Number of Nests per 100 Birds***
40:60	60 (100% production)
50:50	50 (83% production)
60:40	40 (66% production)

Thus, in polygynous species, 100 percent production occurs at any ratio where females make up more than 50 percent of the population (the 40:60 ratio was selected arbitrarily for comparison with production at the same sex ratio for a monogamous species, shown earlier). Indeed, the disparity favouring females might be increased to 30:70 or more for even greater production of offspring per 100 adults.

Eventually, however, the point is reached where males no longer can successfully court and mate with such a large number of females. At such a point, the imbalance becomes so great that the "extra" females no longer contribute offspring and thus become an expendable surplus.

Among penned ring-necked pheasants, McAtee found that some hens remained unmated when the sex ratio reached 12:88. In most circumstances, however, male pheasants can be heavily harvested each autumn without endangering production the following spring.

Age-Specific Birth Rates

The number of births per individual (or, more commonly, per 1000 individuals) in a population is called the *crude birth rate*. The crude birth rate reveals no details about what age groups actually contribute offspring to the population.

Birth rates are by no means fixed within species or within populations, and variations in natality may account for large shifts in the sizes and densities of wildlife populations.

The number of offspring produced during a particular period depends upon the number of females in each age class, the number of these that actually mate, and the fecundity of each age class (the same considerations may apply to males, of course, but females generally govern age-specific production). The number of offspring per female expressed by age classes is called the *age-specific birth rate.*

As an example, a population of brook trout (*Salvelinus fontinalis*) breeding in Lawrence Creek, Wisconsin, showed large age-specific differences in egg production. Reproduction relied heavily on females in age classes I and II (1.5- and 2.5-year-old trout), which together produced more than 98 percent of the eggs.

Three facts emerge from the details of the study. First, egg production per mature female increased with age. Yearling trout produced an average of about 425 eggs per mature female, whereas 2- and 3-year-old females each produced an average of 617 and 906 eggs, respectively.

Second, because not all of the females in age class I were sexually mature, the average egg production for all females (mature and immature combined) in age class I was reduced even further (to 354 eggs). Third, even with lower egg production per female, the individuals in age class I were so numerous that the group still accounted for more than 75 percent of all egg production.

These facts have management implications. In this case, Lawrence Creek is heavily fished, and few trout survive beyond age class III even though the population remains relatively stable. Thus, armed with knowledge of the age-specific reproductive rate, managers can adjust the fishing regulations in ways that will help protect the breeding population (e.g., changes in creel limits, season lengths, size limits, or a combination of these). With reduced fishing pressure, more females would reach the older age classes and thereby would contribute more to egg production.

Table 1.1: Number of Eggs Produced by Brook Trout in Lawrence Creek, Wisconsin, 1955-56.

Age Class (Year)	*Percent Sexually Mature*	*Total Number of Eggs*	*Percent of Eggs Contributed*
I	83.3	1,706,685	76.6
II	100.0	485,756	21.8
III	100.0	32,014	1.4
IV	100.0	2,318	0.1
V and VI	100.0	2,555	0.1
Total		**2,229,328**	**100.0**

Such a shift would result in greater production from the trout population in Lawrence Creek, because older females are all sexually mature and individually can produce larger numbers of eggs than younger females.

In another example, Woolf and Harder (1979) compared age-specific birth rates among white-tailed deer in three states. These data revealed poor reproductive success in the Pennsylvania herd, which was densely populated and maintained with artificial food, in comparison with herds in Iowa and Ohio.

Several hypotheses were explored to explain the poor reproductive performance in the Pennsylvania deer. The factors that were investigated included adrenal stress from heightened social interactions in the populous herd and reduced ovulation rates induced by chemicals in the diet of acorns. Ultimately, however, the low reproductive rates in the Pennsylvania herd were attributed to poor summer nutrition.

This factor extended the lactation period into the autumn breeding season. Thus, fawns were weaned unusually late in the year and were unprepared to breed in the autumn. Moreover, because the older does were still lactating, their nutritional reserves were so low that ovulation and early fetal development were impaired.

These conditions lowered the ovulation rates and induced early mortality in the fetuses of older does. Woolf and Harder (1979) estimated ovulation rates using the common method of examining *corpora lutea*. These structures are the remains of ovarian follicles from which eggs are produced by sexually mature females during the current breeding season. To determine the number of corpora lutea, wildlife managers examine thin cross sections of the ovaries taken from females collected on the research area.

The corpora lutea appear as small, yellowish spheres embedded in the ovarian tissues. Each corpus luteum represents the ovulation of a single egg, and the ratio of young fetuses to corpora lutea thus indicates the fertilization rate. Using these and other techniques, wildlife managers can obtain accurate measures of the reproductive contributions of each age class in a population.

A table of age-specific birth rates thus becomes useful for depicting the reproductive performance of a population. A few examples are shown in Table elsewhere in this chapter.

As an illustration of how reproduction may vary with age structure, consider the population of Canada geese listed in Table elsewhere in this chapter, and two different distributions of breeding birds within the age classes. In the first case, the age structure is represented by 34 percent 1-year olds, 33 percent 2-3-year olds, and 33 percent 4+-year-old birds. Egg production from 100 females would be (34 × 0) + (33 × .20 × 4.6) + (33 × .72 × 6.4) = 182 eggs.

If the age ratio were to change to 40:40:20, respectively, for each of the age classes, then the number of eggs laid by 100 females would be (40 × 0) + (40 × .20 × 4.6) + (20 × .72 × 6.4) = 100 eggs. Thus, with a change in age structure as described—which might easily occur in just a few years-egg production can be diminished significantly [here, by (182 - 100)/182 = 45 percent].

Additive and Compensatory Mortality

Animal mortality—the losses from a population-may be considered as either *additive* or *compensatory*. Numerous environmental factors, including disease, malnutrition, predation, and severe weather, act on members of a population.

Table 1.2: Comparison of Reproductive Performance in Three Populations of White-Tailed Deer.

Area	*Percent Fawns Pregnant*	*Percent Adult Does Pregnant*	*Corpora Lutea per Pregnant Doe*	*Fetuses per Pregnant Doe*
Rachelwood Wildlife Preserve, Pennsylvania	0.0	93.5	1.60	1.40
Plum Brook Station, Ohio	0.0	94.8	1.95	1.77
DeSoto National Wildlife Refuge, Iowa	83.6	100.0	2.23	2.10

For example, given a population of 100 animals, food shortages and disease acting together might have the potential of removing 40 individuals during the course of several months. At the same time, however, predators also might have the potential of removing 40 animals.

If these factors-starvation, disease, and predation—were *additive*, then a total of 80 animals would die from the combined action of these forces. But it is unlikely that the mortality would reach such a level.

Competition for food is reduced whenever predators remove some animals from the population. As starvation lessens, so too does the incidence of disease-related mortality, and fewer animals actually die

Table 1.3: Some Examples of Age-Specific Laying and Birth Rates.

Species and Source						
Brook trout	Age (years)	0.5	1.5	2.5	3.5	4.5
(*Salvelinus fontinalis*)	Percent breeding	0	83.3	100	100	100
McFadden (1961)	Number of eggs per breeding female	0	425	617	906	1196
Canada goose	Age (year)	1	2-3	4+		
(*Branta canadensis*)	Percent breeding	0	20	72		
Cooper (1978)	Number of eggs per breeding female	0	4.6	6.4		
Blue whale	Age (years)	0-3	4-5	6-7	8-11	12+
(*Balaenoptera musculus*)	Number of calves per breeding female	0	0.19	0.44	0.50	0.45
Usher (1972)						
White-tailed deer	Age (years)	0.5	1.5	2.5	3.5	4.5
(*Odocoileus virginianus*)	Percent breeding	16	68	77	81	84
Teer et al. (1965)	Number of fawns per breeding female	0.88	1.32	1.52	1.52	1.52

from malnutrition and sickness because of the interaction with predation. If predators remove 30 animals, only 10 might die of disease. Thus, the mortality factors act in *a compensatory* way.

Errington concluded that mink (*Mustela vison*) preyed on muskrats that were "surplus" members of a crowded population. The surplus muskrats were "social outcasts," because they could not obtain and hold breeding territories.

As such, the outcasts were vulnerable to diseases and predation. If mink did not kill them, the surplus muskrats soon succumbed to disease. As Errington stated, "victims of one agency simply miss becoming victims of another" and many types of mortality are "at least partly intercompensatory in net population effect." Other histories of animal populations involving the compensatory nature of predation are described in Of *Predation and Life*.

Density-dependent factors operate in a compensatory manner. By contrast, severe weather may act in an *additive* way. That is, even though a population may be reduced to low levels, a sleet or ice storm may kill a fixed proportion of the original number of animals, regardless of how many had been taken earlier by predation or disease.

If, however, the storm preceded a period of food shortage, the effects of the bad weather might be compensatory, for the remaining animals likely would experience increased survival.

Hunting is a common form of mortality in populations of game species. Hunting mortality is frequently compensatory, because it usually increases the life expectancy of individuals surviving the hunt, promotes higher reproductive rates, or does both. Swenson compared the reproduction of mountain goats (*Oreamnos americanus*) subjected to different levels of hunting mortality.

One result of the study indicated that the summer ratio of kids to older goats (yearlings and adults) was higher after hunting had reduced the number of older goats the previous autumn. Decreased competition for winter forage explained the increased production of kids. Some caution was expressed, however, because the goats in this study were members of a population that had been introduced 10-20 years before, and the population was still expanding in logistic growth.

Nevertheless, logic suggests that reduced competition in any population will increase the survival of the remaining individuals and will enhance birth rates.

Wagner et al. summarized the compensatory nature of hunting in mathematical terms in this way: The addition of a given pecentage of mortality (from such factors as hunting or fishing) does not add one-for-one with the existing annual mortality from other causes (e.g., disease). Instead, the total annual mortality increases by a much smaller percentage than is measured by the actual pecentage of individuals removed by hunting alone.

The formula for calculating the crude annual mortality rate is

$$a = m + n - mn$$

where

a = crude annual mortality rate

m = mortality rate from hunting or fishing

n = natural mortality rate

In a population with a natural annual mortality rate of 70 percent, the addition of 20 percent mortality from hunting would not increase the total mortality to 90 percent, but only from 70 to 76 percent:

$$a = 70\% + 20\% - (70\% \times 20\%) = 76\%$$

In other words, hunting removes some animals that otherwise would die from natural causes. Errington's ideas about surpluses do not apply here. Instead, the relationship shown in the example emerges simply because an animal can only die from one of the types of causes to which it is exposed: natural mortality or hunting mortality.

The natural mortality rate remains the same with or without hunting, although the actual number of animals dying from natural causes is less where hunting first removes a fraction of the population. Moreover, a given percentage of harvest increases a small annual mortality rate more than a large one.

For example, a 20 percent harvest raises a 40 percent annual mortality rate to 52 percent—a 30 percent increase-whereas, as we have shown, the same 20 percent harvest raises a 70 percent annual mortality rate to 76 percent, for only a 9 percent increase.

Such a relationship, in part, accounts for the more visible effects of hunting species with low mortality such as big game and geese. The relationship supports Hickey's conclusion that the ability to withstand harvest is a function of each species' annual mortality rate.

Life Tables and Survivorship Curves

Comparisons of mortality between populations can be made by use of *life tables* and *survivorship curves. A* life table is a systematic means of describing mortality as it affects various age groups in a population. Deevey published a classic review of life tables for natural populations of animals. Murie described mortality of Dall sheep (*Ovis dalli*) in Mount McKinley National Park, Alaska. Over a period of several years he collected skulls of sheep found in the park.

The horns of sheep grow in annual bursts, leaving a ring between each annual increment so that the age of a Dall sheep can be estimated by counting annual growth segments. From 608 sheep Murie constructed the life table shown in Table elsewhere in this chapter.

The columns of a life table are as follows:

x = An appropriate time interval.

l_x = The number of animals living at the beginning of interval *x*. It is traditional to convert whatever sample size one has to 1000 at the beginning of the l_x column, representing 1000 animals born or hatched.

d_d = The number of animals dying during interval x.

1000 q_x = The proportion of animals that die per interval *x*. It is computed as follows: 1000 *qx*

= $(d_x \div l_x) \times 1000$.

e_x = The life expectancy expressed as the number of additional intervals an individual animal can expect to live at the beginning of interval x.

The derivation e_x involves a few extra calculations, as follows:

$$e_x = \frac{T_x}{l_x}$$

and

$$L_x = \frac{l_x + l_{x+1}}{2}$$

or the average number of animals alive at the midpoint of an interval *x*.

T_x is the sum of the $L_x s$ from the bottom of the table up through the desired x interval.

Biologists often are asked questions such as, "How long does a robin live?" or "How long does a mule deer live?" The answer to such questions depends upon what age the animal has achieved.

The American robin (*Turdus migratorius*) can live to be 7 years old, but the probability of a newly hatched robin doing so is much less than 1 percent. Early mortality, in fact, is so high among songbirds that most life tables for them do not begin until late in the summer or early fall of a bird's first year.

Once a robin has lived to November 1, on the average it will live another 1.37 years. Over half of them will die in the next year. Murie's life table for Dall sheep shows that life expectancy is 7.1 years for a newborn lamb. There was a flaw in Murie's data, however, in that the skulls of very young lambs that died possibly were consumed totally by scavengers or predators.

Thus, young animals would be underrepresented in his life table and life expectancy at birth would be overestimated. Once a sheep reached the age of 6 years one may see that it can expect to live, on the average, another 3.4 years, to reach the age of 9.4 years.

A survivorship curve is constructed by plotting the l_x column of a life table against time. A classic use of survivorship curves in wildlife management was described by Taber and Dasmann for black-tailed deer (*Odocoileus hemionus columbianus*) *in* two habitats in California.

By use of survivorship curves, the researchers were able to compare survival rates of both sexes of five populations of ungulates. All survivorsnip curves were found to decline steeply in the first year, indicating high death rates of young animals.

After that, considerable variation among populations occurred. (The logarithmic scale is used on the abscissa to expand the lower parts of the curve. On a logarithmic scale, the removal of a constant proportion of animals would result in a straight declining line, such as occurs in female red deer (*Cervus elaphus*) from age 3 through 14.

Survival of male black-tailed deer was lower than for females because o(selective hunting of males. Taber and Dasmann noted from their survivorship curves that survival of black-tailed deer was much less for both sexes in shrubland than in chaparral. By examining other population features, they found that fawn production in the shrubland deer was higher than in the chaparral deer (0.76 fawns per adult doe in shrubland to 0.53 per doe in chaparral in December).

This higher production in the shrubland resulted in more intense competition for food, poorer nutrition, and higher mortality. Chaparral is a mixture of woody shrubs, while "shrubland" consists of scattered shrubs and herbs. In the shrubland, deer food was more abundant, and this feature permitted deer to maintain higher densities (25 per km^2) than in chaparral (11 per km^2).

Survival rates in the shrubland, however, were lower than in chaparral, presumably because the shrubland was fully stocked and the higher birth rates resulted in consequent higher losses through starvation. Once the carrying capacity of the shrublands had been attained, a proportion of deer that were not removed by hunting starved, so that the

Table 1.4: Life Table for the Dall Mountain Sheep (Ovis dalli) Based on the Known Age at Death of 608 Sheep Dying Before 1937 (Both Sexes Combined).

x	x'	d_x	l_x	$1000\, q_x$	e_x
Age (years)	*Age as Percent Deviation from Mean Length of Life*	*Number Dying in Age Interval Out of 1000 Born*	*Number Surviving at Beginning of Age Interval Out of 1000 Born*	*Mortality Rate per Thousand Alive at Beginning of Age Interval*	*Expectation of Life: or Mean Lifetime Remaining to Those Attaining Age Interval (years)*
0-0.5	–100.0	54	1000	54.0	7.1
0.5-1	–93.0	145	946	153.0	—
1-2	–85.9	12	801	15.0	7.7
2-3	–71.8	13	789	16.5	6.8
3-4	–57.7	12	776	15.5	5.9
4-5	–43.5	30	764	39.3	5.0
5-6	–29.5	46	734	62.6	4.2
6-7	–15.4	48	688	69.9	3.4
7-8	–1.1	69	640	108.0	2.6

(Table 1.4 Contd.)

(Table 1.4 Contd.)

x	x'	d_x	l_x	$1000\ q_x$	e_x
Age (years)	Age as Percent Deviation from Mean Length of Life	Number Dying in Age Interval Out of 1000 Born	Number Surviving at Beginning of Age Interval Out of 1000 Born	Mortality Rate per Thousand Alive at Beginning of Age Interval	Expectation of Life: or Mean Lifetime Remaining to Those Attaining Age Interval
8-9	+13.0	132	571	231.0	1.9
9-10	+27.0	187	439	426.0	1.3
10-11	+41.0	156	252	619.0	0.9
11-12	+55.0	90	96	937.0	0.6
12-13	+69.0	3	6	500.0	1.2
13-14	+84.0	3	3	1000.0	0.5

growth rate in both shrublands and chaparral was essentially zero.

Taber and Dasmann also pointed out that dynamics of different populations of the same species may vary widely from place to place. It is therefore difficult to say that birth and death rates of a particular population are "typical" of a species; differences among populations of the same species reflect different environmental conditions.

There also is evidence that the genetic makeup of a population may change with the passage of time or in response to some environmental factor. (Such change is the basis for the theory of evolution.) Some changes can take place quite rapidly.

For example, European rabbits (*Oryctolagus cuniculus*) in Australia were in the 1950s intentionally infected with myxomatosis, a viral disease, to control their numbers. The rabbits declined rapidly. There are still rabbits in Australia-not as many, but they are genetically more resistant to the virus than the rabbits in Australia in the 1940s.

Other less noticeable and unmeasured genetic changes possibly occur in many populations, changes that influence their birth rates and death rates, and that may be responsible for population irruptions and crashes for which no external cause may be apparent.

Sources of Population Data

Obtaining accurate information about animal numbers and densities remains one of the more difficult and challenging tasks for wildlife managers. Data are gathered in the form of *censuses*, *estimates*, and *indices*. *A* census is a complete count of individuals in a population.

Some species, particularly those living in open areas, may be counted from aircraft (e.g., pronghorns, *Antilocapra americana*, or winter flocks of waterfowl). Complete counts also are possible in a few special situations. Whooping cranes (*Grus americana*) are large, white birds, and thus are highly visible against a backdrop of marsh vegetation; the small population can be counted accurately in either summer or winter.

A complete count is rarely possible in areas where vegetation or topography conceals animals, or where the population is quite large. In such cases, an estimate may be made on the basis of a statistical sample. A sample may be obtained by counting inanimate objects (e.g., droppings, nests, and dens) or by counting animals.

In either case, the sample is taken on a plot or transect of a known size. Other information often is required before the sample can be interpreted. In the case of dens or burrows, for example, the average family size must be determined, then multiplied by the number of active burrows in the plots. Population estimates for prairie dogs (Cynomys spp.) are made in that manner, as are estimates based on the lodges of beaver (*Castor canadensis*). For droppings, the average number of droppings per day per animal must be known, as well as the maximum number of days since the droppings were deposited.

A common way of sampling living animals is based on a capture-recapture ratio. The estimate requires capturing, marking, and releasing a known number of animals, then resampling the population later. The population size is estimated using the proportion of the marked animals either recaptured (or resighted) in the second sample:

$$\text{No. in population} = \frac{\text{no. marked \& released} \times \text{no. resampled}}{\text{no. marked in resample}}$$

The capture-recapture method, known as the Lincoln or Petersen Index (although the ratio actually is an estimate), often underestimates the population because of a higher likelihood of recapturing (or sighting) marked animals than unmarked animals.

An index is a quantitative measure of a population. However, it seldom provides exact numbers or even an estimate of the numbers or densities of animals in a population. Indices instead compare relative abundance between areas, or changes in abundance from one time to another in the same area.

Counts of displaying male woodcocks (*Scolopax minor*) and ruffed grouse (*Bonasa umbellus*) along established routes are commonly used indices. Others include counts of pheasants (*Phasianus colcbicus*) and red foxes (*Vulpes vulpes*) by rural mail-carriers.

Biologists also obtain sex and age data from various sources. The age structure of fish populations often is determined from a collection of scales; these show annual growth rings known as *annuli*. In autumn, hunters voluntarily submit wings or tails from various kinds of game birds for analysis; quail, grouse, and other birds are sampled for year-to-year changes in the ratio of juveniles to adults.

Waterfowl are among the migratory birds sampled by the U.S. Fish and Wildlife Service, as thousands of duck wings are analyzed each year for age and sex ratios, by species, in what are known as *wing bees*. At roadside check stations, state biologists obtain age and sex information from big game killed by hunters.

Tooth replacement and wear are among the features commonly inspected for age determination in deer and other large mammals. However, the methods for determining age and sex vary greatly by species. Methods range from studying the shapes of feathers among birds to determining the weight of eye lenses for some kinds of small mammals; these methods are reviewed in detail by Larson and Taber.

Sampling theory must be considered when population data are collected. The subject is complex, and an extensive body of literature may be consulted. In its simplest form, however, sampling theory requires that the collected data represent the population at large.

For example, the age distribution shown by scales collected from 100 fish in a lake produces a statistical estimate of the entire fish population in the lake. What is sampled (e.g., 100 fish) in theory represents what was not sampled (e.g., all of the other fish in the population).

However, one or more sources of *sampling bias* may affect the reliability of the samples, and hence the results of the analysis may not be accurate. If the fish population was sampled with a gill net, then the smaller—and thus the younger—fish likely escaped capture. Hence, scales would be collected only from the larger—and older—fish, and the analysis would reflect a population lacking young age classes.

In this case, the bias results from the equipment and methods used in the field. Similarly, both age and sex data collected from deer at roadside check stations are usually biased (i.e., few does and fawns are shot), so those data usually reflect only the adult male segment of the adult population. In this case, the sampling bias is associated with the selectivity of hunters for certain age and sex groups.

However, most population data can be corrected or applied in ways that compensate for sampling bias; alternate field methods or equipment also may reduce the bias to acceptable levels (e.g., electrofishing equipment, or "fish shockers," may yield a better sample of size and age classes than gill nets provide). The important matter here, however, is that bias must be recognized and addressed before population data can produce sound management.

Organization of a Population Management Problem

A wildlife manager charged with solving a problem of population ecology may be faced with a somewhat bewildering array of possible causes of an "unsatisfactory" performance by the animals he or she wishes to manage. The following outline is intended to suggest a means of organizing efforts. The objective, of course, is to identify those factors that are most responsible for preventing the further growth of the population. These factors impede births, increase deaths, or both.

A. Extrinsic Factors

1. Density-independent (primarily weather conditions)
   a. Cause of direct mortality?
   b. Center or periphery of species range?
   c. Does weather have a substantial influence on food quality or quantity-which are density dependent factors?
2. Density dependent
   a. Food
      (1) Quality. Are necessary nutrients present?
      (2) Quantity. Is enough food available?
   b. Cover
      (1) Shelter from elements. Are quality and quantity sufficient?
      (2) Escape or hiding cover-for predators or from predators. Are quality and quantity sufficient?
   c. Refugia available. Are there patches of habitat in the range of the population in which animals have a high likelihood of escaping various mortality factors, such as predators, hunters, parasites, and disease?
   d. Competitors. Is there competition for resources by other species?
   e. Diseases and parasites. Are these factors influencing birth and death rates?
   f. Predators. Are predators controlling the population?
   g. Buffer species. Are other prey species present that absorb some of the impact of predation, particularly when the species being considered is at low densities?
   h. Hunting harvest. Is harvest toll replaced by the next season's production of huntable animals?
   i. Interactions among various factors. What interactions occur? Food supply-disease? Food supply-predation? Food supply-competition? Cover-predation? Buffer species-predation?

B. Intrinsic Factors

1. Genetically stable factors
   a. Litter or brood sizes. What is the inherent potential of

the species to reproduce?

b. Longevity. How long can individuals live?

c. Habitat selection for breeding, feeding, resting. Is it available according to inherent needs of the species?

d. Self-limiting factors. Does the species possess self-limiting behaviour such as territorial spacing, or restricted breeding among selected members of a group?

e. Dispersal. Is there an opportunity for immigration and emigration?

f. Interactions. How do inherent features interact, such as territorial behaviour-food supply, dispersal-food supply, birth rates-food supply?

2. Genetically variable factors

a. Birth rates. Within the physiological limits of the species, does the population show varying birth rates?

b. Survival rates. Does a population differ genetically from time to time in the ability of individuals to withstand stress, or has there been a response to a strong selective factor such as disease or biocides?

As can be seen, answering questions about a population may be a complex task. The most fruitful and simplest approach is usually to examine the more obvious factors first, such as weather, food, cover, and the behavioural nature of the animals. Should such an approach fail to provide satisfactory answers, the more subtle interactions must be examined.

Usually, the talents of a team of researchers, with various forms of expertise, must be called upon. Once the most important factors (key factors) limiting a population are identified, the manager may attempt to modify those factors.

Sometimes nothing can be done, such as when the weather or climate of a particular area is simply unsuitable for the welfare of the species; but most often the application of suitable controls on key factors will result in a desired change in the population being managed.

POPULATION MODELS

When wildlife managers predict how many mallard ducks will be present in the fall population, based upon sample counts of breeding ducks and the number of prairie ponds in the spring, they are using a model. Similarly, an estimate of the number of deer present obtained by sampling and counting pellet groups (droppings) left by the deer is another example of the use of a model. A model, as defined by Walters is any physical or abstract representation of the structure and function of a real system.

In the past decade, attempts have been made to construct models of everything biological, from cellular physiology to entire biomes. These representations are simulation models that trace through a period of time the changes that take place in a system, given some beginning conditions and some circumstances that effect changes in those conditions.

Populations of animals lend themselves reasonably well to the methods of simulation modeling. Owing to the speed with which they perform calculations and the convenience they offer for altering variables at various stages in the operation of a model, computers offer wildlife biologists new opportunities to simulate populations of animals under study and to predict the effects of various management procedures.

The basic tools for doing so are an understanding of FORTRAN or Pascal computer language and several years of data for a population, including age structure, sex ratios, birth rates, death rates, immigration, emigration, and environmental conditions that influence these factors.

Computer models have been developed to simulate wolf (*Canis* lupus)-moose (*Alces alces*) populations on Isle Royale and the projected recovery of whooping cranes (*Grus americana*). An excellent example of a model was constructed to simulate a population of mule deer in Colorado. These authors noted that a model has three basic values:

(1) it forces the researcher to think about population dynamics in new ways (conceptual value);
(2) the researcher must become aware of the usefulness of various types of information necessary to construct an accurate model, and therefore of the information necessary to understand population functions (developmental value); and
(3) the model may be useful in predicting future courses of the modeled population or the effects of manipulation of the population by adjusting rates of exploitation or by altering the environment (output value).

The model of the mule deer population studied by Medin and Anderson utilized the following variables gathered over several years of study: vegetation available as food, weather, food consumption, nutrients in food, other animals as predators or competitors, age, sex, and number of deer present, natural mortality rates, hunter harvest, age structure in the hunter harvest of deer, birth rates as determined by ovarian and fetal analysis, and the condition of the deer.

Only one environmental variable, the amount of precipitation in the April-July period, seemed to have a significant effect on birth rates; it did so by affecting the amount of nitrogen available in winter forage. The density of deer in winter had an inverse influence on their birth rates.

By calculating functions for these variables and feeding them into a computer, Medin and Anderson were able to simulate closely the dynamics of the deer population over 5 years for which reliable data were available. The assumption is then that the model might be projected into the future, given a reasonable assortment of May-July precipitation values.

The authors also tested the effects of different harvest strategies on the model. Then the authors asked some "what if" questions of their model and obtained results depicted in Figure elsewhere in this chapter.

The student can readily see the value of a population model, provided that the model is reasonably realistic. Biologists who develop models also can recognize the frequent inadequacies of field data and assumptions of cause and effect of variables used in the model.

A population model should be only one of many forms of information the wildlife manager may use. At this point in the development of population models, an attitude of informed skepticism seems appropriate.

THE HUMAN POPULATION

It is not possible to consider management of wildlife populations without also considering management of the human population. In 1988, there were about 5.1 billion people on the earth, and this number has been increasing at a rate of 1.7 percent per year.

At such a rate (which has prevailed over the past several decades), a doubling of human numbers will occur in 40 years. Each day, more than 200,000 people are added to those already on the earth. Only 6 of the 170 nations of the world show zero or negative growth rates.

The 1988 U.S. population of 246 million has been growing at a rate of 0.7 percent. Hutchinson (1978) observed that a glance at a newspaper suggests that many people behave as if there were no carrying capacity, no upper limit, to the number of people that the earth can support.

It is true that over the centuries human inventiveness has periodically increased the carrying capacity of the earth, first by changing the way of living from a hunting and food gathering mode of existence to one of agriculture. Later, industrialization, mechanization, and rapid transportation permitted people to trade useful items for food, and fewer farmers were needed to produce human food. The "green revolution," which resulted in the development of high yield grains, further permitted the feeding of even more people.

But agricultural production over the past decade has scarcely been keeping pace with population growth, and an estimated 20-40 percent of the people in the world are underfed.

Most ecologists believe that the carrying capacity of the planet for humans is rapidly being approached, and that resources cannot be produced and processed fast enough to meet the demands of an ever-growing population.

In some places, such as India and Bangladesh, the carrying capacity has already been surpassed. The need to feed, clothe, and house the growing billions of people requires both more extensive and more intensive use of the land and waters. In doing so, humans compete with other animals.

Faced with the necessity of raising crops and trees and mining energy sources of all kinds to supply starving people, many people find that arguments for providing habitat for wildlife lose their strength; and the wildlife management goal of balancing the needs of other animals and those of humans is weighted by the sheer numbers and "humane" priority of our own species.

The influence of the human population is truly global. Lead from the exhausts of millions of automobiles is found in the Antarctic ice pack, and chlorinated hydrocarbon pesticides are infused from the atmosphere into food chains of the tundra, where pesticides have never been applied.

Sulfur and nitrogen oxides emitted from power plants in one country cause acidification of lakes and soils in another. The production and use of resources to support humanity affect the resources for other animals, usually to the animals' detriment. There is no doubt that the human population will stop growing at some point.

The question is only whether human numbers will be controlled by such natural checks as starvation and territorial defense, or by the intelligent application of methods to reduce the birth rate to match death rates, the latter of which have been lowered through medical treatment. The future of wildlife as well as that of humans rests upon such a choice.

MANAGING WILDLIFE

Theodore Roosevelt published *Outdoor Pastimes of an American Hunter* during his tenure (1901-09) as 26th president of the United States. Roosevelt not only reflected on the pleasures of his outdoor experiences, but also issued a call for stemming the destructive tide that was sweeping wildlife and wild lands from the American landscape. His plea marshaled the concerns of others.

The result has been a movement that has continued to the present day-a movement whose goal is the conservation and restoration of wildlife populations and wildlife habitats. And from the context of that movement has evolved the practice of wildlife management.

Wildlife management, as we have defined it, involves the application of ecological knowledge to achieve a balance between the needs of humans and those of wildlife. Ecological knowledge was still in its infancy a century ago, and what we regard as state-of-the-art knowledge today surely will seem primitive and crude a century hence.

Wildlife management developed as a profession in the United States during the 1930s, but attempts at management have a much older history. According to Leopold (1933a), the first game law in North America dates to 1639 when Rhode island closed 'the hunting season for white-tailed deer (*Odocoileus virginianus*) from May to November.

Massachusetts followed with a similar law in 1694. In 1708, the colony of New York protected ruffed grouse (*Bonasa umbellus*), heath hens (*Tympanuchus c. cupido*), and wild turkeys (*Meleagris gallopavo*) during part of the year. Virginia enacted the first "buck law" in 1738, which allowed the legal kill only of antlered bucks.

The concept of curbing the daily kill-known as the bag limit-did not emerge until 1878 when Iowa established a limit of 25 greater prairie chickens (*T. c. pinnatus*) per day. In the 1890s, several states totally protected passenger pigeons (*Ectopistes migratorius*).

Those laws considered the seasonal vulnerability of each species and recognized that game animals might be overhunted. The regulations, however, were made without any assessment of population sizes; nor did the laws consider the reproductive potential of each species in relation to shooting pressure.

Moreover, habitat was neglected by the lawmakers of the day, and no attempt was made to preserve or restore the food, cover, and water needed by wildlife. In short, ecological knowledge and its application did not exist in the realm of wildlife management. The laws protecting heath hens and passenger pigeons were obvious failures.

Restoration of Bison

The mistreatment of American and European bison (*Bison bison* and *B. bonasus*, respectively) was remedied, in part, early in the twentieth century. In 1905, only a few hundred of the once vast population of American bison remained; they were found in zoos and in Yellowstone National Park.

However, their pitiful numbers prompted formation of the American Bison Association at the New York Zoo. Acting under the leadership of the zoo's director, Dr. William T. Hornaday, the Association prodded the conscience of the American public, with the result that bison preserves soon were established.

The Wichita Game Park (now a national wildlife refuge) in Oklahoma was stocked with 15 bison from the New York Zoo, and other refuges for bison were established in Montana, Nebraska, and South Dakota. The population of bison at Yellowstone Park steadily increased without stocking.

During this period, Canada also initiated a protection program for bison. Bison Park in Alberta was established specifically for the species, and by 1920 the sanctuary protected a herd of 5000 animals. Particular concern was focused on a badly diminished subspecies of bison, the wood buffalo (*B. b. athabascae*), which occupied wooded areas in northern Alberta and the Northwest Territories.

Wood buffalo were crossbreeding with the subspecies from the plains, producing hybrids that were highly susceptible to tuberculosis. Fortunately, about 200 pure-blooded wood buffalo were discovered in a remote corner of Wood Buffalo National Park in 1960, and the integrity of the subspecies now seems assured.

In all, estimates indicate that the bison population in North America now exceeds 30,000 animals. A restoration program began in Europe after poaching and the ravages of World War I had eliminated the last of the free-ranging bison herd. Luckily, 56 bison remained in zoos and private game preserves that were scattered across Europe. Dr. Kurt Priemel, a former director of the Frankfurt Zoo, formed the international Association for the Preservation of the European Bison.

The Association developed a studbook that listed the names and genealogies of all pure-blooded animals remaining in Europe. With the studbook, the captive herd could be propagated without indiscriminately crossbreeding the various strains of bison.

The process assured the genetic integrity and the continued evolution of the respective subpopulations from distinctive habitats in Europe.

In 1956, a small herd of bison was restocked in the Bialowieza Forest of Poland, the site where the last wild bison had been shot in 1921. By 1963, the population had grown to 57 animals, of which 34 were born in the wild. A program of winter feeding helps maintain the precious few bison in the Polish herd. Restocking also took place in the Soviet part of the Bialowieza Forest.

These animals in turn produced a wild herd from which biologists learned much about the natural food habits and behavioural patterns of the European bisoninformation never before known to science. Thus, from the dedicated efforts of concerned zoologists and wildlife managers came the successful restoration of a small, but wild, population of bison in eastern Europe.

Nonetheless, Klos and Wunschmann (1972) warn against keeping all animals of a rare species in one place. The dangers of contagious disease, warfare, or fires dictate that separate populations of wild bison should be established in various locations before the species can be considered safe from extinction.

Conservationists take rightful pride in the modest recovery of bison, a success that represents an important milestone in wildlife management. Still, two difficulties persist in the management of bison herds. First, the natural predators of bison are gone from most areas.

The birth rate thus exceeds the mortality rate and produces a surplus of animals. Unlike in the past, an expanding bison population can no longer wander at will across a vast landscape. Farms and ranches claim most of the countryside, and these and other uses of the land are incompatible with free-roaming herds of bison.

Second, and related to the first issue, adequate food supplies are a source of concern in bison management. Expanding herds that are confined by fences soon overgraze the best of rangelands. Artificial feeding is expensive and strains the budgets of conservation agencies.

An obvious solution for these difficulties-hunting-angers some segments of the public, especially when the surplus animals are shot on refuges that were established for the protection of the species. Thus, although the bison population has grown from precariously low numbers, the success of the restoration program has itself raised other issues relevant to bison management.

Whooping Cranes and Foster Parents

Whooping cranes (*Grus americana*) are renowned as a symbol of conservation in North America. Whoopers apparently were never abundant, although they once nested across much of the northern prairies and into the forests beyond. Most of the population wintered on the coast of the Gulf of Mexico. Unfortunately, whooping cranes were affected adversely by agricultural development, and no efforts were made to protect their breeding grounds from the steady turn of the plow across the North American heartland.

Also, many whooping cranes were shot, especially in such places as the North Platte river in Nebraska where the birds concentrated during migration. Perhaps no more than 1400 whoopers survived by the mid-1800s, and by 1941, only 23 birds remained. Of these, 15 birds migrated between their winter quarters in Texas and some then-n breeding grounds in the far north, 6 comprised a nonmigratory population in Louisiana, and 2 were held in captivity.

Initial efforts for managing whooping cranes began in 1918 with enactment of the Migratory Bird Treaty Act. Under terms of the Treaty, whoopers, among other species, gained protection from shooting and other forms of disturbances. However, the population continued to decline in the wake of unabated habitat destruction and limited enforcement of the new law.

A crucial step occurred in 1937 with the establishment of Aransas National Wildlife Refuge in Texas, which protects about 22,000 ha of coastal habitat that forms the core of the wintering grounds for whooping cranes. Still unknown at the time, however, was the location of the nesting grounds for the remaining population of whooping cranes.

Finally, in 1954, nests were discovered in the remote reaches of Wood Buffalo National Park in the Northwest Territories of Canada. The habitat in the park did not require further protection and, at last, studies could begin of the rare birds' breeding habits. Management potentials no longer were limited solely to the wintering area in Texas.

Nonetheless, the population remained unsteady; 6 or 8 young birds might be produced one year, only to have 2 or 3 juveniles (or none) reach Texas the next. Such production barely kept pace with the losses of older birds. The resident population in Louisiana was gone by 1950, and the migratory flock wintering in Texas generally hovered between 25 and 40 birds for many years.

What might be called passive management (i.e., legal protection) by itself clearly was not enhancing the numbers of whooping cranes. Hence, in 1967, a captive breeding program was initiated, using eggs collected from the wild population and from the few whooping cranes held in zoos. The initial idea was to increase production by releasing second-generation birds produced by a nucleus of breeders maintained by the U.S. Fish and Wildlife Service at the Patuxent Wildlife Research Center in Maryland. Despite dedicated and intensive care, however, the program proceeded slowly and lacked much success.

Eggs were produced, and some hatched, but most of the young whooping cranes died before they were ready for release. Then a bold and imaginative method emerged as a second effort. New knowledge of the birds' nesting ecology—gained at Wood Buffalo National Park and from a thorough study of a related but numerous species, the sandhill crane (*Grus canadensis*), together with the strategic protection afforded by two national wildlife refuges-provided the basis for what is known as the *foster-parent* program.

Although each pair of adult whooping cranes usually produces a clutch of 2 (rarely 3) eggs, only 1 of these normally produces a chick able to leave the nest. Both eggs are fertile, but, after they hatch, competition in the nest usually leaves only 1 surviving chick. Meanwhile, studies of sandhill cranes-focusing on incubation activities, brooding behaviour, and the food habits and plumage development of juveniles-indicated strong similarities to whooping cranes.

Researchers believed that young whoopers might fare well under the parental care of sandhill cranes. By 1975, enough information was at hand to initiate the foster-parent program, and 14 whooping crane eggs were moved that year from the nests in Wood Buffalo National Park to Gray's Lake National Wildlife Refuge in Idaho.

The program removed only 1 egg per nest, without causing adverse effects on natural propagation. The sandhill cranes nesting at Gray's Lake overwinter at Bosque del Apache National Wildlife Refuge in New Mexico, and the birds thus follow a migratory route within the historic range of whooping cranes. The migratory route also includes a stopover at Monte Vista National Wildlife Refuge.

Maximum protection therefore could be afforded to young whooping cranes that were successfully reared by sandhill cranes at Gray's Lake. That is, both the summer and winter quarters for the experimental flock, as well as a major resting point enroute, were national wildlife refuges.

As a result, 9 of the 14 transplanted eggs hatched, and 6 chicks grew to flying age in the first year of the experiment. Of these, 4 young whooping cranes survived the fall migration to New Mexico. The foster-parent program has continued each year since 1975. More eggs, including those taken from the captive flock in Maryland, have been added to the sandhill nests at Gray's Lake.

Production in some years is better than others. In 1985, 19 chicks hatched from 27 eggs, and at least 10 of the young birds migrated to New Mexico. However, only 2 chicks survived from 15 eggs the following year. The newly created flock of whooping cranes numbered 19 birds in the autumn of 1986.

The foster-parent program will be evaluated in 1989 by the U.S. Fish and Wildlife Service and the Canadian Wildlife Service; if the whooping cranes at Gray's Lake have mated, other flocks may be started by the same means in northern Michigan or in southern Ontario.

Production has not been lessened in the population nesting in Canada, from which the "extra" eggs are taken for transplant in Idaho. The first year that eggs were removed (14 eggs in 1975), 8 young whooping cranes, or 14 percent of the population, were included in the total of 57 birds wintering in Texas.

In the previous year, when no eggs were removed, the population wintering in Texas consisted of 49 birds, but the total included only 2 juveniles (4 percent). Production reached 12 young (17 percent of 69 birds) in 1976, 9 young (17 percent of 70 birds) in 1977, and 6 young (12 percent of 74 birds) in 1978. Thus, whereas the .year-to-year production still varied, it is clear that removing some eggs from the nests in Canada has not been harmful. Indeed, record numbers were reached in 1986 for both young and older whooping cranes wintering in Texas; 101 birds arrived in Texas, of which 20 (20 percent) were juveniles.

These results are encouraging, but it would be unwise to assume that whooping cranes are at last secure. Nesting has not yet occurred in the Gray's Lake population; fortunately, neither has hybridization with sandhill cranes.

For some unknown reason, more males than females have hatched and survived in the experimental program, and an imbalance in the sex ratio remains a basic concern in the management of monogamous species such as whooping cranes.

Disease recently reduced the small population of whooping cranes held in captivity. Nesting areas for the wild birds seem secure, but in winter, the population in Texas lacks total safety because a few birds stray from the sanctuary of the Aransas Refuge. Further, the Intercoastal Waterway bisects the Refuge, giving boaters easy access to the birds; the waterway also includes heavy barge traffic.

Oil spills and late-season hurricanes remain among the dangers present at Aransas. Collisions with utility lines are a common cause of mortality during migration, and at least one whooping crane was mistaken for a goose and shot during the hunting season. Boyce and Miller anticipate that the goal of 40 nesting pairs should be reached by the year 2000, but they noted that the population dips every 10 years.

Nonetheless, the number of wild whooping cranes reached 120 birds in the autumn of 1986, an eightfold increase from the precariously small population of 15 present in 1941. Wildlife managers and the public thus have reason for applauding the recovery program for whooping cranes.

Return of Wood Ducks

When Congress passed the Migratory Bird Treaty Act in 1918, wood ducks (*Aix sponsa*) were given complete legal protection. The effect was heartening: wood duck populations gradually increased. In 1938, more than 10,000 wood ducks were seen at one time feeding in wheat stubble near Havana, Illinois.

As the population grew, however, it seemed that the number of wood ducks outstripped the availability of suitable nesting sites. Instead of tree cavities, their normal nest sites, some wood ducks nested in chimneys and other atypical settings. Thus, in 1939, biologists in Illinois erected several hundred nest boxes designed specifically for wood ducks.

Nearly 52 percent of the boxes contained nests the first year; by 1942, 65 percent of the boxes were used by wood ducks. Other states in the breeding range of wood ducks followed suit, and nest-box programs soon became the focus of wood duck management in much of the eastern United States.

In 1941, wood ducks once more became legal game during the hunting season in several states. Despite a temporary setback in the 1950s, when strict hunting regulations again were imposed, wood ducks have recovered much of their former abundance.

The annual harvest of waterfowl in the Mississippi Flyway included about 500,000 wood ducks during the late 1960s and 1970s; another 225,000 were shot each year in the Atlantic Flyway during the same period. There was, however, no indication that hunting was causing any decline in the population.

Today, wood ducks rank as the secondor third—most abundant species of waterfowl in the bag of eastern duck hunters. The successful management program for wood ducks can be attributed to several factors: timely recognition of the species' perilous status; adequate legal protection; habitat improvement using man-made nesting structures; and thereafter, careful year-by-year monitoring of the population so that rigorous protection could be forthcoming, as needed, on short notice.

Moreover, wood ducks responded quickly to the management program because they lay large clutches and readily renest if their first clutch fails. Unlike other ducks in North America, wood ducks occasionally rear two broods during a single nesting season. for complete reviews of the ecology and management of wood ducks.

Wild Turkeys: Turning Failure into Success

By the 1930s, wild turkeys had been extirpated from much of their range. As mentioned in other chapter of this book, most attempts at restocking the empty range failed because unfit breeding stock was released. After several failures, however, success was achieved when the stock consisted of wild-trapped birds of the appropriate subspecies (i.e., the stocked birds were of a genetic lineage adapted to conditions in the release area).

Populations of wild turkeys thus were reestablished in much of their former range. Newly established populations of wild turkey also required the protection and effective enforcement of laws. Such protection did not abolish legal hunting, although it was once predicted that the successful release of turkeys in Michigan would not produce a hunting season.

Nonetheless, 11 years after the first birds were stocked in Michigan, hunting began, under a limited permit system that allowed the harvest of any turkey, including immature or adults of either sex. Poor nesting conditions and perhaps indiscriminate harvests in the autumn hunts caused some stagnation in turkey numbers in the late 1960s.

Then, in 1970, Michigan initiated an experimental springtime hunt that was restricted to gobblers (males). A "beard"—the long tuft of bristlelike feathers on the breasts of males-enabled hunters to distinguish between gobblers and hens. Since 1970, turkey populations in Michigan have blossomed under the regime of the spring gobbler hunt.

The annual harvest steadily increased from 91 birds in 1970 to 2361 in 1986, reflecting obvious increases in the distribution and density of the turkey population. Today, no fewer than 40 other states also have reestablished wild turkey populations.

Restoration of Mammals in North America

A pamphlet entitled *Endangered Species, The Success of Wildlife Management in North America* (National Shooting Sports Foundation, no date) summarizes some of the lesser-known cases in which wildlife populations have been restored successfully. In 1900, estimates suggest that no more than 500,000 white-tailed deer lived in the United States.

Less than a century later, in 1980, the herd numbered about 12 million deer. The distribution of the American subspecies of elk (*Cervus elaphus canadensis*) once extended from the Atlantic to the Pacific and from Canada to Mexico. By the end of the nineteenth century, however, the area still occupied by elk was only a fraction of its former size.

Table 1.5: Spring Harvest of Turkeys in Michigan, Gobblers Only, 1970-86.

Year	*Number of Turkeys Shot*
1970	91
1971	96
1972	152
1973	198
1974	238
1975	349
1976	397
1977	476
1978	618
1979	627
1980	844
1981	1033
1982	1760
1983	1746
1984	1458
1985	2016
1986	2361

Perhaps only 40,000 elk remained, most living in Yellowstone National Park. Protection of winter habitat, improved range conditions, and regulated hunting have produced a current population estimated at 1 million animals. Most elk are found in 10 western states, but small herds also live in Michigan, Virginia, and Pennsylvania.

The population of pronghorn (*Antilocapra americana*) numbered less than 13,000 in the 1920s, but increased to more than 400,000 by the early 1980s. Final mention goes to beaver (*Castor canadensis*), a species that has enriched both the history and wealth of North America. Indeed, heedless trapping nearly extirpated beaver from the United States in the 1800s. Today, however, colonies again occur across the nation, even in places where beaver lodges disappeared more than a century ago.

Some Successes with Birds

Leafing through the pages of *Our Varishing Wild Life*, one finds woefully accurate predictions of extinction for several species of birds-unless *effective management activities quickly intervened.* The

"candidates for oblivion" included whooping cranes, heath hens, wood ducks, and California condors (*Gymnogyps cali fornianus*). As we have seen, wood ducks recovered dramatically with intensive management, and the future for whooping cranes is far brighter today than at any other time in recent history.

Heath hens indeed are gone, however, and California condors remain at the brink of extinction. The few condors still remaining in the wild were captured recently for a breeding program at the San Diego Zoo-a controversial action, but indicative of a last-ditch effort for saving the species.

Other candidates on Hornaday's list were trumpeter swans (*Cygnus cygnus buccinator*), roseate spoonbills (*Ajaia ajaja*), upland sandpipers (*Bartramia longicauda*), sage grouse (*Centrocercus urophasianus*), sharp-tailed grouse (*Pediocoetes phasianellus*), and snowy egrets (*Egretta thula*).

Hornaday predicted that the sage grouse would be the first upland game bird falling to extinction. Today, sage grouse are abundant on many western rangelands and, of the others on Hornaday's list, only trumpeter swans and roseate spoonbills remain on the current list of threatened species.

That so many birds once in dire straits are today relatively safe remains a tribute to Hornaday's early call of alarm. The continued existence of these species highlights the successes of wildlife management.

Elusive Measures of Successful Management

An important aspect of wildlife management concerns the maintenance of wildlife populations at levels that approach neither extinction nor excess. Populations of most North American songbirds (e.g., song sparrows, *Melospiza melodia*) are secure and normally fluctuate within acceptable limits with little or no management.

The same is true of most small mammals (e.g., chipmunks,- *Tamias spp.*) although some species exhibit periodic irruptions or cycles (e.g., lemmings, *Lemmus spp.*). Endangered species are notable exceptions that require management.

For game species, however, the ability of managers to maintain populations at levels permitting a reasonable harvest each year is itself a measure of successful management. In that respect, wildlife management has been a long-standing success for many species.

Game animals such as cottontails (*Sylvilagus spp.*) or bobwhites (*Colinus virginianus*) thrive throughout most of their ranges. Indeed, the harvest of some game species numbers well into the millions each year without having a lasting effect on the size of the populations (e.g., mourning doves, *Zenaida macroura*).

Much of the success in the management of these species is attributable to the biological nature of the animals themselves-they exhibit resilient population features and adaptability to human presence. Most of the more abundant species of wildlife thrive in habitats associated with human activities (i.e., habitats maintained in low or midsuccessional stages).

As we have seen earlier, however, even abundant species can suddenly become scarce when they are overexploited (e.g., the passenger pigeon and the bison). Some undertakings of wildlife management are not easily characterized in terms of success or failure. The nuances of changing attitudes often colour our interpretations, as do the revelations of science.

Wolves (*Canis lupus*) were extirpated 200 years ago from the British Isles, an event that was probably hailed as a triumph of progress by citizens of the day. The same, no doubt, was true when mountain lions (*Felis concolour*) no longer roamed the Appalachian, Adirondack, or Ozark mountains.

Hawks, too, were enemies; thousands were killed each year. In the modern world, however, the elimination of any species from large parts of its natural range is no longer regarded as ecologically desirable, and extinction at the hand of humans clearly represents failure.

Abundance is a particularly elusive characteristic against which wildlife management might be judged. In the 1800s, the duck population in North America probably reached 400 million birds, a size about 10 times the number present in 1956. Waterfowl managers decided that the 1956 level of abundance-about 40 million birds—would be the goal of management in the decades ahead. By 1980, the stated goal was being achieved. A higher level of abundance may be unrealistic; humans probably have altered too many wetlands in North America to restore a significantly larger duck population.

The question is, should we regard maintaining 40 million ducks from an original population of perhaps 400 million as a success or failure? Successful wildlife management involves social as well as technical dimensions.

From the technical standpoint, an understanding of the current status of a wildlife population is the first requirement of management. Such knowledge includes the following factors: the size of the population; its growth rate or rate of decline; the reproductive capability of the animals; and the seasonal food, cover, and water requirements of the species.

Only with a grasp of these facts can managers reasonably determine the nature and extent of the biological issues, if any, confronting wildlife populations. From the social standpoint, successful management calls for strong programs of public education, especially in cases where hunting is proposed as a means of regulating wildlife populations (e.g., doe hunts).

Some sectors of the public now express vigorous opposition to all forms of hunting or trapping. Conversely, some management programs require strict protection, and the public must understand why such measures are needed. Protection may be important not just for individual species, but also for larger systems in which two or more species interact.

Black-footed ferrets (*Mustela nigripes*) live in association with prairie dogs (*Cynomys spp.*), and a management program aimed at only one of these species without involving the other would be ecological folly. In still other cases, habitat preservation or modification may be an issue capturing public attention (e.g., designation of wilderness areas or prescribed burning).

Finally, with the social considerations in place, the remedial phases of management can begin, whether they include modified regulations, habitat improvements, or legislative mandates.

2

Aquatic Environment

Water is indispensable to all organisms, yet it is unevenly distributed—in time and space—across the earth's surface. Water also is a simple chemical compound and, unlike most others, it readily appears in liquid, gaseous, and solid forms that act in an immense variety of ecological settings.

It occurs in grades essentially free of minerals as well as in those laden with salts and other materials. Of the immense amount of water on our planet, fully 97 percent occurs in oceans, about 2 percent in glaciers, and less than 1 percent in the combined volume of aquifers, rivers, and lakes.

Many ecological relationships between water and wildlife are direct and obvious; others are more subtle. All are essential. Water management touches the distribution, quality, and quantity of water not only in arid regions, but also where water may be plentiful.

SOME PROPERTIES OF WATER

A high *heat capacity* is among the more important properties of water in relation to living matter. That is, water is able to absorb a great deal of heat without becoming much warmer. For example, if equal weights of iron and water were frozen to absolute zero (-273°C) and then subjected to equal amounts of heat, the iron will have melted at 1298°C, whereas the ice would have just reached its melting point (0°C).

Only liquid ammonia has a greater heat capacity than water, making ammonia-based compounds useful in refrigerators, air conditioners, and other cooling devices. Because water comprises a high percentage of an animal's body weight, its heat capacity helps stabilize body temperatures even under extreme environmental conditions. Water content reaches 67 percent by weight in the bodies of mule deer (*Odocoileus hemionus*) and 82 percent in pronghorn (*Antilocapra americana*).

Homeotherms—those so-called warm-blooded animals with self-regulating body temperatures—take special advantage of this property; birds and mammals live under the most extreme temperature regimes on earth. Even poikilothermic, or cold-blooded, species such as fishes survive under a wide range of climatic regimes because the temperature of their habitat (i.e., water) changes relatively little between tropical and polar climates.

Adaptions of many kinds, of course, delimit most animals to more specific ranges on land or in water, but water's high heat capacity is fundamental to each species' overall tolerance for ambient temperatures. Water also is a universal solvent altering the chemical state of an unusually large number of other substances.

This property makes essential nutrients available for life processes while concurrently serving as the medium of their transport. Thus, dissolved materials from fundamental sources such as bedrock may be transferred to the living components of ecosystems everywhere, first externally and then internally, within each organism. Indeed, Leonardo da Vinci noted that "water is nature's carter," clearly referring to its importance as a life-giving transportation system.

Water's action as a solvent may change the carrying capacity of wildlife habitat. Inundation of soils otherwise above the water table leads to a rapid, if temporary, increase of available nutrients that may greatly expand both the numbers and growth rates of plants and animals at the flooded site. Conversely, water may dissolve or carry harmful materials.

In modern times, the solvent properties of water have fostered man-made disasters. Pollution of many kinds has ruined entire aquatic systems and destroyed the biotic communities they supported. Closed watersheds continually receive an ever-larger concentration of salts that steadily accumulate to the point that many forms of life are harmed or excluded.

This phenomenon is accentuated where evaporation exceeds precipitation. The Great Salt Lake in Utah and the Dead Sea bordering Israel are classic examples of closed watersheds naturally affected by salt accumulations, but immense numbers of lesser sites are similarly affected throughout the world. In Kenya, after the traditional breeding area of lesser flamingos (*Phoeniconaias minor*) suddenly was flooded, the huge flock-perhaps 2 million birds-quickly moved en masse to Lake Magadi, a shallow lake with no outlet that is fed by saltwater springs.

The intense heat caused rapid evaporation, further concentrating the salts in the lake. After the birds hatched, the legs of the young flamingos built up anklets of encrusted salt deposits as they waded in the mineral-laden water.

Few could survive the burden of the encrustations. Fortunately, a group of conservationists happened on the scene and began the arduous task of removing deposits from the doomed birds. In all, some 27,000 young flamingos were freed from their shackles. The flamingo colony returned to their original breeding areas the following year, avoiding the lethal waters of Lake Magadi.

Similarly, heavy encrustations of sodium salts killed or immobilized about 300 Canada geese (*Branta canadensis*) and other waterfowl on a hypersaline lake in western Saskatchewan. Some of the birds were encrusted with at least 3 kg of salt crystals. The dead geese showed evidence of acute muscle degeneration and had aspirated lake water.

The encrustations apparently occurred when the lake water cooled rapidly, resulting in the supersaturation and crystallization of the dissolved salts. Most of the immobilized geese (155 birds) survived after being captured and relocated on nearby freshwater wetlands.

Human disturbances also can increase the salinity of water, of which the case at Mono Lake, California, has attracted wide attention. The city of Los Angeles diverts the streams feeding Mono Lake, which not only lowers the lake's water level, but also further concentrates the already saline water. Mono Lake, famous for its mineral towers, lacks fishes but produces immense numbers of brine shrimp and brine flies that feed hundreds of thousands of migrant birds traveling in the Pacific Flyway.

If the current lake level falls by 3 m, the brine flies will lose 40 percent of their habitat. Further drops will impair reproduction of the brine shrimp, again impairing the food supplies for birds. Lower lake levels also mean that predators could gain access to birds nesting on the lake's islands. Mono Lake already has fallen about 11 M, and conservationists worry that continued losses will trigger the collapse of the lake's food chain.

Some Ecological Influences of Water

Light penetration into water interacts with depths and clarity to support the basic productivity necessary for aquatic food chains. Birge and Juday recorded light penetrations of 67 percent full intensity and 10.5 percent full intensity at 1-m and 10-m depths, respectively, in the usually clear waters of Crystal Lake, Wisconsin.

However, wave action, erosion, or other factors may inhibit light penetration, causing diminished productivity in disturbed systems. Robel reported a negative relationship between water turbidity and the biomass of submersed vegetation important as food for waterfowl. Carp (*Cyprinus carpio*) and other so-called rough fishes contribute to turbidity in soft-bottomed marshes, often to the point where vegetation may be affected and the carrying capacity for waterfowl may be reduced.

Water clarity increased from a transparency of 15 cm to more than 90 cm after rough fishes were removed from a North Carolina lake. Water exerts a powerful physical force on the landscape. The natural phenomenon of geological erosion has created the canyons, valleys, escarpments, and other features of the landscape that have much to do with wildlife habitat.

Topography, of course, thereafter may influence the amount and quality of water available to fishes and other wildlife. The same water supporting trout and other cold-water organisms at high elevations later produces very different aquatic communities as it moves to lower elevations.

Oxygenation and clarity as well as temperatures are transformed as water velocities respond to topographical gradients. Rivers meandering across flat terrain cut new channels so that water eventually flows in newer, self-made courses. Old river channels thus separated from the new riverbed are known as oxbow lakes in North America and as billabongs in Australia.

Horseshoe Lake Game Refuge in southern Illinois was developed around a 485-ha oxbow of the Mississippi River. Some 30,000 Canada geese, about half the region's winter population, once used the refuge each year, establishing the oxbow lake as the most important winter goose habitat in the Mississippi River Valley.

More recently, the refuge has supported an even larger winter population of about 100,000 geese. The numerous billabongs developing from the old river systems in Australia are crucial breeding, feeding, and refuge habitat for ducks and other waterbirds. Like oxbow lakes, billabongs become progressively shallower, develop aquatic vegetation, and lose many of their original riverbed characteristics.

Mature billabongs are among the most important waterfowl habitats in Australia. Whereas these and other processes are natural phenomena

Table 2.1: Relationship of Water Turbidity to Submersed Plant Production.

Relative Turbidity Rating	*Water Turbidity (Colorimeter Units)*	*Plants (kg/ha)*	
		Range	*Mean*
Low	0–50	1680–3585	2297
Medium	51—100	18—1064	448
High	101—150	6–560	140

of a maturing landscape, water also erodes immense amounts of soil when humans are careless. Sheet, gully, and riparian erosion each have forceful implications on soil, vegetation, wildlife, and human resources.

Large-scale patterns in rainfall distribution are influenced by air currents moving across mountain ranges. Warm, moisture-laden air moving upward over mountainous terrain cools at the higher elevations and can no longer retain its moisture. Rain or snow falls on the windward side of the slope.

However, little moisture remains by the time the air currents have passed over the mountains, and a dry "rain shadow" develops on the lee side of the range. The Great Basin of North America, encompassing much of Nevada, Utah, and southern Idaho, lies in the rain shadow of the North American cordillera, in part, creating an arid environment suitable for chukar partridges (*Alectoris chukar*).

In the form of ice, water during the glacial epochs shaped lakes, rivers, and terrain as the ice sheets advanced, and then retreated, across much of North America. The numerous prairie potholes dotting the northern plains claim glacial origins. Some were formed by gouging and others resulted when ice chunks calving from the glacier's leading edge were forced downward under the immense weight of the advancing glacier.

When the glaciers eventually retreated, a myriad of water-filled potholes remained that became the heartland of breeding habitat for waterfowl in North America. At least 50 percent of the North American duck population is produced in this region-aptly known as America's "duck factory"—even though these wetlands make up only 10 percent of the total breeding habitat.

On May 29, 1986, an ice dam formed by a surge of Hubbard Glacier closed off Russell Fiord, Alaska, and impounded about 5.3 km^3 of fresh water. The new lake stratified; a layer of dense salt water lay beneath an accumulating layer of fresh water. The lake level rose nearly 30 cm per day and, had the water continued rising, drainage patterns in local rivers would have changed radically, no doubt impairing the migrations of Pacific salmon (*Oncorhynchus spp.*) and threatening the economy of neighboring villages.

When the ice dam broke open on October 8, 1986, the discharge was about 14 times the amount of water cascading over Niagara Falls each second. In places, erosion removed the alluvial soils down to bedrock and produced a 200-300 m retreat in the shoreline.

Until then, however, marine life was trapped behind the ice dam, largely depending on food and oxygen in a layer of salt water buried beneath the deepening layer of fresh water. About 170 seals and sea lions (Pinnipedia) were among the marine mammals confined in "Lake Russell."

Rescue efforts, organized by the California Marine Mammal Center, received widespread coverage in the news media, but only a few of the entrapped animals were captured and released before the ice dam ruptured and Russell Fiord returned to a marine environment. Geologists, however, believe that Hubbard Glacier again will close Russell Fiord, forming an even larger freshwater lake and once more producing a rapidly changing environment for marine wildlife.

Bruemmer has described the ecological importance of permafrost, the stratum of icebound ground that underlies about one-quarter of the earth's land surface. Thick layers of permafrost develop wherever annual freezing exceeds annual thaw.

In Barrow, Alaska, permafrost is about 400 m thick, and in Siberia, maximum depths of nearly 1500 m are known. In summer, the Arctic becomes waterlogged and green with a rich carpet of vegetation. About 900 species of vascular plants occur in areas with permafrost, yet the average precipitation (20 cm) is less than occurs in the Mojave Desert.

Permafrost explains the paradox of a watery land with an arid climate. The scant rainfall and snowmelt cannot seep into the frozen soil and the water thus remains in the root zones of the vegetation. Without permafrost, most of the tundra would become a lifeless desert.

With permafrost, the food web includes herbivores such as caribou (*Rangifer tarandus*), muskox (*Ovibos moschatus*), and Arctic hares (*Lepus arcticus*). Some appreciation of the shaping force of water can be gained when estimates of soil carried annually by some of the world's great rivers are considered: the Yellow River, 2080 million tons; the Ganges River, 1600 million tons; the Amazon River, 400 million tons;

the Mississippi River, 344 million tons; the Colorado River, 149 million tons; and the Nile River, 122 million tons. The Yellow River in China and the Colorado ("red," in Spanish) in the United States, among others, derive their names from the colored burden of soil they carry.

Some of these loads are, of course, man-caused, resulting from abusive practices upriver, but much of the burden is the normal result of water's geological erosion. In the form of glacial ice, water discharges even larger amounts of sediments. Friedman and Sanders (1978) estimated that glaciers in Antarctica discharge 35-50 billion tons of sediments annually at a rate of 2500 to 3570 tons per km^2 of ice (versus about 13 billion tons or 260 tons per km^2 of watershed for the world's rivers combined).

Sedimentation in such vast amounts often has produced large deltas such as those at the mouth of the Mississippi and Nile rivers. The delta at the mouth of the Mississippi River is expanding at a rate of about 90 m per·year. These deposits are rich, carrying with them a nutrient-base of continental proportions.

The marshes of the lower Mississippi Delta in Louisiana, for example, are renowned for the populations of muskrats (*Ondatra zibetbicus*) and other wildlife they support. Conversely, when the Aswan High Dam impeded the Nile's nutrient discharge, the Mediterranean Sea's sardine fishery quickly collapsed. Before completion of the Aswan High Dam, Egyptian fishermen harvested 16.3 million kg of sardines from the shallow waters just beyond the Nile Delta, but shortly after the dam began restraining the nutrient-enriched floodwaters of the Nile, the sardine harvest dropped by 97 percent.

Water, Distribution, and Isolation

The configurations of water, past and present, play a role in the geographical distribution of organisms. Perhaps the best-known example is Wallace's line, a zoogeographical boundary coinciding with a deep trench in the seabed between the small islands of Bali and Lombok in the East Indies.

The narrow trench remained an effective barrier to faunal dispersal even when sea levels were lowered during the glacial ages of the Pleistocene. Conversely, the islands between Bali and the Asian mainland were surrounded by much shallower seas; the islands joined as a contiguous land mass with Asia when the ocean receded.

Faunal dispersal occurred between the mainland and the islands up to and including Bali, but not beyond. The gap between Bali and

Lombok, although less than 32 km in width, still marks the terminus for the Oriental fauna, even for such mobile groups as birds.

Fisher (*Martes pennanti*) and some other mammals living in the montane forests of northern Utah are barred, in part, by the Green River from moving eastward into similar habitats in Colorado; conversely, the range of Abert's squirrels (*Sciurus aberti*) does not extend westward from Colorado into northern Utah for the same reason.

However, for reasons that remain unclear, the Columbia River has not been a similar barrier to mammalian distributions; most of the species on the northern side of its course also are present on the southern side. Nonetheless, some mammals have extended their ranges westward or eastward across the Cascade Mountains because of the gorge cut through the mountains by the Columbia River.

Two species of western squirrels moved eastward through the gorge, whereas white-tailed deer (*Odocoileus virginianus*) and muskrats moved westward into Washington and Oregon along this "highway" through the mountains.

The swimming abilities of terrestrial animals clearly influence their predisposition to cross water, and hence expand their ranges; the width and velocity of rivers are other factors in this matter. Some animals confronted with water barriers successfully expand their distributions by "rafting."

That is, where tangles of vegetation and soil break away from one side of a river, small animals thereon may be transported to the opposite side, but rafting as a means of transporting larger animals probably is rare. Ice bridges are another means for animals to cross water barriers. Wolves (*Canis lupus*) reached Isle Royale by crossing 29 km of ice on Lake Superior, thereafter establishing a predator-prey interaction with the island's moose (*Alces alces*) population.

Fuller and Robinson recorded the movements of deer and predators across ice on the St. Mary's River between Ontario and Michigan; deer seldom crossed more than 1000 m of ice, whereas the predators did so more readily. Lack (1954) noted that eiders (*Somateria mollissima*) breeding on small Arctic islands delay nesting until after the surrounding ice melts, after which Arctic foxes (*Alopex lagopus*) cannot reach the islands and destroy their nests; a similar defensive mechanism is employed by gulls nesting on islands in Finland.

More than 250 goose nests on Arctic islands were destroyed when foxes crossed ice bridges during a late spring. However, because geese normally abandon breeding areas where successful nesting is thwarted repeatedly, it seems probable that such large losses are rare occurrences.

Water barriers also serve as isolating mechanisms leading to the development of new forms by adaptive radiation. The isolating function of water may be either real, in terms of distance or physiology (e.g., intolerance to salt water), or psychological. Hawaiian geese (*Branta sandvicensis*) apparently evolved from Canada geese that were isolated, perhaps by the misadventure of a Pacific storm, from their North American homeland.

The species is the only goose endemic to an island and, in isolation, it has adapted uniquely to a terrestrial lifestyle in the lava fields of Hawaii. Trappers apparently introduced blue foxes-a colour- phase of the Arctic fox-onto some Aleutian Islands to assure inbreeding, and hence perpetuation of the more valuable blue-phase pelage of these animals for commercial purposes.

Ground-nesting birds, among them Canada geese, have been virtually eliminated from certain islands where the foxes were released. Perhaps the most heralded instance of adaptive radiation concerns the water-related isolation of certain birds in the Galapagos Islands. Charles Darwin (1845) immortalized these birds in his journal as "a most singular group of finches."

Known today as Darwin's finches (Geospizinae), their common ancestral stock arriving from South America subsequently evolved into 14 species having the lifestyles of warblers, woodpeckers, and, of course, ground-feeding finches. The water between the islands was of sufficient distance to allow time for the development of reproductively isolated populations before additional colonizers invaded from other islands in the Galapagos archipelago.

Conversely, Mayr described species and subspecies of land birds in the Solomon Islands that easily could cross the small water gaps separating the islands, but do not, apparently because of the strong psychological barrier presented by the water itself.

Fishes have obvious problems crossing land barriers, although walking catfish (*Clarias batrachus*) are remarkably adapted for overland movements. The distributions of many fishes are limited by their inability to tolerate either salt water or fresh water, whereas others, such as Atlantic salmon (*Salmo salar*) seasonally visit each type of regime.

Vast geological changes also have produced unusual distributions-and problems-for certain species. Among these is the former occurrence of immensely large lakes that subsequently disappeared, leaving only remnant waters with isolated fish populations. In late Pliocene-Pleistocene times, a lake of nearly 52,000 km^2 with a maximum depth of about 300 m covered much of what is now Utah. Known as Lake Bonneville, it drained northward via the Snake River into present-day Idaho, ultimately connecting to a vast network of river drainages.

Subsequent geological and climatological events diminished the lake so that, today, only a few isolated lakes dot the ancient lakebed. No less than 7 endemic species of fishes evolved in the isolated remnants of Lake Bonneville and their immediate drainages.

Springs in desert regions are as isolated as oceanic islands, but, unlike islands, their faunas are derived from past ages rather than by chance invasion and subsequent adaptive radiation. The Devil's Hole pupfish (*Cyprinodon diabolis*) perhaps is the best-known case of a highly isolated, relict species threatened by civilization.

This species—one of several in the family of killifish with restricted distributions-evolved in a single spring in Nye County, Nevada. Unfortunately, demands for irrigation water lowered the spring's level to the point that spawning habitat along the pool's periphery was no longer inundated, and the population at times has numbered no more than 125 breeding adults.

More recently, the spring has been protected and an artificial spawning platform was installed just below the water's present level. Also, a population of Devil's Hole pupfish now is maintained artificially in a refugium located near the foot of Hoover Dam.

Water-influenced environments also may effectively have an impact on animal distributions. Historically, pronghorns failed to cross the Missouri River eastward from Nebraska into Iowa, not so much because of the river itself, but because the riparian forests bordering the river are unsuitable habitats.

Farther north in the Missouri's drainage, the forests diminished and pronghorns ventured successfully across the river into the eastern parts of the Dakotas and beyond.

Conversely, riparian forests extended the range of white-tailed deer westward into the prairie states; forested river corridors reach like fingers into grasslands where the deer otherwise would not have found suitable habitat in presettlement times.

Similarly, woodchucks (*Marmota monax*) moved westward across the Flint Hills using the riparian corridors along tributaries of the Kansas River.

WATER AND WILDLIFE POPULATIONS

Water's impact on wildlife populations takes many different forms. For many animals, successful breeding is directly or indirectly related to water, usually in the form of precipitation. For example, the harvest of cottontails (*Sylvilagus floridanus*) in New Jersey on the first day of the hunting season was related to the combined amounts of rain falling during March and September.

Higher amounts of rainfall in these months diminished the number of cottontails killed per hunter . In this relationship, the March rainfall probably influenced the survival rates among the first litters of the year, whereas rainfall in September likely governed the late-summer breeding production from jubenile cottontails. Several species of common game ducks, particularly in the genus *Anas*, depend largely on semipermanent wetlands for nesting habitat.

Much of the North American population of mallards (*A. platyrbyncbos*), pintails (*A. acuta*), and other ducks breeds on the prairie potholes of the northern Great Plains. Potholes are capable of producing more than half of the game ducks available for hunting. However, as is typical of a prairie ecosystem, the northern plains commonly experience droughts.

The result is a regime of wet-dry periods that directly affects the nesting habitat available for waterfowl. With drought and the lack of spring runoff, the potholes are diminished temporarily in their carrying capacity, and breeding waterfowl experience reduced production or are

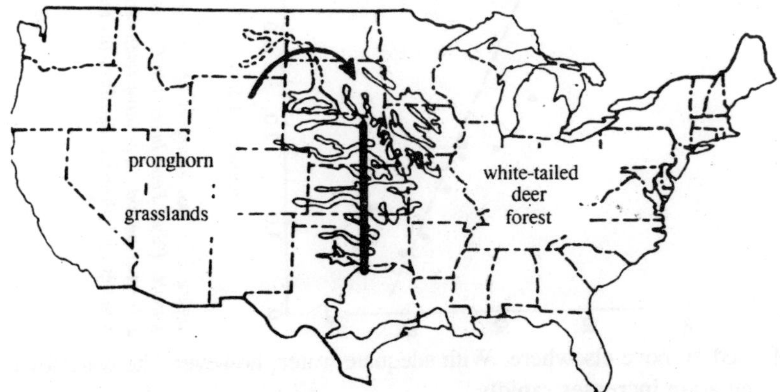

Figure 2.1: Generalized map of riparian forest intrusions into North America's grassland interior.

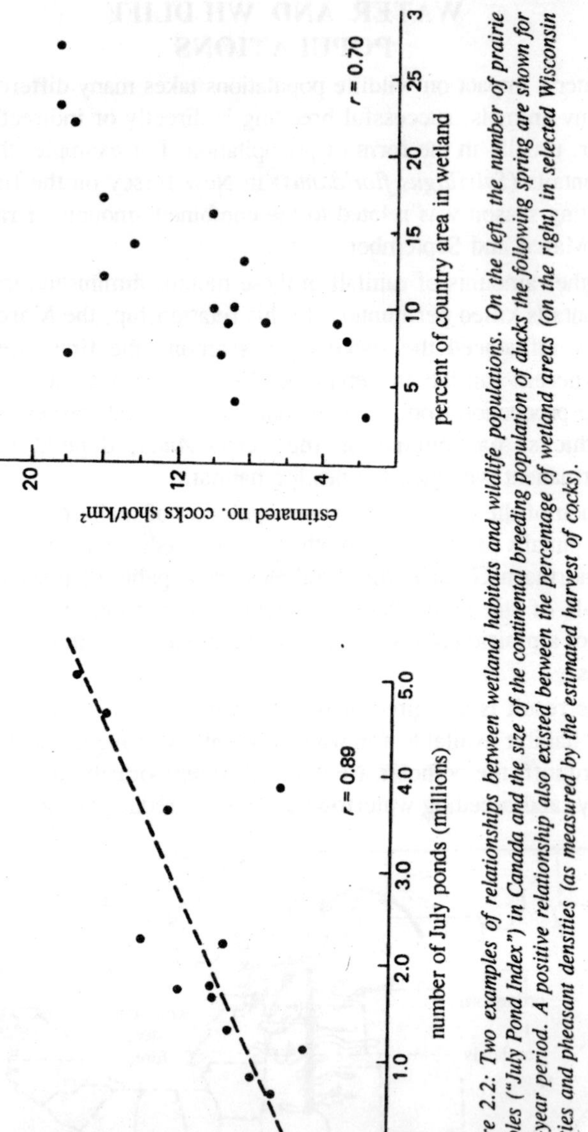

Figure 2.2: Two examples of relationships between wetland habitats and wildlife populations. On the left, the number of prairie potholes ("July Pond Index") in Canada and the size of the continental breeding population of ducks the following spring are shown for a 10-year period. A positive relationship also existed between the percentage of wetland areas (on the right) in selected Wisconsin counties and pheasant densities (as measured by the estimated harvest of cocks).

forced to move elsewhere. With adequate water, however, the waterfowl population increases rapidly.

Thus, a census known as the *July Pond Index* was developed to assess the availability of prime breeding habitat for ducks. Crissey

(1969) subsequently plotted numbers of breeding ducks against the numbers in July ponds available the previous year.

The strong statistical relationship that resulted underscores the value of habitat assessment as a useful indicator of wildlife populations and, of course, the immense value of potholes as waterfowl breeding habitat. Also shown in Figure elsewhere in this chapter is a similar correlation between the area of wetlands in Wisconsin and pheasant (*Phasianus colchicus*) densities.

Bobwhites (*Colinus virginianus*) are widely distributed in the United States and are among the most popular of game birds. Millions are harvested each year by sportsmen, making bobwhite management of paramount importance for many state conservation agencies.

This concern has resulted in comprehensive studies of bobwhites (Stoddard 1931 is a classic, but, more recently) and hundreds of other research reports. The volume of data available clearly illustrates that bobwhite populations are highly responsive to climatic patterns, particularly as measured by rainfall.

In the heartland of South Carolina's best bobwhite habitat, for example, drought reduced the number of juvenile quail per adult female to 4.9 versus an 11-year average of 9.1 and a maximum of 13.2. Similarly, Kiel (1976) found a linear relationship between rainfall and the age ratios of bobwhite on the King Ranch in Texas.

Bobwhite populations thus have remarkable shifts in abundance, responding with "boom or bust" years. Of four types of weather patterns monitored along with bobwhite populations for 25 years, Stanford (1972) found that quail are most severely reduced by droughts and high temperatures. The following condensed list reflects the variety of effects produced by limited rainfall.

1. Pairing, covey breakup, and nesting are delayed, limited, or fail to occur at all.
2. Smaller clutches are laid and incubated; high nest abandonment occurs among normal-sized clutches.
3. Females are emaciated and die incubating; eggs spoil from high ground temperatures before incubation begins; desiccation traps hatching chicks in their eggshells; uneven hatching prompts females to leave their nests prematurely with fewer chicks.
4. Large percentage of adults lack broods in the summer; above average number of males alone care for small broods.
5. The normal second hatching peak (in August) does not occur.

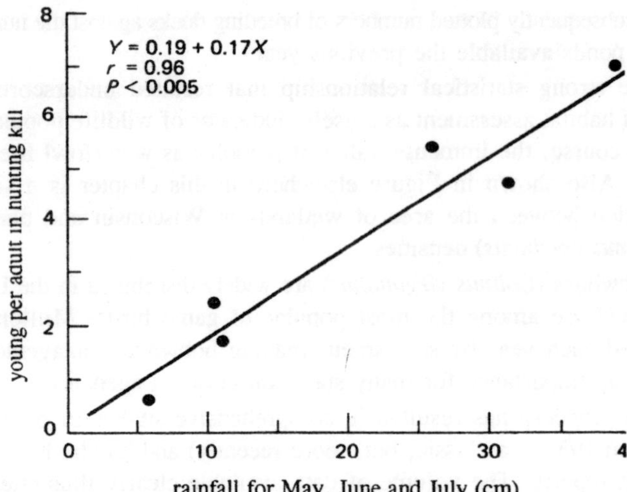

Figure 2.3: Relationship between rainfall in late springearly summer and the ratio of young to adult bobwhites bagged in south Texas.

For California quail (*Lophortyx californicus*), McMillan (1964) found only 35 percent young in the harvest when rainfall averaged 16 cm, whereas 70 percent young occurred in years when rainfall averaged 30 cm. The difference between good and poor reproduction for California quail is based largely on the annual increment produced from renesting efforts; in years of low rainfall, renesting is limited and the overall production of young is reduced greatly.

The western limits of bobwhite distribution are irregular and fluctuate locally with precipitation and perhaps other environmental factors. Rainfall patterns in the Rolling Plains of Texas, for example, vary annually from about 18 cm to more than 127 cm, and cause major fluctuations in bobwhite populations.

In describing these conditions, Jackson emphasized that this problem for wildlife managers is not unlike a similar situation in agricultural management. Dry years inflict crop losses, too, but these failures ultimately have stimulated better methods of land management. This lesson should not be missed in quail management, as repetition of outdated techniques such as predator control, stocking, and closed or reduced hunting are ineffective responses when rainfall shortages temporarily depress quail densities.

The flux of quail densities at the periphery of their distributions also was suggested in Oklahoma where Schemnitz studied a sympatric population of bobwhites and scaled quail (*Callipepla squamata*). During

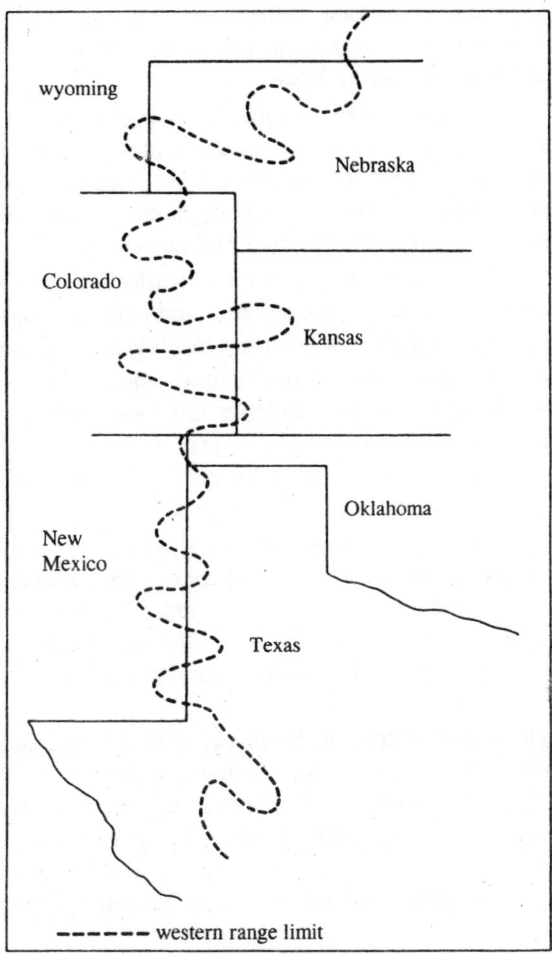

Figure 2.4: Approximate western limits of bobwhite. The irregular nature of the boundary reflects year-to-year changes in precipitation.

3 consecutive years of drought, bobwhite rapidly declined, with juveniles making up less than 48 percent of the autumn population. In contrast, young scaled quail made up nearly 75 percent of the fall population during the same period, and the population increased.

On a long-term basis, the distribution of these species, as reflected by their densities, swings back and forth with extremes in precipitation. Bobwhite breed with a minimum of 40 cm of rainfall , whereas scaled quail experience successful reproduction with as little as 15 cm.

Production of wild turkeys (*Meleagris gallopavo*) likewise depends on seasonal rainfall. Remarkable differences in juvenile-adult age ratios-from 0 to 576 poults per 100 adult hens-were recorded for a 10-year period on the King Ranch in Texas.

Beasom and Pattee (1980) explained nearly all of this variation with models primarily based on soil moisture storage and rainfall from the preceding late summer and autumn months. Egg production, rather than nesting activities or poult survival, apparently is the critical phase in the reproductive cycle determining productivity in wild turkeys.

And, whereas the causative agent directly affecting egg development is unknown, the influence of late summer and autumn rainfall prior to the breeding season triggers a mechanism involving vegetational quality.

Similarly, Francis (1967) formulated an equation based, in large measure, on precipitation and available soil moisture that accurately predicted the productivity of California quail. Teer et al. (1965) found that population densities of white-tailed deer in Texas were related to the precipitation occurring in the previous year.

In drought years, the relationship was especially close and lessened only when rainfall again occurred in average or above-average amounts. *Sowls* (1961) reported strong indications of reduced reproduction among javelina (*Tayassu tajacu*) in Arizona following uncommonly dry years. Such relationships suggest that precipitation controls the populations of some game species.

The significance of control, however, is manifested largely under extreme conditions (e.g., drought) rather than when precipitation falls at or near its long-term mean. Barring such extremes, most species seem geared to normal precipitation patterns. For example, jackrabbits (*Lepus californicus*) have two peaks of reproduction during the year, apparently coinciding with the two rainy periods normally occurring in Arizona.

Physiological and Behavioural Responses

That some wildlife populations may respond to water in positive or negative ways has been shown in the preceding discussions. How this happens is not always clear, although the why seems more certain. Namely, it makes little sense for eggs to hatch successfully if the habitat's carrying capacity is so diminished by water shortages that there follows little or no chance for the young to survive.

Even waterfowl nesting on dry land-that otherwise might successfully produce and hatch eggs in years of drought-require aquatic habitat for rearing their broods. Reproductive efforts for water-dependent species, if proceeding routinely in dry years, thus would remain only

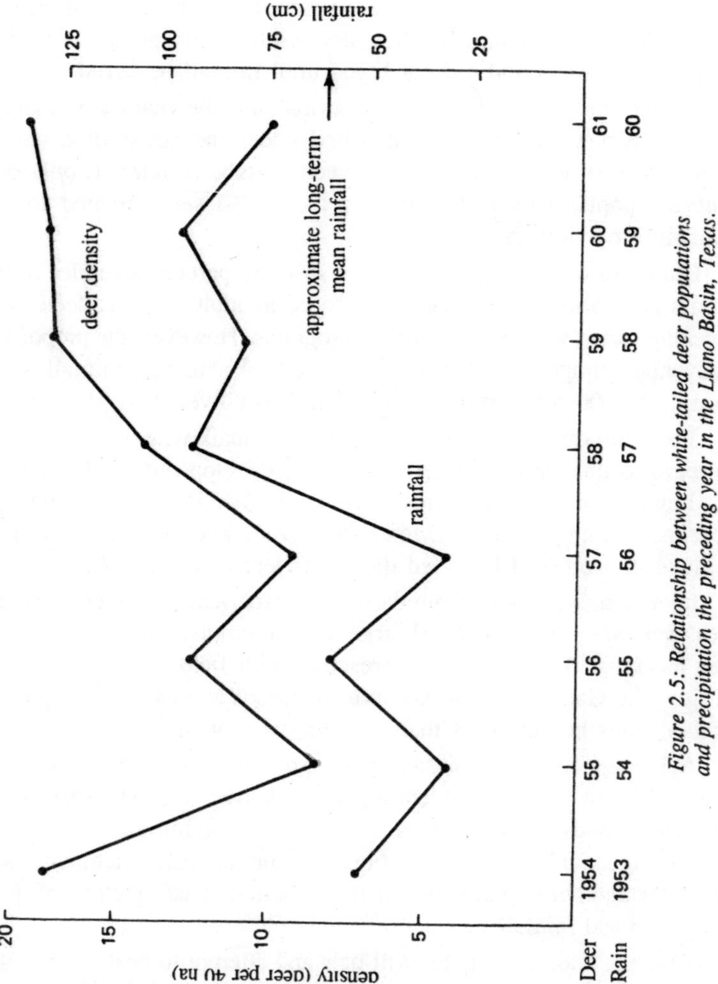

Figure 2.5: Relationship between white-tailed deer populations and precipitation the preceding year in the Llano Basin, Texas.

fruitless exercises, costly in energy, and contrary to the overriding dictum of natural selection.

Returning to quail for the moment, we find that these game birds apparently have evolved a trigger mechanism for breeding that is dependent on rainfall. Lehmann found a high correlation between rainfall and bobwhite reproduction, and suggested that reduced amounts of vitamin A in dry years limit breeding.

Carotene is the precursor of vitamin A, and normally is contained in green foliage. As the succulence of green vegetation usually is a function of precipitation, the amount of carotene varies with rainfall.

Thus, in droughts, carotene levels are reduced and vitamin A ultimately is not available to quail. With a dry winter and spring, bobwhite remained in coveys and did not breed until rainfall occurred.

Winter mortality also was above normal, and the vitamin A reserves in their livers were greatly diminished under the stress of drought. Similar results were recorded between Gambel's quail (*Lophortyx gambelii*) populations and rainfall ; these also seem related to the availability of vitamin A.

Hungerford (1964) recorded only 19 to 28 percent juveniles in the autumn population when vitamin A stored in adult livers collected the preceding spring was less than 400 micrograms. However, the proportion of juveniles jumped to 74 percent in a year of abundant rainfall when more than 1600 micrograms of vitamin A per liver were stored.

The reproductive organs of Gambel's quail with less than 550 micrograms of stored vitamin A failed to develop during the normal breeding season, but adult birds were not harmed by the deficiency. In experiments with penned bobwhites, Nestler showed that fewer juveniles survived in broods of hens fed diets deficient in vitamin A.

Interestingly, broods from these hens experienced higher mortality rates even when they were fed large dietary supplements of vitamin A after hatching. These results correspond with field studies indicating that juvenile Gambel's quail are more vigorous and experience greater survival rates in wet years than in years of drought.

A linkage between rainfall, plant growth, and reproduction was indicated by an analysis of plant hormones known as phytoestrogens in the green foods of California quail. The physiological action of phytoestrogens inhibits reproduction in some domestic mammals, and may offer another explanation for the "boom or bust" pattern of quail production and rainfall.

Whereas California quail will pair and attempt to nest even in dry years, these efforts result in as few as 25 young per 100 adults. In one study, the crop contents of adults collected before and during the breeding season in a dry year revealed reduced volumes of foods, but the food contained detectable amounts of phytoestrogens. The plants were no less available, but their growth was stunted and poor.

In the following year, when rainfall was generous, large amounts of green foods were consumed from the vigorous growth of forbs and grasses. Phytoestrogens in these samples were virtually absent, and 325 young per 100 adults subsequently were produced. In an accompanying experiment with penned quail, birds receiving a diet containing phytoestrogens initiated laying 2 months later and produced 81 percent fewer eggs than did those fed a phytoestrogen-free diet.

Based on these studies, Leopold et al. concluded that the presence or absence of phytoestrogens in the foliage of annual vegetation may well coordinate quail reproduction with the prospective food resources later available for broods. In Australia, the seasonal flooding in the MurrayDarling drainage normally stimulates breeding in local fish populations.

These fishes respond to a temperature threshold, below which breeding is inhibited. Above the threshold, however, flooding is required to induce breeding activity. Unfortunately, water impounded behind Murray-Darling dams is thermally stratified, so that cold water released from the bottoms of the dams depresses the temperature and inhibits breeding downstream for considerable distances.

Another striking relationship occurs among some species of Australian waterfowl. Frith reported that breeding in grey teal (*Anas gibberifrons*) develops directly in response to rising water levels. In inland Australia, where most of these birds normally nest, there is no regularly defined breeding season.

Grey teal initiate courtship and nest whenever the billabongs and other depressions are rapidly filled; breeding might occur in midwinter one year, in midsummer the next, and may be skipped altogether in years when water supplies are inadequate. As shown in Figure elsewhere in this chapter, gonadal development closely parallels the pattern of the steadily rising water, although the nutritional status of the birds affected this response.

Sexual activities begin almost immediately with virtually every male at once seeking a mate in a highly compressed period of courtship. Eggs may be produced in as few as 10 days after the water begins rising, and nests occur in every conceivable site throughout the affected area.

If the rise in water levels is not great, only the local population breeds, but if a major flood develops, immense flocks of nomadic teal appear and breed also. Flooding initiated from rainfall or melting snow occurring at distant sites suffices to initiate breeding: when the water travels downstream, the flooding stimulates breeding of grey teal even in the absence of local rainfall.

Local rainstorms that are insufficient to change the water levels fail to trigger breeding. Recently, Chrome (1986) suggested that the massive production of invertebrates when the dry wetlands refill is responsible for the onset of breeding in grey teal, rather than the rainfall and rising water levels per se.

Wildebeest (*Connochaetes taurinus*) and perhaps some other grazing species in Africa exhibit a remarkable response to rainfall. Because a premium exists for fresh grass, wildebeest rapidly abandon their grazing areas for those where rain stimulates new growth. Talbot and Talbot (1963) found that every major movement of wildebeest herds was associated with rainfall.

Herds of 100,000 animals may turn in their tracks to move toward a rainstorm, covering distances of 50 km or more a day. The sound of thunder or the smell of rain may trigger these movements, but sight seems the primary sense attracting wildebeest to a distant storm.

Rainfall on the African plains is localized during the dry season, and dark columns of clouds 80 km distant are seen easily. The stimulus of rain is strongest when the plains are dry; at such times, wildebeest even leave areas of adequate forage when rains fall elsewhere on the plains.

Once there, the wildebeest mill about for a day or two until fresh grass appears. Occasionally mistakes occur, and wildebeests move long distances only to find that the rain fell on wooded hills instead of on the plains. On balance, however, this response remains an adaptation that gives wildebeest the best chance of finding fresh grass in a semiarid environment.

Some animals can manufacture water within their digestive systems. Reliance on metabolic water has freed some animals from the necessity of drinking (e.g., kangaroo rats, *Dipodomys* spp.). The manufacturing process, simply stated, is the recombination of the carbohydrates available in the diet.

Seeds are a common source, with each molecule of a simple carbohydrate ($C_6H_{12}O_6$) potentially producing 6 molecules of H_2O for the animal's needs. Metabolic water contributes 18 percent of the total daily water requirements for kit foxes (*Vulpes macrotis*) and, because kit foxes live in areas devoid of free water, the balance is obtained as preformed water in the bodies of their prey.

Kit foxes thus require at least 175 g of prey daily to meet their needs for preformed water, and more prey is needed for this purpose than for energy demands. Animals producing metabolic water often have concomitant adaptions for water conservation.

These include highly effective kidneys or other mechanisms that wring virtually all usable water from the urine before it is eliminated, and behavioural patterns that reduce water loss. Sand grouse (*Pterocles* spp.) inhabit some of the most arid regions on earth, including the Sahara and Kalahari deserts in Africa.

Because the nests of sand grouse are often located several kilometers from the nearest water, ornithologists have long questioned how the chicks drink. In answer, Cade and Maclean (1967) described a remarkable adaptation whereby the male sand grouse carries water to the young in its feathers.

The male's abdominal plumage is highly specialized for this purpose and, in fact, holds more water than a paper towel or a cellulose sponge of equal weight. Water in the feathers will, of course, evaporate in flight, but even so, tests indicate that a sand grouse beginning a 32-km flight with 25 g of water can deliver 10-18 g to the brood per trip.

On arrival, the male stands erectly, allowing the young birds to strip water from the specialized feathers. In the past, the small number of natural water sources undoubtedly restricted sand grouse populations, but, more recently, man-made water developments have enhanced the birds' distribution and numbers in parts of their overall range.

Sand grouse are obligate drinkers surviving in water-poor environments, and thus demonstrate model examples of the ways evolution involves adaptive compromises. It was once thought that nasal glands rinsed away salt water entering the sensitive nasal membranes of seabirds. Later, research determined that the glands secrete highly concentrated saline fluids, functioning in effect as an extrarenal mechanism for eliminating salts.

Technau (1936) showed that the development of the nasal (or salt) glands in seabirds was highly correlated with each species' association with seawater. Not only do seabirds have large nasal glands when compared with terrestrial species, but the glands' development also varies within subspecies of seabirds, depending on their use of salt water.

Terrestrial birds have rudimentary nasal glands but are unable to secrete salts. Among aquatic species, the development and function of the glands depend on each individual's exposure to salt water. In ducks, for example, nasal glands of individuals emanating from freshwater marshes show little development, whereas those of the same species raised on saline lakes have well-developed, functional glands.

There may be racial differences in other cases. Among mallards, a resident race living on the coast of Greenland exhibits a well-developed nasal gland, whereas those of the European race are much reduced. Thus, the development and function of nasal glands in birds depends on two factors, a primary genetic factor (i.e., marine versus terrestrial species) and a secondary environmental effect of salt stress.

Individual aquatic birds possessing the genetically adapted nasal glands may show temporary function when they are confronted with salt-water environments, only to have the gland regress when the birds move on to freshwater habitats (and vice versa).

Cooch (1964) examined the possibility that impairment of nasal glands in ducks was related to avian botulism. In a series of experiments, it was determined that sublethal dosages of *Clostridium botulinum* toxin (type C) can cause mortalities in ducks drinking salt water.

Ducks drinking fresh water, but given the same dosages of toxin, showed improved survival. With little or no toxin, salts in the water were excreted by the birds' nasal glands. Massive dosages of the toxin, of course, remain lethal, but more moderate exposure to the toxin seems to impair the functional ability of the gland, and leads to death when the osmolarity of the blood plasma can no longer be regulated.

Table 2.2: Percent Survival of Pintails Subjected to Five Doses of Clostridium botulinum (Type C) Toxin in Association with Three Levels of Water Salinity.

	Toxin Doses				
Water Type	2000	1500	1000	500	250
Fresh	67	67	100	100	100
5 percent NaCl	17	50	50	83	100
10 percent NaCl	0	33	50	67	83

In effect, these experiments suggest that Wetmore's early (1915) implication of "alkali poisoning" may describe botulism-induced mortality more accurately than supposed.

The physiological compatibility—or incompatibility—of some organisms with regional precipitation regimes has implications for some management strategies. Wild turkeys belong to a single species but exhibit six reasonably well-defined races.

A constellation of environmental factors undoubtedly contributed to the formation of these races, but rainfall patterns influence at least the Rio Grande race and its distribution. An isohyet of 81 cm of rainfall coincides well with the eastern edge of this race's distribution, beyond which, in wetter areas, it does not survive and another race occurs. Glazener (1967) thus suggested that the efforts of past decades to transplant Rio Grande turkeys from Texas into the southeastern states were doomed from the onset.

These restoration efforts simply used the "wrong" race, one ill-adapted to the rainfall regime of the wetter release sites. On the other hand, successful transplants in Kansas, Oklahoma, and New Mexico were made within the precipitation limits tolerated by Rio Grande turkeys.

In fact, some of these and other transplants, especially those in Nebraska and North Dakota, were established well outside the race's original distribution. The Russian ecologist Formozov formulated a classification for mammals and their relationships with snow: *chionophobes*, those avoiding snow; *cbioneupbores*, those adapted to snow; and *chionophiles*, those highly specialized or restricted to snow.

Pruitt (1959) considers New World caribou (*Rangifer tarandus*), unlike Old World reindeer, as chionophiles because they spend two-thirds of their annual cycle in snow and because of their behavioural and morphological adaptations to snow conditions. In fact, "snow caribou" seems a more appropriate name for the species than barren-ground caribou.

Caribou in Canada are confined in winter by snow having certain characteristics. Soft, thin snow is preferred, and, as harder snow conditions develop, the animals progressively travel to sites where winter forage is more accessible. Snowfall and topography interact so that the winter migration routes of caribou likely are governed by these features, indicating a behavioural reaction to favourable pathways through snowfields perhaps not unlike the flyways of birds.

Within their wintering habitat, caribou progressively forage more on upland areas as snow depths increase on lower-lying sites. The energy expended by caribou digging ("cratering") in snow for lichens increased proportionately with the density of the snow cover.

About twice as much energy was required for cratering in dense snow with a thin crust, compared with a light, uncrusted snow, and increased fourfold in snow compacted by a snowmobile. Thus, snow depth and density interact on the energy caribou expend when feeding; the energic cost of obtaining food must remain low or be offset by the energy derived from the forage.

The altitudinal migrations of moose in British Columbia also are correlated strongly with snow depths. Spring migration upward to higher elevations is marked by rapidly decreasing depths of 46 cm or less, whereas downward movements in winter coincide with increasing accumulations of snow at higher elevations.

Under these conditions, the winter range of moose is dynamic. Snow depths, density, and hardness are important features interacting with the winter activities of moose, but unless snow depths exceed 70 cm, moose experience little or no serious restrictions of movement. Telfer and Kelsall (1984) have discussed the adaptations, including track loads, of some large North American mammals for survival in snow.

Ice also is important in the breeding behaviour and management of several polar species. For example, harp seals (*Phoca groenlandica*) whelp in the rough ice near the interior of ice floes where there is some degree of shelter. Female harp seals mate again soon after whelping, but the embryos do not begin development for 11 weeks afterward.

Both the breeding schedule and the phenomenon of delayed implantation are responses to ice patterns; mating takes place when the herd is congregated in the floes, and the pups are born a year later when ice conditions again are optimal. The pups' white coat, lasting only for about 2 weeks after birth, is a valuable fur, promoting passionate controversies about harvesting the young animals while they are still nursing their mothers.

The pelts' whiteness makes it difficult to photograph the pups aerially against a background of snow and ice for inventories governing the annual harvest. However, the white pelt absorbs ultraviolet radiation, so that special film produces a black image of the pups against the white background, and a useful census of production now is possible.

WATER, DISASTERS, AND HARD TIMES

Water-related disasters befalling animal populations, even if occasional, may require management action, as occurs in the aftermaths of flooding, blizzards, storm tides, or droughts. Virtually nothing can be done, of course, about the disaster per se, but harvest regulations may be tightened when large segments of wildlife populations are killed or fail to reproduce because of a short-term calamity.

Severe winter drought contributed to massive losses in Texas when 21,000-30,000 deer died between January and August, 1962, within part of a single county. Densities before the die-off were 26 deer per 40 ha and about 15 per 40 ha afterward, indicating a 44 percent reduction in the population.

With the return of normal rainfall, the deer population recovered in 1 year's time to about the same level that existed prior to the die-off. Spevak (1983) recorded decreasing species diversity within a community of desert rodents during a drought, followed by recovery to predrought levels when rainfall patterns returned to normal; densities also decreased for nearly all of the rodents during the drought.

In 1982-83, an 11-month drought reduced kangaroos (*Macro pus* spp.) by 40 percent across more than 1 million km^2 of eastern Australia. Such droughts and their impact on kangaroo numbers may be intrinsic to the ecology of kangaroos, thereby counterbalancing much of the rapid population growth that occurs between droughts.

Heavy snowfall can limit populations of deer and other ungulates. Deep snows may entrap animals for extended periods, and starvation follows when local food supplies are exhausted. In the Adirondack region of New York, Severinghaus (1947) recorded mortalities of 21 deer per 2.6 km^2 when snows were deep, long-lasting, and late in the year.

Deep snows lasting 5 weeks significantly affected deer mortality, and those exceeding 10 weeks caused severe losses. Snow depths in excess of 50 cm retard movements, especially among fawns. In Utah, snows up to 90 cm in depth caused mortalities of 9 to 42 percent, depending on the available forage, within segments of that state's mule deer herd.

Such conditions often bring forth public pressure for artificial feeding programs, but this short-sighted remedy usually further elevates deer populations above the carrying capacities of winter ranges. In fact, herds kept in proper balance with winter forage supplies suffered only slightly higher than normal mortality in deep snow.

Conversely, on depleted ranges, losses were magnified several times over. The condition of the snow, particularly its density and water content, interacts with the amount of snow on deer mortality. Light, fluffy snows are troublesome as the legs of deer penetrate deeply, making movement extremely difficult and energetically expensive. Conversely, wetter snow packs may develop a crust that enables deer to move rather easily on the snow's surface.

Snows accumulating in burned-over or clearcut forest limit elk (*Cervus elapbus canadensis*) distributions in winter; with 60 cm or more of snow, elk seek out coniferous cover or sites at lower elevations even at the expense of leaving better forage behind. In the central Rocky Mountains, mule deer follow a snow-imposed rotation in their grazing pattern, moving on to other areas as the snow depth increases above 46 cm; in severe winters, more than 90 percent of the winter range may be excluded because of deep snows.

The concentrations of deer eventually crowding into sites with less snow (usually southern-facing slopes) severely deplete forage supplies, and as many as 381 carcasses were located in about 5.2 km^2 of overbrowsed winter habitat. Snow depths affect the movements and interactions of both predators and prey.

Einarsen (1948) found a herd of nearly 1,000 pronghorns concentrated on 26 km^2 of land during a severe Oregon winter, and described a scenario where pronghorn vulnerability to coyote (*Canis latrans*) predation was increased by deep snows.

Moose on Isle Royale seek dense cover along the lake edges when snows are deep, and wolf (*Canis lupus*) packs run on the ice bordering the shoreline at these times. Thus, Peterson (1977) located significantly more moose kills near shorelines when snows were more than 50 cm deep, but at lesser snow depths, more kills occurred elsewhere on the island. Snow depths also influenced the age structure of moose killed by wolves. Losses of calves increased from 30 percent to 47 percent when snow depths exceeded 76 cm.

Within the adult segment of the Isle Royale moose population, the vulnerability of "prime-aged" animals changed with snow depth. Normally, adults between one and six years of age avoid significant wolf predation, but kills of adult moose in these younger age classes increased dramatically with deeper snowfall.

Snow depths also have important implications for wolf ecology as well as for prey populations. In Minnesota, wolf kills of white-tailed deer increased in winters with greater snow depth. Deep snows influenced the vulnerability of deer by acting as a physical impedance for escape and by reducing fat reserves (i.e., restricted feeding and increased energy costs from travel).

Thus, to a large extent, the food supply of wolves is determined by an external factor, snow depth. Wolves breed in midwinter and whelp in spring; hence, litter size and pup survival may be affected by the vagaries of winter snowfalls.

The results of severe winters, including deep snows, on the age-specific mortality of deer may be pronounced. Of 323 black-tailed deer (*Odocoileus hemionus sitkensis*) starving in southeastern Alaska,

Table 2.3: Percent Age Distribution of Adult Moose Killed by Wolves in Relation to Snow Depth.

Adult Age Classes	*Snow Depth*		
	Less than 51 cm	*51-76 cm*	*More than 76 cm*
1—3	5.9	18.2	29.7
4—6	8.8	10.2	13.5
7—9	38.2	25.0	27.0
10—12	35.3	30.7	13.6
13—16	11.8	15.9	16.2

56 percent were fawns, 8 percent were adults less than five years old, and 36 percent were older adults.

The heavy losses of fawns were further reflected in changes in the age ratio before and after a critical 15-day period when snow depth increased to a maximum of 210 cm; the ratio dropped from more than 45 fawns:100 adults to about 15:100 when warmer weather and rains finally ameliorated the severe conditions.

Snow depths in the winter preceding the birth of Dall sheep (*Ovis dalli*) were correlated strongly with lamb:ewe ratios about one month after the lambing season in Mount McKinley National Park. The inversity of this relationship probably results from a combination of reduced rates of pregnancy, natality, and/or neonatal survival in years of heavy snowfall.

Snow cover during the nesting season in Spitsbergen was associated with the percentage of young barnacle geese (*Branta leucopsis*) present in the autumn population; a good correlation existed even though the population data were obtained four months after the nesting season ended.

In this case, snow cover influenced the proportion of adults nesting successfully; brood size was not affected. Hence, the percentage of juvenile geese varied from less than 3 percent in years with prolonged snow cover to 25 percent in years when snow did not persist as long.

Similarly, the date when snow cover was 50 percent cleared correlated with several parameters associated with the breeding activities of Canada geese nesting on the tundra of the Northwest Territories. Among these was a strong association between the persistence of snow cover and the percentage of eggs failing to hatch.

In Alaska, Hansen (1961) underscored the effects that storm tides might have on nesting black brant (*Branta nigricans*); these and other waterfowl often adapt to rising water by elevating their nests, but the

Table 2.4: Changes in Age Ratios (Fawn: Adult) of Black-Tailed Deer with Snow Depth.

Date	*Fawns Per 100 Adults*	*Snow Depth (cm)*
December 15	48	25
February 26	57	46
March 1	46	76
March 8	29	178
March 10	36	137
March 13	33	117
March 16	50	71
March 19	13	58
March 20	8	53
March 21	17	48
March 23	14	41
April 10	14	30

hatching success of eggs was limited under flood conditions. Whereas most other waterfowl attempt second nestings when their first nests are destroyed, brant are physiologically unable to renest, and large-scale flooding may cause major population depressions.

A torrential rain of 61 cm in 5 hours followed 2 years later by the heavy rains of Hurricane Carla flooded 3000 ha of prime habitat of Attwater prairie chickens (*Tympanuchus cupido attwateri*) on the Texas Gulf Coast; prior to these floods, the site had the highest-known density of this endangered species, whereas none was seen there in the years afterward.

Cultivation of the better-drained lands at this site forced the prairie chickens into lower areas, thus magnifying the impact of these floods on their population. Fire, as well as cultivation, also may influence the effects of flooding on ground-nesting birds. Low, wet sites escape fire, so that when bobwhites were attracted to these remaining patches of nesting cover, their nests were flooded by the next heavy rain.

Changes in the thermal structures of the Pacific Ocean at equatorial latitudes initiate what can become one of the most disastrous events on earth. South Americans call the event El Nino ("The Child") because of the coincidental timing with the Christmas season; episodes are irregular but recur at an average of about 4-5 years.

The phenomenon is an anomalous incursion of warm water in the eastern Pacific that may unleash droughts, floods, and other powerful forces across the globe. The results sometimes produce widespread suffering and losses of human and animal life but always affect the abundance and distribution of marine organisms on the Pacific coast of South America.

The precise causes of El Nino are unclear, but the mechanics of an episode include surges of warm water—known as Kelvin waves—flowing toward the western coast of South America, and a deep surface layer of warm water developing offshore. Normally, the currents flow in the opposite direction, leaving only a shallow layer of warm water at the surface along the western coastline of the Pacific basin.

The usual pattern also includes an upwelling of nutrient-enriched cold water off the coasts of Peru and Ecuador. Upon reaching the surface, the enriched cold water supports an immense base of plankton and, in turn, a huge pyramid of marine life. With El Nino, however, the upwelling is contained within the thick layer of warm water, thereby interrupting the flow of nutrients to the surface and collapsing the food web.

The consequences of El Nino may disrupt socioeconomic conditions as well as biological communities on both land and sea. In one episode, the catch of anchovies (*Engraulis ringens*) in Peru and Chile fell from 13 to 2 million tons, thereby sharply reducing foreign trade and initiating a wave of high unemployment.

Conversely, tropical species of marine organisms for a time may invade the coastal zones as a consequence of the switch from cold to warm water during an El Nino. These include several species of sharks, marlin, and other fishes, as well as sea turtles; these events may produce temporary changes in the fishing and dietary habits of Peruvians. Fishermen as far north as California have been confused by catches of unfamiliar species, and millions of small tropical crab (*Pleuroncodes planipes*) clogged the pipes at the San Onofre Nuclear Power Plant during a recent El Nino.

Because of food shortages, some seabirds moved as much as 1600 km from their normal range. The reproductive success of seabirds as far north as Oregon was reduced because of the abnormally high water temperatures associated with a recent El Nino.

The stress of El Nino also alters the depositional pattern of new shell material on some species of mollusks. Because the shells expand in increments similar to tree rings, it seems possible to detect El Nino events in the archaeological record from shells unearthed in ancient middens.

The El Nino of 1982-83 was particularly severe; it caused major perturbations in much of the world, including epidemics of typhoid fever, fires, crop losses, mudslides, and invasions of snakes and insects. Barber and Chavez (1983) reported as much as a 20-fold decrease in the biomass and productivity of phytoplankton resulting from the diminished upwelling of nutrients.

At the time, anchovy stocks still were depleted from an earlier El Nino and the overfishing that followed. Thus, the consequences of the 1982-83 episode were catastrophic for marine organisms dependent on these and other food fishes.

Colonies of Humboldt penguins (*Spheniscus humboldti*) in Peru suffered reduced breeding success and increased mortality as a result of the 1982-83 El Nino; the population declined 65 percent-from 6000-8000 birds prior to 1982 to 2000-3000 birds in 1984. Seabirds of several other species also experienced wholesale reproductive failure in the 1982-83 episode, as witnessed at Christmas Island.

Instead of reaching an expected breeding population of about 10,500 pairs, frigate birds (*Fregata spp.*) gave up nesting and departed for areas where small fish, squid, and other food still flourished. Abandoned nests and dead or starving nestlings were all that remained on Christmas Island from the impact of El Nino.

Torrential rains associated with El Nino also thwarted nesting efforts. A variety of terns (*Sterna spp.*), shearwaters (*Puffinus spp.*), and boobies (*Sula spp.*) experienced similar fates. In this instance, the adult birds responded to the adversities of El Nino by dispersing, thereby channeling the limited food resources into their own survival rather than continuing the energy-demanding activities of nesting and rearing young.

Because most seabirds are long-lived species, the strategy of skipping a breeding season for the short term is an appropriate evolutionary adaption to food shortages. In extreme situations, however, adult birds sometimes starve and their carcasses begin littering the beaches . Overall, only 150,000 seabirds, or less than 2 percent, of an estimated population of 14 million returned to their nesting sites on Christmas Island at the end of the 1982-83 El Nino.

Major declines in seabird populations also occurred in the Galapagos Islands from the same episode. On Isla Daphne Major, the exceptional rainfall produced thick vegetation, which greatly diminished the suitability of some nesting sites formerly used by boobies—a habitat limitation posing long-term effects.

Similar evidence for the stress of El Nino on the food web can be found among marine mammals. According to Barber and Chavez (1983), all of the pups of the Galapagos fur seal (*Arctocephalus galapagoensis*) born during 1982 died before the end of the 1982-83 episode; juvenile mortality also occurred during the same period in three other species of seals and sea lions.

The seal pups probably died from the lack of adequate milk resulting from the poor foraging success of their mothers. As an indirect measure of the poor food supplies, the female seals foraged at sea for an average of 5 days during the El Nino, whereas 1.5 days is the typical foraging period.

Reptiles in the Galapagos Islands also were vulnerable to the extreme conditions of the 1982-83 El Nino . The surge of flood waters displaced giant tortoises (*Testudo elephantopus*) from highland habitat on the Tortoise Reserve on Santa Cruz Island. The circumstances perhaps explain how these plodding terrestrial animals colonized other islands in the Galapagos archipelago: the violence of the El Nino floods swept the tortoises into the ocean.

Also, because of changes in water temperature, larges areas of algae died on the Galapagian coast, thus eliminating the staple food for marine iguanas (*Amblyrhyncbus cristatus*). Starvation soon killed thousands of iguanas.

Reservoir Effect and Management

Organic matter accumulating in the upper horizons of exposed soils normally undergoes oxidation; this chemical process is enhanced further by the action of microbial and other biological agents. The net result-a steady release and recycling of nutrients-is essential for virtually all food chains in terrestrial systems.

In newly flooded aquatic systems, however, the impounded waters may be enriched rapidly by the sudden incorporation of plant and soil nutrients. The reaction is not unlike the explosive organic activity within a hay infusion. Production at virtually all trophic levels usually is increased substantially, although local factors such as water temperature affect the rates at which productivity accelerates.

The initial flush of nutrients may enrich the waters of larger impoundments for several years. Thereafter, further oxidation of soil organic matter is curtailed and the system eventually stabilizes at a lower nutrient level. Such dynamic enrichment of water following impoundment is known popularly as the *reservoir effect*.

Reservoir effects occur naturally on many ephemeral wetlands, among them the prairie potholes and playa lakes of the North American Great Plains. These wetlands are maintained by precipitation that is characteristically unpredictable; they accordingly undergo frequent but irregular wet-dry fluctuations promoting high biological activity after drought periods end.

A microcosm involving the reservoir effect important to waterfowl develops when melting snow forms temporary wetlands on the northern prairies. Blue-winged teal (*Anas discors*) and other ducks feeding on the invertebrate populations irrupting in the temporary wetlands derive the protein sources critical for successful breeding.

The seasonal flooding of riverbottom forests is another natural reservoir effect. These habitats remain rich, productive ecological zones because of the wet-dry cycles they experience. Among the benefits for wildlife is the availability of mast-primarily acorns-for wood ducks (*Aix sponsa*) foraging in shallowly flooded timber.

Pin oak (*Quercus palustris*) is among the more valuable producers of mast in the Mississippi Delta country, and flooding of this species in its dormant season does not affect acorn production. Pin oak stands are subject to water and other management practices leading to improved hunting success.

In addition to waterfowl, such species as swamp rabbits (*Sylvilagus aquaticus*) are associated with lowland hardwood forests, and their distribution in Missouri suggests that forests of more than 100 ha may be necessary to sustain sizable populations. A rich community of wildlife makes seasonal or permanent use of lowland forests and adjacent uplands.

However, impoundments stabilizing water levels in bottomland forests interrupt the normal flooding regime and destroy the community; trees begin falling after 3 years of flooding, reaching a maximum at 8 years. Whereas waterfowl utilization of permanently flooded bottomlands may increase for a time, the effect is temporary and declines as the man-made system matures.

Regrettably, no more than 25 percent of North America's original lowland hardwood forest remains today, a result of wholesale drainage and food-control projects. Although the area of forest lost directly to these activities may not be great, drainage promotes conversion of forested bottomlands into farmland.

Runoff from these croplands further limits the remaining forest system when siltation reduces root aeration, a primary mortality factor in lowland forests. That basic productivity can be increased temporarily when land is periodically flooded suggests that water levels might be manipulated to accrue certain advantages.

Indeed, the concept is not new, as periodic drying of ponds in Europe was considered an essential element of fish culture in 1883. Production in the ponds responded to the flush of nutrients available first to microorganisms and, ultimately, to the fishes after each dry period in the management rotation.

This strategy is well known to rice farmers as a fundamental method for increasing yields. During the dry, fallow period, the soil is enriched naturally before reflooding and the planting of the next crop. Thus, reservoir effects influence both the plant and animal components within aquatic systems. In the 1930s, reservoirs constructed by the Tennessee Valley Authority initially furnished excellent fishing.

Increased fish yields, both in numbers and in poundage, from new impoundments supported active sport and commercial fisheries. Turner (1971) recorded a doubling of fishing success (measured as the catch per man-hour) between a pre- and postimpoundment fishery in Kentucky. Fishing success was greatest in the year immediately after impoundment; it then declined in each of the following 4 years.

The weights of many species steadily increased in the same time period. Jenkins and Morais (1971) reported a negative relationship between the ages of 103 reservoirs and the biomass of bass and sunfish harvested; as the impoundments aged, catches decreased. In some impoundments, the nutrient flush and subsequent increase in benthic fish foods are supplemented by the cover afforded to young fish from submerged trees and shrubs.

The deliberate, seasonal drying of wetlands is known as *drawdown;* it, too, relies on the reservoir effect. Wildlife managers have applied drawdowns for the production of waterfowl food and cover plants, control of succession, and improvement of the interspersion of vegetation in

Table 2.5: Average Weights In Grams of Selected Fishes Harvested Before and After Impoundment, Rough River, Kentucky.

		Postimpoundment (Years)			
Species	*Preimpoundment*	1	2	3	4
Black bass	520	540	560	610	630
Sunfishes	20	40	50	50	50
Catfishes	150	180	350	560	710

wetlands. These management goals depend on the control of water supplies into and from the wetland, a feature of intensive management at many state and federal wildlife refuges.

Elaborate water-control structures and diversion schemes have been developed for such manipulations; these usually are individually tailored to meet a variety of local conditions and needs. Fredrickson and Taylor (1982) described the benefits of drawdown management and the production of moist-soil vegetation for many kinds of songbirds, shorebirds, and mammals, as well as waterfowl.

The scheme they proposed recognizes four categories of water depth: deep (more than 15 cm); medium (15 cm); shallow water and mudflat; and dry. Ideally, as many units as possible should be developed, each held at a water depth attracting different groups of wildlife.

The moist-soil management plan offers an alternative to the common practice of producing row crops as wildlife food; grains are suitable food only for waterfowl and a limited number of other species, whereas the diversity of foods encouraged by drawdown management supports an equally diverse community of wildlife.

Row crops also offer little cover and often are nutritionally incomplete, whereas natural vegetation generally overcomes these deficiencies. Furthermore, drawdown management maximizes production of most invertebrates, thereby providing a ready source of proteinaceous food required by many kinds of birds.

Midge (Chironomidae) larvae respond favourably to water-level manipulations and, as a major food of renesting pintail hens, increase the renesting efforts of these birds. A population of midge larvae in a Utah salt marsh managed for waterfowl was 18 times larger after a drawdown cycle than that of an adjacent site inundated continuously for three years .

Green-tree reservoirs are managed units of bottomland forest that are temporarily flooded during the fall and winter months; the object is to make mast crops on the forest floor available to wintering waterfowl. This system duplicates the natural flooding experienced in hardwood bottomlands in much of the South and Midwest, but, because flooding is controlled, the practice assures that water is applied in years of diminished rainfall.

The idea originated in Arkansas' pin oak bottomlands among duck hunters wishing to maintain their legendary hunting in dry years. Green-tree reservoirs offer two management values: first, unlike permanently flooded reservoirs, the trees are not killed, so that timber resources are not lost; and second, the acorn crops important as foods for wintering waterfowl remain available each year regardless of rainfall. Dramatic results were achieved, and the concept spread to other states; a duck population on one southern refuge immediately doubled, and ultimately expanded from 21,000 to as many as 100,000 birds.

Whereas several species of waterfowl respond to green-tree reservoirs, mallards and wood ducks are the principal targets for this water-management practice in the Atlantic and Mississippi flyways. In the Northeast or other regions where timber is not adapted to seasonal flooding, preliminary management schemes suggest that waterfowl use may be improved when impoundments are created, even though flooded trees may be killed.

The dynamic nature of green-tree reservoir management also affects the invertebrate foods necessary for breeding ducks. Drobney and Fredrickson (1979) recorded a shift from 33 percent invertebrate foods in the fall diet of wood duck hens to 54 percent for prelaying hens, 79 percent for laying hens, and 43 percent for postlaying hens in a large block of water-managed hardwood forest in southwestern Missouri. Depressions within green-tree reservoirs in Illinois remaining permanently flooded harbored 10 times more biomass of invertebrates in the spring than in the autumn.

BEAVER, WATER, AND WILDLIFE

Beaver (*Castor canadensis*) are renowned for their manipulation of water. Their dams alter the movement of water and, in doing so, produce significant changes in the local ecosystems. Trees flooded by beaver impoundments generally die, although in southern bottomland forests the distribution of cypress (*Cupres*sus spp.) often seems associated with the ponds beaver create.

For a time, the dead trees offer habitat for cavity-nesting birds, fungi, and a host of wood-boring insects. In the absence of foliage, the amount of light penetrating through the canopy is increased greatly. The impounded water is warmed, both from the increased amount of solar radiation and from the reduced rate of stream flow.

Siltation also is more rapid behind the dam-what once might have been a gravelly streambed becomes a mud-bottomed pond. Subtle but profound differences also occur in such basic phenomena as nitrogen cycling in streams where beaver have impounded water. Naiman and Melillo (1984) showed that nitrogen accumulations were about 1000 times greater in a subarctic stream after beaver dams modified the environment. Immense numbers of beaver once were widely distributed in North America. Estimates suggest that 60 million beaver ranged over 15.5 million km^2 at a density of about 4 animals per km^2, with a carrying capacity varying between 0.9 and 1.25 colonies per km of stream.

As much as 30-50 percent of the smaller streams within the current range of beaver may fall under the direct influence of their activities. Marked differences in the biota develop between beaver impoundments and unaffected downstream communities. A comparison in California showed that beaver ponds supported a less diverse assemblage of bottom organisms than did the more heterogeneous habitats in the stream.

However, both the numbers and the biomass of organisms in the impoundment were significantly greater. The reservoir effect, described earlier, likely explains much of the increased production both for invertebrates and fishes in beaver ponds. Knudsen (1962) reported increased production of brook trout (*Salvelinus fontinalis*) after new beaver ponds were established, but trout habitat in the ponds deteriorated a few years later.

Active beaver ponds on a small stream in Colorado provided at least 200 people with fishing recreation each summer; each person stayed an average of 2 days and caught 5 trout per day.

Some studies have uncovered few differences in the numbers of trout between beaver ponds and comparable lengths of unaltered stream, but as much as a fourfold increase in trout populations has been recorded for beaver ponds in New Mexico.

Despite these differences in fish numbers, comparative research consistently has shown that significantly larger trout (individual length and/or weight) occur in beaver ponds. Such differences may be dramatic when expressed in total weight. On the basis of a 4-year average, Gard (1961) found that trout biomass in beaver ponds reached 217 kg per ha, whereas only 36 kg per ha occurred elsewhere in the same stream.

The composition of the trout community also may be altered under the influence of beaver impoundments. In at least some instances, beaver dams present complete or partial obstacles to trout movements within streams. Upstream movements are usually more restricted than those downstream, and this limitation may have consequences when trout are denied access to their spawning habitat.

Beaver impoundments often provide nesting habitat for waterfowl. Production estimates vary between 1.6 and 3.0 ducklings per ha on

Table 2.6: Composition of a Trout Community Before and After Removal of Beaver Dams.

Species	*Composition (Percent)*	
	Before	***After***
Brown trout	74	31
Brook trout	23	16
Rainbow trout	3	53
Totals	100	100

beaver impoundments in Wisconsin and New York, -respectively. Beard (1953) identified six major components of marshlands created by beaver that favour waterfowl. These are (1) interspersion of cover with water, (2) composition of cover types, (3) water depth, (4) amount and types of food resources, (5) freedom from human disturbances, and (6) the proximity of nesting cover to brood habitat.

With these components at their best, the average number of young produced each year reached 11.4 ducklings per ha. Collins (1974) attributed the increase in duck populations during a 20-year period in Ontario to the increased numbers of active beaver ponds. In Maine, beaver ponds offer black ducks (Anas rubripes) nesting and feeding habitat, and also serve as effective waterfowl refuges during the autumn migration.

Also, black duck broods showed definite patterns correlating with active beaver ponds, largely because of suitable cover produced by stabilized water levels.

Beaver are, of course, a manageable resource in their own right. But prices for beaver pelts fluctuate somewhat cyclically in the marketplace, so that trapping efforts also vary. In off-years, beaver populations expand, often causing timber losses, flooded roadways, and diversion of man-made drainage systems. At other times, high fur prices place considerable pressure on beaver populations.

The beaver's own practice of water management may affect other wildlife such as otter (Lutra canadensis) or ruffed grouse (Bonasa umbellus), but the implications of their activities on two groups-trout and waterfowl-clearly suggest that orderly management is possible. For example, the age of beaver ponds is an important influence on waterfowl production, with newer impoundments normally having greater use than older ones.

Regularly conducted aerial surveys thus permit determinations of each pond's status so that older ponds might be identified. Artier (1963) found that the temporary drainage of beaver impoundments, followed by the seeding of millet (Echinochloa crusgalli), produced large amounts of food for ducks wintering in Alabama. Impoundments managed in this way created substantial income for landowners when they were leased for duck hunting.

Because of the unique influences beavers exert on the landscape (e.g., raised water tables, upstream sedimentation, nitrogen accumulation, and transfer of biomass from terrestrial to aquatic systems), their widespread removal undoubtedly altered watercourses throughout North America. Brayton (1984) thus described how beaver restored severely eroded riparian habitats on streams in Wyoming.

Biologists stocked the eroded areas with beaver and, because the sites were denuded of suitable vegetation, logs and branches were cut and delivered to the beavers for constructing their dams. Three years later, the silt load declined by 90 percent, erosion stopped as vegetation again stabilized the banks and, not incidentally, various kinds of wildlife returned to the restored streamside communities.

At one site, spring floods washed away the dams, so stronger building materials were added to the delivery of logs: old truck tires. The beavers immediately incorporated the tires into the log dams and, as a result, the strengthened dams withstood the spring floods. These examples of "beaver engineering" understandably have attracted the interest of land managers concerned with the restoration of damaged riparian habitats.

ALLIGATORS AND MARSH ECOLOGY

Just as bison (*Bison bison*) once dominated the ecology of the American plains, so have alligators (*Alligator mississippiensis*) assumed an influential role in southern marshes. Nowhere are these relationships more prominent than in the Everglades, where alligators shape the structure and survival of plant and animal communities.

As always, many factors are involved, but even a cursory look at the ecology of "gator holes" underscores the importance of a single species in maintaining the integrity of a larger, complex biota.

Gator holes overlay natural depressions in the limestone floor of the Everglades. Alligators clear marsh vegetation from the depression, then move the debris to the rim, forming a pool surrounded by a levee of plants and mud. *Willows* (*Salix caroliniana*) are the first woody plants that invade the elevated rim, but bald cypress (*Taxodium sp.*) characterizes the trees that eventually grow on the levees.

Understory vegetation on the levees consists of grasses, sedges, ferns, and other plants tolerant of shade. Of the herbaceous plants, flag (*Thalia geniculata*) *is* conspicuous, reaching heights of 3 m in the fresh water inside the gator hole (these plants are intolerant of the salt-water tides sometimes flooding the marshes outside the rim protecting gator holes).

Indeed, the large bananalike leaves of flag turn brown at the beginning of the winter dry season and, because they stand out against the green background of other marsh vegetation, unfortunately may guide poachers to alligator dens. The vegetation developing on the levees offers diversity otherwise lacking in much of the Everglade's "sea of grass," and hence several kinds of birds, mammals, and reptiles find food, cover, and breeding habitat on the levees.

Perhaps of greater importance, however, is that gator holes become miniature refuges of fresh water during the winter dry season, maintaining not only alligators but also other creatures dependent on water. As many as 23 species of fishes concentrate in gator holes when the water in the marshes recedes each winter, as do large numbers of crustaceans; recorded densities reach 1600 fishes and crustaceans per m^2.

Such a readily available prey base establishes food chains for predators, whereas the organic waste left by the predators, in turn, maintains a nutrient base for organisms serving as food for the fish populations.' Thus, a largely self-sustaining system develops at a critical season and, when the winter drought ends, organisms harbored in gator holes rapidly repopulate the surrounding marshes.

A particularly interesting relationship exists between gator holes and wood storks (*Mycteria americana*). These large wading birds have developed a breeding cycle coinciding with the normal dry season each winter and hence with the prey concentrated in gator holes.

Large quantities of food are required by nestling storks, and the adult birds capitalize on the dense fish populations in gator holes to meet the demands of their young. For example, wood storks and other wading birds reduced the biomass of fishes concentrated in dry-season ponds by 76 percent and their numbers by 77 percent, perhaps assuring survival through reduced competition for the remaining fish stocks during the rigors of the dry season.

Conversely, in years of exceptional rainfall, wood storks postpone or cease breeding altogether because fish populations then are dispersed throughout the marshes and cannot be harvested efficiently as food. Wood storks and other marsh birds attracted to gator holes are prey for alligators, but, as one biolgist remarked, for every bird eaten by an alligator, another 10 birds survive on food and water in gator holes during the dry season.

These interactions have clear importance for the management of wetlands inhabited by alligators. If poaching significantly reduces alligator populations, then an entire chain of events is interrupted to the detriment of a large number of organisms in a carefully arranged ecosystem. In short, protection of one resource, alligators, becomes a means of assuring continuation of an entire wetland community adapted to seasonal patterns of rainfall.

Oil, Water, and Birds Don't Mix

Among uie pollutants contaminating water resources and the wildlife associated with aquatic habitats are agricultural chemicals, heavy metals, and a complex of industrial wastes (e.g., polychlorinated biphenyls).

All of these can, and do, affect wildlife, particularly birds. In recent years, however, public attention has been captured by the sensational impacts, real and potential, of large-scale oil spills. Supertankers, far larger than any battleship, carry immense tonnages of petroleum, and modern capabilities for offshore drilling have developed sizeable oilfields around the globe.

In marine environments alone, some 6 million tons of oil are introduced each year. Misfortunes besetting tankers and other oil facilities have produced some major wildlife disasters, among them the Santa Barbara and Ixtoc I blowouts, and the wreckage of the *Torrey Canyon* and *Argo Merchant*.

Large numbers of waterbirds were lost in these and other disasters, although there is not necessarily a positive correlation between the size of the spill and the number of birds affected. Location of the spill and the time of year are more critical factors causing high mortality.

Reactions of birds confronted with oily water seems species-specific, with surface-active taxa such as diving ducks (Aythyinae) or penguins (Spheniscidae) more susceptible than others. In 1985, for example, oil spills in the heavily traveled shipping lanes around the Cape of Good Hope threatened colonies of jackass penguins (*Spheniscus demersus*).

In the worst spill, about 1180 penguins-probably an underestimate-

were oiled when the bulk carrier *MV Kapadistrias* ran aground near the birds' feeding grounds. The number of penguins oiled in this spill exceeded the total population of smaller breeding colonies elsewhere on the coast of South Africa.

Conversely, fewer than 100 Cape gannets (*Sula capensis*) in a nearby colony of 140,000 birds were oiled, thereby illustrating the vulnerability of penguins to oil spills. Unfortunately, no effective means have been developed to treat oil-damaged birds on a large scale.

In fact, most oiled birds cannot be captured easily for even cursory treatment until they are already debilitated by starvation, toxicity, or exposure. Methods currently employed rely in part on removing oil with solvents or detergents on a one-bird-at-a-time basis that usually requires holding the birds for long periods afterward.

Even so, only a small percentage (5-10 percent) of the treated birds survives this costly process and, of these, perhaps only a fraction thrives after they are released.

Oil in aquatic environments directly affects birds in one of two ways (or, more likely, with both acting simultaneously). The first result is a loss of insulation when plumage is fouled with oil. More than most terrestrial species, aquatic and semiaquatic birds rely on their plumage as a protective medium against heat loss.

Even small amounts of oil, especially on a bird's underside, effectively render the plumage useless for this purpose; less than 1.0 g of oil has caused the death of ducks. Hartung found that ducks undergo rapid increases in their metabolic rates to overcome heat losses when their plumage is oiled.

Since oiled birds usually stop feeding, they must draw on their body reserves, and when these are exhausted, they experience greatly accelerated starvation. Second, oil is ingested as the birds preen their plumage. If, as reported by Hartung and Hunt (1966), ducks acquire about 7.0 g of oil on their plumage when exposed to spills, they ingest about 1.5 g the first day and about half of the total on their feathers within 8 days after exposure.

Subsequent effects vary somewhat with the type of oil (e.g., diesel, lubricating, etc.), but each of the oils tested induced at least lipid pneumonia, gastrointestinal irritations, fatty livers, and adrenal cortical hyperplasia, and indicated that toxicity is a definite factor in the mortality of oiled birds.

The interaction of heat loss and starvation with toxicity in settings where birds may already be experiencing environmental stresses from food shortages, cold, disease, or even migration is not difficult to imagine. Hunt (1961) reported the deaths of 12,000 wintering and transient ducks on the lower Detroit River where more than 60,500 liters of waste oil entered the system daily.

An indirect effect of oiling concerns reproduction. Ducks ingesting 2.0 g of lubricating oil ceased laying immediately and did not resume egg production until two weeks later. Furthermore, fertile mallard eggs exposed to small amounts of mineral oil experienced 68 percent less hatching success than untreated eggs; this experiment was designed to simulate eggs contaminated by oil washed up on shore (as might occur among gulls, terns, and other shorebirds nesting near the water's edge).

In still another experiment, this one simulating the application of oil to eggs from the breast of an incubating bird, Hartung (1965) found that none of the eggs hatched, in turn suggesting that prolonged incubation of the dead eggs lessened the chances for a second nesting attempt. Whereas a coat of oil might interrupt the normal gaseous exchange through an eggshell and thus induce death of the embryo, Albers (1977), Hoffman (1978), and Szaro et al. (1978) determined that it was the toxic components of oils that drastically reduced the hatching success of eggs oiled on as little as 20 percent of their surface.

The toxic action works rapidly, as 82-94 percent of the embryos were killed within 96 hours after exposure. Lewis and Malecki (1984) showed that weathered No. 2 fuel oil (common home-heating fuel) remained as toxic as fresh oil to the embryos of gulls (*Larus* spp.). Only after a month of weathering was the composition of the oil altered enough to pose little or no threat to the hatching success of gull eggs.

Birds also are trapped in oil pits and sumps constructed near oil fields, refineries, and petrochemical factories. Most of the victims are ducks and other waterbirds, which apparently mistake the oil for water, although songbirds are killed in summer.

Oil pits in arid zones are particularly dangerous, especially during droughts and in winter when freshwater ponds are frozen. Oil sumps in the San Joaquin Valley of California claim an estimated 150,000 birds each year and, in New Mexico, Glover estimated an annual loss of 225,000 birds in crude oil pits. After placing carcasses of various-sized birds in oil pits, Flickinger and Bunck (1987) concluded that the rates of sinking and disappearance of the birds were related positively to body size, and the carcasses disappeared more rapidly in summer when oil temperatures were hot and more slowly in winter when the oil was cooler. Thus, frequent counts of birds killed at oil pits in winter may overestimate mortality, but the losses of songbirds in summer may be greater than reported. Depending on body size and season, bird carcasses in oil pits can be counted with reasonable accuracy every 1 to 3 weeks.

Water and Raw Sewage

Few streams are exactly alike in their unaltered state, but it is possible to illustrate some generalized results experienced when a stream is polluted by raw sewage. Bartsch and Ingram (1959) described a model stream with a flow of 2.8 m^3/second and a water temperature of 25°C receiving sewage from a community of 40,000 persons.

Upstream from the point of contamination, the water is high in dissolved oxygen (DO), and low in its biological oxygen demand (BOD). Upon entry, however, the sewage causes radical changes in these parameters of water quality.

BOD increases markedly, reflecting the depletion of dissolved oxygen by the demands of an immense bacterial population in *a zone of degradation*. This is followed by *a zone of active decomposition* where ciliates and other somewhat higher forms adapted to sludge deposits and oxygen famine exist. Downstream, nearly 80 km distant, *a recovery zone* begins, marked by a replenishment of DO and a greatly reduced BOD resulting from the stream's ability to reaerate itself.

Here the bacteria-eating ciliates give way to rotifers and microscopic crustaceans, and a full range of aquatic life again begins. However, the stream's recovery takes 8 days of flow and covers a distance of 154 km from the point of contamination.

The theoretical model of the foregoing example largely was realized when the fish fauna was examined upstream and downstream from a sewage disposal plant in Illinois. Pollution reduced both the density and composition of the fish community downstream from the sewage plant, although, in this instance, local conditions permitted recovery within a lesser distance than is shown in the model.

The zones of biological degradation, decomposition, and recovery are more or less collapsed into a single ongoing process in sewage-treatment ponds and lagoons. The degree to which sewage materials recover depends on the type and extent of treatment (e.g., aeration, filtration, BOD in subunits), but virtually all of the systems are water-based operations. Although not planned for such purposes, construction of sewage-treatment plants often creates wildlife habitat for a number of aquatic species. For waterfowl, the lagoons are unusual habitat because the water is often deep, and the edges lack emergent vegetation and, in fact, may be covered with rock or other hard-surfaced materials.

Instead, the attractive component seems to be the abundant invertebrate food supplies available in nutrient-enriched ponds. Uhler (1956, 1964) perhaps was the first to describe waterfowl usage and production on sewage lagoons, underscoring the abundance there of midge larvae and other invertebrates-more so than in natural wetlands.

Midges are particularly well-known sources of protein required by nesting hens and ducklings, and in sewage-treatment lagoons in Missouri, their numbers-sometimes exceeding 16 per cm^2-made up more than 94 percent of the total insect population. Maxson (1981) recorded waterfowl usage of a sewage lagoon in North Dakota and noted that this habitat served migrating and premolting birds as well as those raising broods.

More than 60 waterfowl broods were recorded on the 263-ha lagoon each year, or one brood per 183 m of shoreline. Conversely, sewage environments possibly may promote avian diseases, feather-wetting from detergent accumulations, or poisoning from blue-green algal toxins.

However, Maxson (1981) did not observe significant mortality of either adults or ducklings from these or other factors. Swanson's (1977) summary of brood usage of lagoons showed a range of 2.9 to 19.3 ducklings per ha of surface. Dornbush and Anderson (1964) found that lagoons had more than twice as many broods per ha as natural wetlands in South Dakota. Thus, within the confines of their primary purpose, sewage lagoons may offer a variety of management and research opportunities, including those associated with urban wildlife management.

"ACID RAIN": A CHANGING ENVIRONMENT

Combustion of fossil fuels, particularly coal, leads to chemical reactions in the atmosphere. Acids form when sulfur dioxide (SO_2) and nitrogen oxides (NO.) released from smelters, power plants, or other industrial installations combine with atmospheric moisture. Environmental damage occurs when the moisture, now infused with sulfuric and nitric acids, falls as precipitation.

In principle, any acid-sensitive environment subject to acid precipitation may be harmed. Cowling and Linthurst (1981) warned that acid precipitation may damage terrestrial ecosystems more than is supposed. For example, rain falling in forests is intercepted by several tiers of foliage before reaching the ground, so that contaminated rainwater can alter the structure and function of leaves well before the rainwater can be buffered, possibly by a neutral soil. Addison and Jensen (1987) recently analyzed the complex setting regarding air pollution for forest ecosytems.

Nonetheless, the effects of acid precipitation currently are most apparent in lakes. The acidity steadily increases as runoff from watersheds accumulates in lacustrine systems. Prevailing air currents dictate the deposition of acids formed in the atmosphere so that lakes far removed from the sources of combustion are affected.

Hence, oxide-bearing smoke from industries in Ohio or New Jersey eventually may damage lakes in Canada. Because both rainfall and snowfall act as vehicles, the phenomenon is described correctly as acid precipitation. However, the term "acid rain" has been used widely in the public media and now seems established beyond recall.

In fact, "acid rain" was the term initially used in 1872 when British chemist Robert Angus Smith noticed that rainfall in industrial England was eroding the surfaces of buildings. Unfortunately, acid rain is a subtle form of pollution that initially did not attract the same notoriety as did smog. Today, the biological implications of acid rain strain international politics as well as aquatic environments.

The formation of acid rain has been heightened by recent economic development and, ironically, by some environmental efforts promoting clean air. America's vast coal reserves promise to alleviate, in part, the nation's dependence on foreign oil, and numerous industries accordingly have altered their fuels.

New smokestacks, heightened to reduce pollution at ground level, actually disperse the oxide-bearing gases high and wide into the atmosphere. Treatments for one set of ills, it seems, have become the cause of another. That rain and snow were gaining widespread acidity was first noted in Europe and later, in eastern North America.

Changes in hydrogen ion concentration are measured exponentially by a pH scale of 0 (acid) to 14 (alkaline) around a neutral point of pH 7. A decrease from pH 5 to pH 4, for example, represents a tenfold increase in acidity. Precipitation relatively free of man-made sources of contamination normally would register about pH 5.7, and values below this point define acid rain.

Thus, the apparently small decline in pH to 4.0-4.5 recorded for 1972-73 in eastern North America actually represents an alarming increase in the acidity of the region's precipitation. Acid rain also contains higher amounts of lead, cadmium, mercury, and other heavy metals than does unaffected precipitation.

The transfer of the methyl form of mercury from aquatic systems into fish-eating wildlife is particularly efficient because methylmercury is readily absorbed and slowly eliminated in birds and mammals. Moreover, methylmercury biomagnifies in aquatic food chains; thus the tissues of fish-eating species such as otter (*Lutra canadensis*) are contaminated at levels greater than are found in the fishes on which they feed.

Although conclusive data are lacking, acid rain potentially threatens human health because heavy metals and other contaminants increase in drinking water. With great acidity, for example, the concentration of dissolved aluminum in water increases massively, and aluminum has been implicated in the pathogenesis of several human diosorders, including kidney disease, Alzheimer's disease, and amyotrophic lateral sclerosis ("Lou Gehrig's disease").

Regional and local properties of watersheds affect the impacts of acid rain. If limestone is the dominant parent material, then the acids often are neutralized as they pass through the ecosystem. On the other hand, where parent materials lack this buffering effect, watersheds are susceptible to increased acidity from the contaminated precipitation.

Unfortunately, the latter is true in much of eastern North America where granitic bedrock predominates. More than 50 percent of the high-elevation lakes surveyed in 1975 in New York's Adirondack Mountains had pH values of less than 5.0, whereas earlier (1929-37) only 5 percent of these lakes were that acidic.

Lakes in Nova Scotia originally surveyed in 1955 all exhibited increased acidity after 21 years of exposure to acid rainfall, and in Ontario, the acidity of lakewater gained at rates of up to 0.16 pH units per year. Loucks (1980) reported estimates suggesting that more than 48,000 lakes in Ontario alone will experience significant acidification by the year 2000.

Whereas acid rain can damage all levels of aquatic food chains (beginning with single-celled organisms), fish populations are often the first vertebrates stressed by increased acidity. McNicol et al. (1987), for example, reported fewer species and reduced biomass among minnows (Cyprinidae) in lakes with a pH of 5.5 or less.

Conversely, yellow perch (*Perca flavescens*) are among the few fishes relatively tolerant to acidification. Brown trout (*Salmo trutta*) populations now are gone in about one-third of the lakes in parts of southern Norway, and several species have disappeared from some lakes in Ontario. Fish losses may be dramatic, as when snowmelt or heavy rains suddenly flush aquatic systems with acidic water, but more often the increased acidity inhibits reproduction.

Thereafter, fish populations gradually diminish as older cohorts expire. Egg fertility, hatching, and juvenile survival are each limited by reductions in pH.

In addition to losses of eggs and fry, fishes of some species fail to spawn when acid rain lowers the pH of lake water. The acidity also seems linked with skeletal deformities and with major reductions in the biomass of fish populations. Spawning may be limited or terminated when the calcium in the serum of female fishes reaches such levels that ovarian maturation no longer occurs.

Reproductive failure of this type apparently occurs when pH ranges between 5.2 and 4.7. As shown in Figure elsewhere in this chapter, the same acid stress probably demineralizes the skeletons of fishes, leading to deformities when pH drops below 5.0. Thus, when acid rain lowered the pH of lake water below critical levels, fishes of several species experienced poor reproduction, reduced numbers and size, and physical deformities.

Increasing acidity also may disrupt the form and function of gill filaments. Acid rain also may inhibit the sense of smell in salmonids, and therefore may modify the normal migratory behaviour of Atlantic salmon. Acidification of pH 4.5 or less kills adult salmon, their eggs (pH 3.5), and immature forms (pH 4.0), but reductions in salmon populations also occur in rivers where the pH is above lethal concentrations.

Hasler (1960) determined that the migration abilities of salmon are controlled largely by olfaction; hence, the upstream migrations of spawning salmon may be thwarted in rivers with increased acidity. That is, if low pH alters the manner in which salmon return to their home streams, adults may no longer locate suitable spawning sites and the population will diminish accordingly.

Royce-Malmgren and Watson (1987) thus demonstrated that the olfactory responses of juvenile salmon were impaired when pH was lowered from 7.6 to 5.1. The effects were reversed when the pH returned to 7.6. These findings have important management implications, especially for programs designed to reintroduce salmon: in acidified rivers, stocked fish may not find their way back to sites where they were released.

Other wildlife directly dependent on aquatic systems also may be affected by acid rain. Freda (1986), for example, noted the high mortality of amphibian embryos reared in acidic water. As we have seen, acidification clearly damages fish faunas, and thus fish-eating birds also are affected.

In Sweden, Eriksson (1986) reported declines of ospreys (*Pandion baliaetus*) in areas with acidified waters; this probably occurred because nestling survival was affected by the reduced foraging success of adults. However, other associations are somewhat more subtle.

Longcore et al. (1987) evaluated the risks to which birds may be exposed as a result of acidified wetlands. For example, mergansers (*Mergus spp.*) and loons (*Gavia spp.*) normally return to natal areas for nesting and, if these waters become barren because of acidification, future breeding efforts may be fruitless.

That is, the adults may continue nesting at sites where there is little chance of successfully raising a brood. Acidity also eliminates clams and snails, each an important source of dietary calcium required by birds during egg laying. Calcium shortages thus may affect such species as black ducks (*Anas rubripes*). Fish-eating birds can obtain calcium from the bones of fish-but only as long as fish are available.

Acidity also affects the abundance and diversity of the invertebrate fauna required by young birds as a source of protein. Compared with less acidic wetlands in Maine, brood survival for ring-necked ducks (*Aythya collaris*) was lower on wetlands where pH was less than 5.5.

The differences appeared in broods of older ducklings in which the growth of feathers and body mass required high levels of dietary protein. However, invertebrate numbers may increase and become more available to waterfowl when acidity reduces fish populations (i.e., fish and waterfowl may compete for invertebrate foods).

Hence, contrary to the situation with ringneck broods, Pehrsson found that more foods were available for mallard ducklings on acid lakes than on those unaffected by acid rain. Ericksson found that alternate prey foods for juvenile goldeneyes (*Bucephala clangula*) may be more difficult to catch and also may be less palatable.

McNicol et al. (1987) thus noted that increased acidity may influence predator-prey relationships between fish and waterfowl and their foods. Some invertebrates are more sensitive than others to acid environments. Mayflies (Ephemeroptera), which are four times more common than any other food in the diets of young black ducks, are among the sensitive groups and thus may be eliminated when wetlands become acidified.

Such data seem significant since nearly all of the breeding range of black ducks lies within the northeastern region affected by acid rain. Thus, how do black duck broods fare in acidified wetlands, and in what ways does the presence of competitors-fish-interact with the availability of invertebrate foods?

DesGranges and Hunter (1987) addressed such questions with data pooled from three sets of experiments (e.g., comparisons of various combinations of lakes and experimental wetlands with and without fish and acidity). Data from these experiments suggested that the quality of lakes as habitat for either fish or black ducks declines steadily with increasing acidity.

However, in acidified lakes, fish are affected by both direct toxicity and diminished food supplies and thus are more sensitive to acidity than ducklings. Virtually all fish disappear below pH 5.0, and the sharp decline in fish density means more food for ducklings, at least for a time.

Eventually, perhaps at pH 4.5, so few invertebrates survive that ducklings are deprived of food and succumb to the effects of acidity. The study concluded that acidification has a negative effect on black duck broods and could be disastrous in extreme cases. Thus, concern for waterfowl is yet another reason for controlling acid rain.

WATER DEVELOPMENTS AND WILDLIFE

The uneven distribution of fresh water necessarily gained the attention of early civilizations. Campsites were associated with available water of suitable quality, but as civilization advanced, methods to move water were developed. At first, crude wells were constructed, but subsequently dams and aqueducts altered the distribution of water for man's advantage.

The technology of modern civilization developed the large-scale wonders of Hoover Dam and the California water scheme, among countless others. The Murray-Darling river system is Australia's largest, draining more than 1,036,000 km^2, yet the average depth of runoff in the system is only 1.3 cm annually.

However, 84 major dams built on the system divert about half the natural flow of the rivers for irrigation and urban uses. The region's mammalian fauna, already largely displaced by livestock, was little affected by the widespread irrigation scheme, but wholesale displacement of birds adapted to semiarid conditions did occur.

These birds were largely replaced by introduced species such as starlings (*Sturnus vulgaris*) and house sparrows (*Passer domesticus*) that are adapted to an agricultural regime. However, the Murray-Darling irrigation scheme provides some benefits for waterbirds during dry periods, and depressions filled by tailwater runoff have become the principal habitat for the otherwise declining populations of freckled ducks (*Stictonetta naevosa*).

In the main, however, control of the flow in this river system will lead to diminished waterfowl populations, in part because wildlife requirements were not part of the planning for the irrigation scheme.

Water also has been diverted for other reasons, most notably to "reclaim" wetlands for agricultural production and other developments. Wetland reclamation has occurred on both large and small scales, involving everything from the establishment of major cities such as Leningrad and Mexico City to the farming of prairie potholes.

In the case of prairie potholes, the figures are staggering. Estimates of the original number of potholes in Prairie Canada vary from 6.7 million to 10 million. Some 1.2 million more potholes occur in the United States. A recent summary underscored the drastic impacts of agricultural and other activities on these wetlands in the United States.

By 1950, only 50 percent of the potholes remained; and during the period 1943-61, more than 405,000 ha of pothole habitat were lost. Some 64,000 potholes were drained in the Dakotas and Minnesota in 2 years, and losses continue at a rate of more than 2 percent per year. As a direct result, waterfowl production on the prairies, once estimated at 15 million ducks annually, now totals only about one third that number.

In some areas, however, blasting offers a useful management tool for creating or reclaiming small wetlands. Blasting may be used effectively in bogs and marshes where succession has advanced to the point that vegetation encroaches on open water, thereby reducing the carrying capacity of the site for waterfowl and other wildlife.

In many areas of the United States, streambeds have been straightened as a means of reducing floods. This process, *channelization*, often destroys riparian zones bordering the stream, and hence alters the size and composition of wildlife communities associated with streamside vegetation. Possardt and Dodge (1978) recorded 636 birds of 62 species associated with a stream in Vermont, but in channelized sections of the same stream only 387 birds of 53 species were present.

In particular, warblers and vireos were reduced because of their dependence on insect foods gleaned from under- and overstory vegetation.

In Iowa, Stauffer and Best (1980) predicted that removal of woody vegetation in a riparian community would eliminate 78 percent of 41 species of breeding birds even though herbaceous cover remained; another 12 percent would decrease in numbers, and 10 percent would increase under these conditions.

Conversely, a much greater percentage of birds could continue breeding if channelization were conducted so that a part of the riparian canopy remained intact. Geier and Best (1980) developed similar predictions for nine species of small mammals confronted with channelization and other disturbances of riparian habitat.

Entire watersheds and the wildlife population therein also may be degraded by channelization for an extensive review). For one example, Shapiro et al. (1982) summarized the aftermath of channelization of the Kissimmee River basin in Florida.

In all, nearly 16,500 ha, or 78 percent, of the marshland in the basin were drained, producing devastating effects on productivity and faunal associations in these wetlands. Sport fisheries were reduced and probably other segments of the fish fauna were limited as well.

Waterbirds declined by 93 percent from prechannelization levels. Furthermore, wholesale disruption of the aquatic ecosystem reduced the prey base available for bald eagles (*Haliaeetus leucocephalus*), producing a 74 percent reduction in the number of active eagle territories in the basin even though suitable nesting sites remained in place after channelization was completed.

In another case, Erickson et al. (1979) found that a 40-km channelization project in North and South Dakota stimulated a nearly fourfold increase in the rate of wetland drainage. In other words, the presence of a channel prompted landowners to drain wetlands that otherwise would have remained intact as valuable wildlife habitat. Channelization also contributed to the dislocation of blackbirds (Icteridae) in Tennessee.

When streams were channelized and the bottomland forests destroyed, as many as 10 million birds started feeding in agricultural areas. If future land-use patterns are similar, then man-bird conflicts of this type can only become more intense.

A classic case of biological disruption resulting from manipulation of water occurred when the Welland Canal was enlarged in 1932. The canal bypassed the formidable barrier of Niagara Falls between lakes Ontario and Erie. Its reconstruction permitted sea lampreys (*Petromyzon marinus*) access to the upper Great Lakes and their tributaries (only 3 adult lampreys were recorded in Lake Erie prior to 1932, suggesting that the original canal, completed in 1829, itself was something of a barrier for marine lampreys).

The adults breed in rivers, depositing about 60,000 eggs per female in their single breeding effort before dying. Filter-feeding larvae hatch from the eggs and remain in their natal streams for several years before transforming into parasitic adults.

Equipped with suckerlike mouths, adult lampreys attach themselves to fishes and rasp through their victim's skins with rings of concentric teeth; they then feed on body fluids and blood of a variety of hosts, but lampreys have been particularly devastating to the lake trout (*Salvelinus namaycush*) fishery in the Great Lakes.

Production of lake trout in Lake Michigan under the impact of lampreys fell from nearly 1.95 million kg in 1935 to 155,000 kg in 1949. As lake trout populations collapsed, complex changes occurred in other fish populations, resulting in alterations of basic predator-prey relationships and an unstable fishery for all species of commercial value.

Millions of dollars have since been spent controlling lampreys using mechanical traps, electric wires, and, more recently, selective larvicides. The latter have successfully controlled sea lampreys in Lake Superior. Despite these and other disruptions, other kinds of water development have proven beneficial for wildlife even though their construction was for other purposes.

Among these are flood-prevention lakes. These are impoundments of various sizes designed to reduce floods by confining excess water in the upper reaches of watersheds. Construction was authorized by federal legislation (most recently, by the Flood and Agricultural Act of 1962) and is carried out by the Soil Conservation Service.

The impoundments, however, remain the property of the owner. Depending on the region, warmwater or coldwater fisheries often may be initiated in flood-prevention lakes with stocking programs. For waterfowl, the attractiveness of these impoundments seems self-evident under the presumption that any new wetland areas have some habitat value.

However, because the impoundments remain in private ownership, no recommendations were formulated by public conservation agencies for managing these-habitats. Hobaugh and Teer (1981) accordingly studied 55 flood-prevention lakes in Texas to determine features that might influence their value as waterfowl habitat. The lakes they surveyed supported more than 42,000 wintering and migrating ducks, especially where the impoundments had large areas of surface and abundant aquatic vegetation.

Because lakes with clear water attracted more ducks than those with turbid water, practices for reducing erosion were recommended, including livestock fencing and the seeding of annual grasses on disturbed sites around each lake. Furthermore, the importance of the watershed projects as waterfowl habitat demonstrated that wildlife values should be incorporated in the planning and construction phases of each project, rather than have them emerge as random or incidental benefits afterward.

In part, the losses of prairie potholes as crucial waterfowl habitat are offset by the existence of ordinary stock ponds. Stock ponds, of course, are not designed primarily for waterfowl or other wildlife requiring aquatic habitat, but their presence nonetheless has produced benefits. Bue et al. (1952) studied waterfowl production on stock ponds in South Dakota, finding that more than 20 ducks were raised per pond.

The implications of these data are clear when they are expanded to include all of the 1850 stock ponds then available in a single county: production varied from 36,000-43,000 ducks in each year of the study. Later, Ruwaldt et al. (1979) estimated that 88,600 stock ponds made up 14 percent of the total wetland area in South Dakota, again indicating the importance of these man-made structures as auxiliary habitat.

Perhaps of greater importance is what might be done if stock ponds were managed for wildlife in keeping with the concept of multiple use. Hudson (1983) suggested that only slight modifications would be needed to increase waterfowl production on stock ponds.

For example, much might be done to increase the amount of shoreline length per area of surface water in the design and construction of stock ponds without compromising their primary purpose. Mack and Flake (1980) found that shoreline length had a strong relationship to the presence of waterfowl broods on stock ponds in South Dakota.

Futhermore, stock ponds should cover more than 0.5 ha with about 40 percent of the area less than 61 cm deep, indicating that minor shifts in the initial selection of the site may provide these features. Better grazing practices, and hence more vegetation suitable for nesting, probably would produce even more broods on stock ponds.

Stock ponds also represent an underutilized resource for riparian and other species. Menasco (1986) recorded 115 species of wildlife, including 3 endangered species, on ponds in the Tonto National Forest in Arizona. With fencing, stock ponds can be managed as riparian communities while still providing water for livestock. Ekblad and Crockford (1983) suggested the construction of "no-freeze" water troughs as another improvement in regions where winter temperatures cause the ponds to ice over.

Water is piped through the pond's embankment to a trough partially buried for insulation in the backslope. Regulated by a valve, the water runs continuously, and hence does not freeze. Because the trough is a separate source of water, the pond can be fenced to reduce the risk of cattle breaking through the ice and drowning, while also protecting wildlife cover on the shoreline.

Specific water developments for wildlife encompass a variety of structures, many of which are one of a kind, designed to match a local setting. For example, seeps may be impounded to collect water for desert bighorn sheep (*Ovis canadensis*) as Halloran and Deming (1958) described for refuges in Arizona and Nevada. Other kinds of water developments increase the carrying capacity of arid and semiarid habitat for various kinds of big game.

Horizontal wells are particularly useful where declining water tables no longer make vertical wells or , other surface-water developments practical or possible for livestock and wildlife. In California, for example, Weaver (1973) noted the extirpation of bighorn sheep from arid regions where springs and seeps no longer reached the surface. Additionally, horizontal wells flow ' by gravity, are unlikely to become contaminated, and require little maintenance and no operational costs.

Development costs are minimal except when drilling equipment must be hauled by helicopter to remote areas. Sites for horizontal wells are selected on the basis of (1) former occurrence of springs or seeps, (2) suitable geological formations, especially dike or contact aquifers, and (3) presence of indicator plants known as phreatophytes. Some common phreatophytes include willow (*Salix spp.*), reed (*Phragmites communis*), and salt cedar (*Tamarix spp.*). McKenzie (1985) has provided a state-of-the-art review of solar-powered and other systems for pumping water on rangelands.

The original self-filling water basins were designed for desert quail, and led to their popular identification as "*gallinaceous guzzlers*". Guzzlers consist of (1) a collection basin having at least one side gently sloped or stepped for access, (2) a cover to reduce evaporation, and (3) an apron serving as a watershed for the collection basin.

Most guzzler units are fenced so that the installation cannot be damaged by livestock. The surface area of the apron is dependent on (1) the capacity of the collection basin and (2) the minimum amount of rainfall expected at the site each year. A surprisingly small artificial watershed is needed because virtually all of the precipitation falling on the apron is collected.

For example, in a region receiving only 2.5 cm of rainfall annually, a 2650-liter collection basin can be filled to capacity by 105 m^2 of runoff surface; a circular apron only 11.5 m in diameter fulfills this requirement.

Roberts noted that distribution patterns and consumption rates should be determined if wildlife is to benefit from guzzlers. His summary showed that the home ranges of mule deer are larger in arid environments so that managers space guzzlers at intervals of about 1.5-5.0 km, depending on local conditions.

Water consumption also varies according to the setting. Mule deer in Oregon consume an average of 3 liters per visit, whereas their average consumption in Arizona is nearly twice as much. Hence, water developments must be designed in a manner appropriate to each environment.

For instance, where drifting snow can be expected, proper placement of the apron will catch the melt water and greatly enhance the unit's function, whereas, lacking such a natural situation, snow fences may be used to enhance drifting in the watersheds of guzzlers.

Guzzlers, while effectively improving habitats where water is a limiting factor, sometimes may produce new management concerns. Vegetation surrounding guzzlers may be overutilized and damaged by grazing species attracted to these or other water developments. In fragile desert communities, recovery of overgrazed vegetation may be extremely slow, if it occurs at all.

Mule deer moving to guzzlers in Arizona severely hedged palatable shrubs within 180 m of the structures to the extent that many plants were killed. Predation rates also may be higher than normal at man-made watering sites. If this seems likely, guzzlers should be constructed near appropriate escape cover.

Also, fenceposts should be pointed on top to discourage avian predators from perching near guzzlers where small animals might be expected to visit. The location of guzzlers or other water developments should not encourage poaching. Water developments situated near roads, for example, may prove unwise.

Finally, once guzzlers are functional, other factors besides water availability will become limiting, thus requiring new assessments of the desired size and density of wildlife populations, including measurements of hunting pressure.

3

INFLUENCE OF SOIL

Soils affect the basic nature of aquatic and terrestrial environments. The distribution and abundance, as well as the quality, of organisms are influenced by the soils associated with ecosystems. Some systems are poor and nearly sterile, whereas others are immensely rich. In the thoughts of Allen, farmers gauge their land in yields of crops, but it makes little difference if we measure the productivity of land in bushels of wheat or in coveys of quail.

Each is in some way a product of the soil and its capacity. These relationships may be complex, but they are no less true for songbirds than for quail, for minnows than for bass, for Africa than for North America. In this chapter, we shall examine both direct and indirect interactions between soil and wildlife.

The focus highlights the fundamental importance of soil as a component of wildlife habitat. Each soil type has an inherent capability for producing biomass in some form. But unless these capabilities-or limitations-are understood, the best management of farm or forest, plain or mountain, remains unfulfilled.

In short, soil management is an investment for the future, and its renewability as a natural resource must be maintained by stewards of the land. Abuse of the soil resource clearly diminishes the capacity of an ecosystem to function as fully as it should.

SOME FEATURES OF SOIL

Soils are classified by texture, based on their content of sand, clay, and silt. These materials vary from coarse grains to particles resembling powder. Because of the different nature of each textural

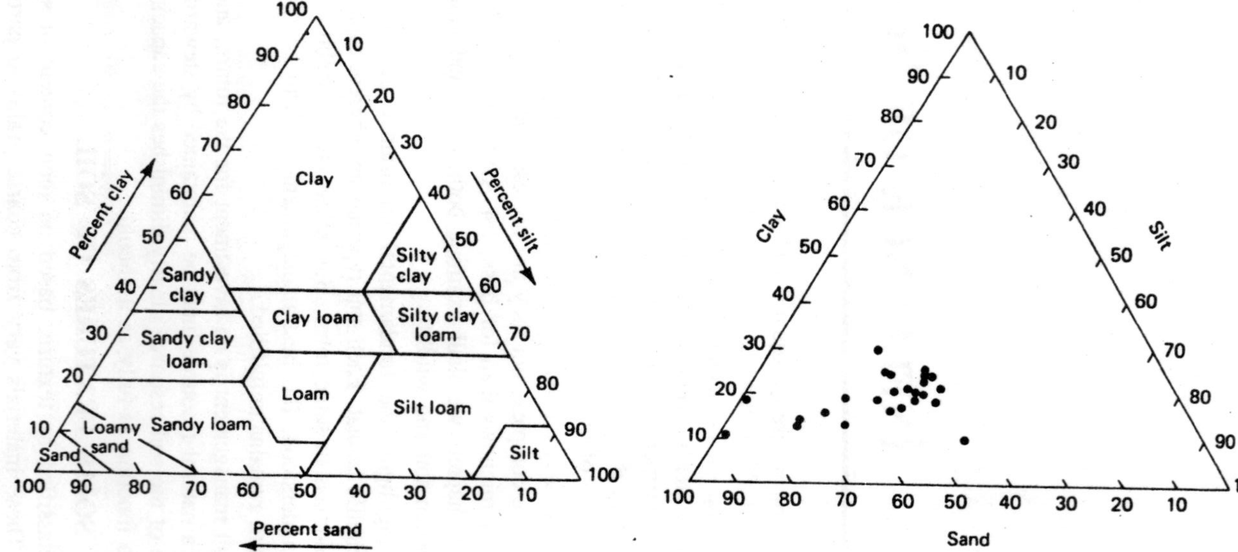

Figure 3.1: Classification guide for soil texture employed by the U.S. Department of Agriculture (left). As an example, a soil with 30 percent clay, 40 percent silt, and 30 percent sand is classified as a clay loam. If more than 20 percent of the soil materials are larger than 2.0 mm, the classification is modified accordingly (i.e., as gravelly clay loam). The distribution of pocket gophers in eastern Kansas (right) coincides with loams low in clay and silt and high in sand.

group, many kinds of wildlife have developed associations with certain soil conditions.

Many of these relationships are indirect and usually concern vegetation, and hence form a link with wildlife seeking food and cover. For others, the associations are more direct. Sidewinder rattlesnakes (*Crotalus cerastes*) offer a clear illustration of an adaption to the loose, granular texture of desert sands; movement would be difficult for sidewinders without their peculiar but effective twisting and sliding means of locomotion.

Some evidence suggests that at least two species of desert rodents locate more buried seeds as the soil moisture in sand increases. In their native range in Europe, gray partridges (*Perdix perdix*) show an association with sandy or other well-drained soils, but their distribution in the United States is not so uniformly related to soil texture. "Buffalo wallows" formed by the dust-bathing of bison (*Bison bison*) support a flora un-like the surrounding grasslands, thereby increasing habitat diversity on the plains.

Soil texture and soil moisture are among the differences between wallows and nearby sites. The texture of soils on streambanks may influence the channel profile, which in turn influences water temperature, stream velocity, and cover availability for fishery resources. Streambanks with high silt-clay contents generally form deep, narrow channels, whereas those with more sand develop wide and shallow channels.

In Australia, Wood (1980) studied a rabbit (*Oryctolagus cuniculus*) population located on an area of small sand dunes where the length of the breeding season-from 4 to 14 months-was related to soil moisture. Soil texture also limits the natural distributions of some animals and sometimes influences the ways in which wildlife and their habitats are managed.

Pocket gophers (Geomyidae) and moles (Talpidae) have elongated skulls, small eyes, reduced tails and ears, and short fur capable of lying forward or backward in keeping with their fossorial habits. These adaptations clearly have evolved for life underground, and it is not surprising that soil texture strongly influences where they might occur.

Soil texture was second only to the availability of food in determining the distribution of the plains pocket gopher (*Geomys bursarius*) in Kansas. In Minnesota, most burrows of Richardson's ground squirrels (*Spermophilus richardsonii*) were located in loams instead of in other soils. Clay loams were too wet for the squirrels, whereas the higher sand content of other soil types in the study area may have limited the stability of the burrows. Similarly, pine snakes (*Pituophis melanoleucus*) burrowed in a narrow range of sandy soils in the Pine Barrens of New Jersey; the limits were defined by a soil soft enough for penetration for digging and, at the other extreme, not soft enough to collapse the burrow or nest.

The safety of the eggs and, later, of the emerging hatchlings is of obvious importance in relation to soil type for pine snakes and other kinds of burrowing reptiles. Gophers were found only in soils with low clay content and more than 40 percent sand. Soil texture also limited the distribution of pine voles (*Microtus pinetorum*) in Pennsylvania.

These rodents are semifossorial in their habits and lack specialized morphological adaptations for digging or living permanently in burrows. Nonetheless, soil texture peculiar to their distribution suggested methods limiting the injury pine voles cause to fruit trees (root and bark damage).

New orchards might better be located on soils unsuitable for pine voles. In established orchards, poison and other direct controls can be concentrated only on those soil types preferred by the animals instead of more widespread and costly treatments on areas where soil texture already acts as a deterrent.

On the other hand, prairie dogs (*Cynomys ludovicianus*) show less selectively and dig their burrows in several kinds of soil. King (1955) reached a similar conclusion but noted that only exploratory tunneling occurred in rocky ground or loose sands; no successful burrows were established in soils of these textures.

Crawford and Bolen (1976) found correlations between the amount of deep sandy soil and populations of lesser prairie chickens (*Tympanuchus pallidicintus*) in west Texas. The relationship provided indirect evidence of the reliance of these birds on native vegetation adapted to these soils. Denney (1944) and Crawford (1946) called attention to several other soil-wildlife associations and their relationship to management; Wilde (1946), Cronemiller (1955), and Allan et al. (1963) proposed ways that soil data might be applied to managing wildlife habitat.

Managers thus often can locate areas suitable for habitat improvements directly from soil maps or, conversely, they can rule out sites where management might be inappropriate. In aquatic environments, the ecological conditions influencing the occurrence of lead poisoning include soil texture. Waterfowl feeding in silty-bottomed wetlands largely avoid contact with expended shotgun pellets, whereas the pellets remain more available on clays or other hard-bottomed substrates where shot does not settle rapidly. In terrestrial environments, however, the availability of lead shot seems independent of soil texture, and upland birds may mistakenly ingest pellets lying on the surface of moist soils.

Pheasants (*Phasianus colchicus*) ingest lead shot and quail also may experience lead poisoning. Locke and Bagley (1967) suggested that lead poisoning in mourning doves (*Zenaida macroura*) may occur more frequently than supposed.

Doves collected from game management areas in the mid-Atlantic states contained lead shot and/or elevated lead concentrations in their livers; up to 11 percent of the samples showed these traits, indicating that doves have a high degree of exposure to lead.

More than 50 percent mortality occurred in mourning doves experimentally fed as few as two pellets, and females ingesting only one pellet hatched fewer eggs. Hence, management may be required on all soil types in terrestrial habitats where accumulated shot might pose a hazard to feeding birds. Two days after the hunting season opened for mourning doves on a public hunting area in Tennessee, Lewis and Legler (1968) recorded a 300 percent increase in shot on the soil surface, or a total of about 107,500 pellets per ha.

If hunting areas such as this also are managed with food patches-and lead shot still is used-then disking or plowing soon after the hunting season is over may be required to reduce the risk of lead poisoning in birds seeking seeds or grit.

Unusual soil conditions at a wildlife refuge in Texas once caused the deaths of about 500 ducks. The birds died of exhaustion after being shackled by sticky balls of mud weighing between 400 and 740 g. Gray partridge chicks also have died when their feet were encumbered by mudballs formed from wet clayey soils.

With accelerated losses of wetlands, biologists have tried to improve the remaining areas as a means of enhancing waterfowl and other wildlife habitat. One technique, dynamiting, is used to blast heavily vegetated areas so that open-water "potholes" are created for feeding and other benefits.

An evaluation of these structures 20 years after they were blasted revealed that soil type greatly influenced their longevity as waterfowl habitat. Potholes blasted in coarser-textured soils retained greater depths over time than those with finer, more erodable soils, even though their original depths were greater in finer soils. Accordingly, soil texture should be considered when planning wetland blasting programs.

Soil chemistry also interacts with wildlife. Some soils are alkaline, some are acidic, and still others are neutral in their pH. The percentage of soil samples with a pH above 6.0 correlated positively with the litter size of cottontails (*Sylvilagus floridanus*) in five soil regions of Alabama; litters increased from 3.6 to 4.7 with increasing pH. Soils in some places are laden heavily with salts of many kinds.

Areas with high evaporation, low precipitation, and high water tables have soils encrusted with soluble salts that support sparse vegetation of unusually high salt tolerance known as *halophytes*. We have noted in Chapter 11 that the granite-based soils of the northeastern United States lack the buffering capacity to offset the devastation of acid-bearing precipitation.

Soils vary in their nutrient content. Phosphorus, nitrogen, potassium, and other major nutrients are present in various amounts and may be deficient for the welfare of plant and animal communities. Farmers, of course, regularly add fertilizers to enhance crop production, at times providing better nutritional values for wildlife as a beneficial side effect.

However, wildlife managers seldom are able to fertilize soils solely for the crops of animals they produce. Fertilizers are expensive and often remain outside the economic realm of wildlife management. In general, most wildlife habitat is associated with low-quality soils that are unsuitable for cultivation. Albrecht (1944) was among the first to herald associations between soil fertility and its effects on wildlife.

He stressed the importance of nutrients passing from the soil into the diets of animals instead of continuing the old belief that wildlife can thrive merely with ample vegetative bulk irrespective of its nutritional qualities. Indeed, most trophy-sized big game come from sites rich in nutrients, especially where calcium and phosphorus are abundant.

Phosphate deficiencies in some soils of Hawaii affect livestock and, presumably, the exotic pronghorn (*Antilocapra americana*) population there as well. After introduction, the pronghorn herd on Lanai split into smaller units and frequently ventured into habitats other than grasslands.

Among other symptoms, insufficient phosporus promotes easily broken bones, disturbances in sexual functions, and appetite irregularities. In the first hunting season, more than one-fifth of the pronghorns shot as game in Hawaii indeed had bones so brittle that they broke in the hands of hunters.

The animals also did not reproduce as expected, and this, along with their wandering into atypical habitats (for food?), suggests that pronghorns cannot prosper on Hawaii's phosphatedeficient soils. Some minor elements also are necessary for the normal growth and development of plants and animals. These are known as *micronutrients*, including boron, cobalt, copper, zinc, and iron, among others.

Most serve as catalysts for complex physiological processes, and thus only small amounts need be present in soils to satisfy these functions. When deficiencies occur, however, organisms commonly exhibit altered growth patterns or other abnormalities.

When there is less than 0.05 ppm of selenium, for example, in the diets of grazing animals, they regularly acquire nutritional muscular dystrophy or "white muscle disease". Selenium may be deficient in several types of soil, but this most often occurs in those of volcanic origin. Mountain goats (*Oreamnos americanus*) in British Columbia showed symptoms of white muscle disease after they were captured, and some died shortly after they were confined in pens.

An analysis of 13 species of forage plants from their range showed that 11 species contained less than 0.05 ppm of the element, and that two salt licks also had little selenium. Strangely, no evidence of white muscle disease occurred in the mountain goat herd before these individuals were captured.

This suggested that the stress of capture and confinement may have triggered the disease. If so, Hebert and Cowan speculated that stresses from heavy hunting or predator pressure could lead to an outbreak of white muscle disease in the herd still living on soils with marginal amounts of selenium.

Selenium also can be too abundant for the welfare of wildlife, thereby illustrating the principle that "the dose alone determines the poison." Irrigation runoff supplies the water for the Kesterson Wildlife Refuge in California, but the soils in the surrounding San Joaquin Valley are mineral-rich deposits from an ancient seabed.

The refuge in effect is a settling basin for irrigation water laden with selenium and other toxic elements (e.g., cadmium, arsenic, lead, mercury). The ever-increasing concentrations of selenium eventually produced abnormalities in the embryos of waterbirds: missing legs, feet, wings, or eyes, as well as other kinds of disfigurements.

Fully 41 percent of the nests of aquatic birds at Kesterson contained at least one dead embryo, and 20 percent included at least 1 embryo or chick with an obvious abnormality. Reproduction in waterfowl and other birds breeding at Kesterson thus remains poor because of the high rate of embryonic mortality. In response, a three-part management plan was initiated to reduce the hazard: waterfowl are hazed and frightened away; selected habitat on the refuge was made unattractive; and safer habitat elsewhere in the area was improved to attract the displaced birds.

Selenium contamination in the watershed of the San Joaquin River in California also exceeds those concentrations that can impair the development and maturation of chinook salmon (*Oncorbynchus tshawytscha*). Another illustration was found in a Minnesota deer population associated with iodine-deficient soils. This herd experienced a high incidence of goiter.

Thyroid glands from these deer were about three times heavier than normal, and their thyroxine levels were onehalf to one-third of normal. When members of the herd were given iodized oil, a significant increase in thyroxine levels followed. Testis size also increased in response to the hormonal stimulation of the additional thyroxine.

This study suggested the potential of management geared to specific soil deficiencies as opposed to more general nutritional shortcomings related to poor soil fertility.

Some Influences of Soil on Wildlife

Fossorial animals, as we have already seen, depend on soil features for the integrity of their tunnels and dens. Some soils may crumble easily, whereas others may resist digging by even the strongest of the burrowing species. Of 50 red fox (*Vulpes vulpes*) dens examined in central New York, all but four were dug in fine sandy soil. *Soil* structure also influences the distribution and internal features of fox dens in Eurasia.

Dens in clay soils were shallow with many branches, whereas those in sandy soils were deep and lacked extensive branching. Moss found that the woodchuck (*Marmota monax*) burrows closely coincided with the occurrence of sandy loam on a study area where loam and fine sandy loam also occurred; 100 of 115 burrows were restricted to sandy loam and, given the accuracy of the soil map used in the study, the remaining burrows also may have been located in soils of that texture.

Bank-dwelling muskrats (*Ondatra zibethicus*) exhibit some selection for soil types, usually choosing clay-based soils for their burrows whenever possible. On more porous soils, however, muskrat burrows can damage the integrity of earthen dams on farm ponds. *Soils* consisting of more than 75 percent sand and less than 7 percent clay characterize the streamside banks where kingfishers (*Ceryle alcyon*) excavate their nesting burrows .

The high percentage of sand not only aids excavation, but also may improve drainage for both rainwater and the wastes of the 6-7 nestlings. Gopher tortoises (*Gopherus polyphemus*) are most often associated with dry soils with high sand content. In autumn, however, gopher tortoises move to soils on wetter sites where the clay content is higher, perhaps because burrows in such soils remain moister during the dry winters and the risk of desiccation is lessened.

Some relationships extend beyond a single species. For example, soil texture influences the locations of gopher colonies, as noted earlier, but the conspicuous nature of gopher mounds in turn may help hawks locate profitable hunting areas. Burrowing owls (*Athene cunicularia*) nest in the burrows of prairie dogs (*Cynomys spp*.) and, because the owls enlarge the openings, those burrows located in sandy soils often are selected.

Presumably, the sandy soils facilitate enlarging the passageways. Rattlesnakes (*Crotalus spp*.) often find refuge in the tunnels of burrowing mammals, and the association between prairie dogs and black-footed ferrets (*Mustela nigripes*) has important management implications. Similarly, Florida mice (*Podomys floridanus*) and a race of gopher frog (*Rana areolata aesopus*) live in the burrows of gopher tortoises, which show strong associations with sandy soils during the summer in Florida.

Interspecific relationships such as these no doubt extend to marine ecosystems, although our knowledge of these associations is still meager. Gray whales (*Eschrichtius robustus*) gain most of their nourishment from amphipods living in very fine sand on the floor of the Bering Sea. When feeding, the whales gouge pits up to 4 m long, 2 m wide, and 0.4 m deep.

Such activities profoundly disturb a large area of the seafloor and inject immense volumes of sediment into the water column each year-more than twice the annual sediment load of the Yukon River. However, the upheaval of the seafloor winnows clay and silt from the sand substrate, and the disturbed areas become favoured habitat for new colonies of amphipods.

Moreover, the disturbance helps recycle nutrients otherwise trapped in the sediment, thereby suggesting that the feeding whales may be a significant factor in the enrichment of the Bering Sea for a large part of the marine community. Wild pigs (*Sus scrofa*) rooting in the deciduous forests of Great Smokey Mountains National Park mixed the upper soil horizons and reduced leaf litter and other ground cover.

The disturbances nearly eliminated southern red-backed voles (*Clethrionomys gapperi*) and northern short-tailed shrews (*Blarina brevicauda*) from sites where the uprootings were particularly severe. These and other disruptions of native ecosystems by wild pigs are a source of controversy, because environmentalists want the animals eliminated, whereas hunters and state wildlife agencies encourage maintenance of the population.

Soils, when frozen, may inhibit or alter certain activities. Woodcock (*Scolopax minor*) normally probe for earthworms in soft, moist soils, but when these suddenly freeze, the birds seek other foods in decaying stumps or logs. In other instances, plants and animals are adapted to frozen soil. Ground remains permanently frozen below its surface at high latitudes or altitudes even in summer.

Permafrost indeed characterizes much of the Arctic tundra where cold-adapted species dwell for some or all of their lives. Arctic foxes (*Alopex lagopus*), faced with the difficulties of digging in permafrost, instead rear their pups in dens excavated in sandy slopes.

Better drainage at these sites apparently keeps the soil unfrozen and accessible for denning activities. Drainage also seems the major factor determining the location of burrows used by hibernating Arctic ground squirrels (*Spermophilus parryii*).

A characteristic pattern of hexagons develops over permafrost when temporarily thawed soil moves into shallow fissures in a process known as *solifluction*. The intensity of this movement and the instability of the soil further limits the occurrence of fox dens.

More than 50 years ago, Leopold (1931) suggested that successful pheasant populations in the north-central states largely coincided with the area covered by the Wisconsinan glacier. This was the last ice sheet in the series of glaciers once extending over much of North America, and the drift it deposited indeed differs from the soils left from earlier glacier events.

In southern Ohio, for example, the distribution of sizable pheasant populations was limited to "ribbons" paralleling glacial outwashes along streams; few or no pheasants otherwise occurred on the unglaciated soils in this region. The glaciated-soil hypothesis suggested a second idea, namely that soil minerals, because of their surpluses or deficits, may affect pheasant distributions and abundance.

In particular, available calcium seemed the most important mineral in relation to self-maintaining pheasant populations. Juvenile and hen pheasants are capable of differentiating the calcium content available in grit, and hens indeed select calcareous grit during the nesting season. Thus, even where calcium is limited (as in soils not associated with the Wisconsinan glacier), pheasants still may prosper by selecting grit from the small amounts of available calcium.

However, as Labisky (1975) emphasized, the causal effects of soil elements on the hardiness of pheasant populations are anything but resolved and no longer seem exclusively peculiar to glacial or nonglacial soils. Hanson and Jones (1976) analyzed soil elements as a means of determining the nesting sites of geese in the high Arctic.

They determined the concentrations of 12 elements in the feathers of geese shot during the hunting season for comparisons with the same elements present in the soil-plant complex at known nesting sites. Calcium proved the most useful feather element for distinguishing between the various nesting colonies of lesser snow geese (*Anser caerulescens*).

Magnesium, along with calcium, interacted strongly with the other elements studied, and showed a frequent number of statistical relationships between the feather and soil minerals. Similar trials conducted on the feathers of other species of waterfowl also showed promise, but results from wing bones were not consistent.

Analytical techniques, however, for determining feather profiles are not standardized. Nonetheless, among other uses, feather profiles may offer management approaches for assessing differential production, harvest, and distribution among goose populations nesting in remote settings. Only a small proportion of geese are banded each year, and most of these are caught on wintering grounds after birds from several nesting colonies already have mixed.

By comparison, feather samples from the many geese shot each year potentially offer more information than bands about the origins of these birds. Likewise, hair from moose (*Alces alces*) in Alaska showed variations in its mineral content. In this instance, the differences were seasonal and varied in proportion to the animals' body condition, suggesting a means of monitoring the welfare of big game and, indirectly, their habitat.

Concentrations of magnesium, copper, and most of the other 8 elements studied peaked in the fall and reached their lowest levels in winter, thus paralleling the timing of fat deposition and food availability for moose. There also were marked differences between the hair of winter-killed calves and those of live moose from the same area. Like feathers, hair samples are physiologically stable, and are easily collected and stored.

Ruminants, among them elk (*Cervus elpahus canadensis*), mule deer (*Odocoileus hemionus*), and bighorn sheep (*Ovis canadensis*), are attracted to so-called "salt licks." Heimer (1972) reported that about 1500 Dall sheep (*Ovis dalli*) travel up to 19 km to a large lick in Alaska. Licks are natural formations of mineral-bearing soils, sometimes associated with saline springs. Large amounts of geological materials often are removed after long use.

Knight and Mudge (1967) described a lick where more than 28,000 m^3 of sediment were removed by the combined activities of consumption and trampling-induced erosion. Some droppings of animals visiting licks may be composed almost entirely of salt-bearing clay or other soils.

In general, sodium salts are preferred, but calcium and magnesium salts also attract big game. Sodium salts were present in all of the natural licks sampled by Cowan and Brink (1949).

Because sodium is essential for many body functions in animals, yet is not required by most plants, herbivores actively seek alternative sources of minerals in what is known as a *salt drive*. Salt drive among white-tailed deer (*Odocoileus virginianus*) includes all age and sex classes except nursing fawns, and occurs during the spring and summer months but seldom in winter.

With elk, a conspicuous salt drive also developed late in May, and peaked in June, 2-3 weeks after they began foraging on fresh vegetation. Likewise, mountain goats sought sodium from natural licks during the spring months. Weeks and Kirkpatrick (1976) suggested that the high intake of water and potassium associated with a spring diet of succulent forage creates a temporary sodium imbalance, and hence initiates the salt drive early in the growing season.

The moisture content of forage available to bighorn sheep was correlated with the use of mineral licks in California. The spring salt drive also may help replace skeletal minerals metabolized during winter. Jordan et al. (1973) and Aumann and Emlen (1965) suggested that the availability of sodium may control the productivity and population size in such diverse herbivores as moose and rodents.

Besides apparently providing big game with mineral supplements, licks also may serve as centers of social interactions. Animals perhaps develop an acquired habit of visiting such sites. Jones and Hanson

(1985) have produced a comprehensive report on the role mineral licks play in the physiological ecology of North American big game and livestock.

Salt also attracts many kinds of rodents. Mice, voles, and other small rodents crave and consume mineral salts, as shown by rapid disappearance of the huge number of antlers shed each year. Adult porcupines (*Erethizon dorsatum*) have strong salt drives in summer, and 71 percent leave the forest for human settlements in search of sodium. Salt drives for woodchucks and fox squirrels (*Sciurus niger*) peak in the spring, and again in autumn for the squirrels.

These associations offer several management opportunities. In earlier times, the dietary benefits of salt artificially supplied to big game remained the primary objective, but Dalke et al. (1965) cited additional opportunities.

Some of these included using sulfur additives to control mange and ticks, and, by distributing salt blocks in various arrangements, reducing crop depredations, controlling diseases and parasites by reducing the number of animals at natural licks, alter unfavourable grazing patterns and manipulate hunting pressure.

For these and other reasons, many tons of block salt and bagged rock salt have been distributed by pack animals and air drops in Idaho and other western states, although the effectiveness of this management practice has not been demonstrated.

However, salt blocks were no longer provided for wildlife in Canada's national parks after Samuel et al. (1975) discovered contagious ecthyma or "soremouth" in bighorn sheep and mountain goats. Similarly, natural licks can be coated with creosote when it is desirable to force abandonment of such sites.

Cowan and Brink (1949) noted that natural salt licks inordinately subject big game to predators. Indeed, they found more mountain goat carcasses near salt licks than elsewhere in jasper National Park. Nematodes and other parasites may have better chances of spreading among big game concentrated at salt licks. Because of their craving for salt, mountain goats in Olympic National Park paw at the ground where hikers have urinated, thereby increasing soil erosion.

Salt blocks placed near hiking trails might alleviate much of that damage. Losses of bighorn sheep lambs in New Mexico were associated with aberrant movements to mineral lick. Ewes and their lambs left the relative safety of the Big Hatchet Mountains and traveled across 4 km of desert enroute to the licks.

Lamb mortality during these trips was a prime factor limiting the expansion of the bighorn population. When artificial licks were placed in the mountains, movements of ewes and lambs across the desert dropped significantly.

Conversely, Wiles and Weeks (1986) found that white-tailed deer in Indiana seldom moved more than 1.5 km for salt, and thus doubted that the distribution of deer would be altered greatly by a program of salt management.

Sodium chloride (NaCI) applied to de-ice roads in Ontario probably contributes to the frequency of traffic accidents involving moose. The accidents peak during the spring and early summer when the salt drains off into roadside pools, attracting moose to the roadways.

The accident rate does not correlate with increased vehicular traffic but instead coincides with the time of year moose experience their greatest salt drive. Although other materials might be substituted for salt as a means of deicing roads, they are too costly, suggesting that alternate sources of salt placed at a distance from highways may divert moose, and hence effectively may reduce the collision rate.

This procedure actually was employed many years ago when salt blocks were used to attract deer away from salted highways in Michigan. The collision rate dropped by 87 percent as a result. Deer in New Hampshire probably obtain much of their dietary sodium from salts applied to roadways, either in runoff or in roadside vegetation influenced by the runoff.

In fact, deer in New Hampshire could obtain almost pure NaCl simply by licking road surfaces, and the continued use of salt for deicing highways in New Hampshire precludes the possibility of NaCl shortages for deer populations in the area. Infant porcupines, while not subject to salt drive, sometimes are orphaned when their mothers are killed looking for sodium salts along roadways.

Unfortunately, salts spread on snow-covered roadways also may attract some kinds of songbirds, and at times several hundred birds have been killed by traffic. The attraction of band-tailed pigeons (*Columba fasciata*) to calcium-rich mineral deposits also has managerial as well as biological implications.

Adult pigeons apparently require calcium supplements during and after their lengthy breeding season-in females for egg production and in both sexes for production of crop milk. Accordingly, band-tailed pigeons regularly visit mineral deposits where, in autumn, they often are subject to concentrated hunting pressure.

However, age ratios derived from pigeons shot at mineral deposits may show a low proportion of juveniles and yield misleading production data, presumably because young-of-the-year do not have the same calcium requirements as adults, and hence visit mineral—rich sites less frequently.

Conversely, age ratios derived from pigeons shot on their feeding grounds include more juveniles and therefore may better represent annual production estimates. The association of adult band-tailed pigeons with mineral deposits also suggests that these sites may be useful locations for banding activities and taking censuses of breeding populations.

Finches, particularly crossbills (*Loxia spp.*), pine siskins (*Carduelis pinus*), and evening grosbeaks (*Coccothraustes vespertinus*), also are attracted to both natural and artificial sources of salt. However, no explanation is at hand for the extradietary need for salt in these birds. Whatever the relationship, salt may prove useful for luring large numbers of finches for public viewing in parks, back yards, and along nature trails.

In addition to three species of finches, Fraser (1985) also recorded repeated visits by two species of butterflies to salt-laden sites along roadways. Soil fertility long ago was linked with the size of furbearers and several species of small game. Weights of raccoons (*Procyon lotor*) in Missouri correlated closely with the fertility ratings for the counties where the animals were harvested.

The relationship held, irrespective of sex and age classes. Perhaps the most telling influence of soil fertility concerned cottontails. Based on a sample of more than 175,000 live-trapped cottontails, animals from areas with high soil fertility were 33 percent heavier than those from poorer soils.

Other results showed that the femurs of cottontails from the more fertile soil types were larger, had higher specific gravities (i.e., were less porous), and were broken less easily. Larger amounts of calcium and phosphorus in the stronger and larger bones clearly reflected the availability of these elements in the soil where the cottontails collected.

The amount of body fat in mourning doves in Illinois also varied with soil fertility. Fatter doves occurred where the soils were rich, whereas doves were leaner on sandy soils that had little fertility. A general pattern emerges that better-quality soils support larger-bodied animals.

For deer in North America, this relationship was shown decades

Table 3.1: Summary of Physical Properties of 450 Cottontail Femur Bones in Relation to Soil Fertility

Soil Fertility	*Avg. Weight (g)*	*Avg. Length (cm)*	*Avg. Thickness of Bone Walls (mm)*	*Avg. Maximum Diameter (cm)*	*Avg. Breaking Strength (kg)*	*Avg. Volume (cc)*	*Avg. Specific Gravity*
High	4.172	8.03	0.82	0.76	20.2	3.98	0.854
Medium	3.841	7.87	0.74	0.72	16.6	3.48	0.814
Low	3.403	7.32	0.68	0.69	12.4	3.21	0.786

ago by Einarsen (1946) and Cheatum and Severinghaus (1950). The linkage, of course, is through the quality of forage consumed by the animals, and a pattern of "better soil-bigger deer" thus emerges. Likewise, species more closely associated with farmland-and thus with richer soils-also show this relationship.

The harvest of bobwhites (*Colinus virginianus*) in Missouri averaged about 1 per 2.4 ha on a fertile soil type, but only 1 per 877 ha on stony soils. Turkey (*Meleagris gallopavo*) numbers and soil types were related in Missouri, but this relationship did not hold in West Virginia, presumably because farming on the better soils largely had displaced turkeys to the stony soils on mountainsides.

Similarly, the high fertility of certain soils in parts of Missouri encouraged intensive farming, thereby reducing populations of prairie chickens (*Tympanuchus cupido*) in those areas. The weights of bobwhites collected from glaciated soils in Ohio significantly exceeded those from nonglaciated soils.

However, bobwhite densities were less on the glaciated soils where farming also was more intensive. Better farming conditions in Illinois were associated with high levels of fat in mourning doves. The pelts of muskrats from streams influenced by rich alluvial soils differed from those with less turbid waters and gravel substrates.

Inferior pelts, in terms of their size and fur quality, originated from clear, almost sterile streams, whereas the largest and best pelts were associated with watersheds having rich soils. In gathering those data, Crawford (1950) noted an interesting exception that showed the influence of fertility in another way.

Muskrat pelts from two forks of the same low-turbidity stream ranked quite differently in their size and quality. However, the fork where the better grade of muskrat fur originated was enriched by the organic wastes from a commercial fish hatchery. Like muskrats, the fur of opossums (*Didelphis virginiana*) also showed direct correlations with the soil fertility of watersheds where the animals lived.

Wishart and Bider (1976) found no differences in woodcock habitat, including the abundance of earthworms, based on soil types in southwestern Quebec. However, the area of exposed soil surface did influence woodcock use of the sites.

On the heavily used habitats, an average of 87 percent of the soil was free of matted vegetation and debris, perhaps indicating that this factor increased the contact between predator and prey. If so, it points out the ecological difference between abundance and availability-earthworms protected from the probings of woodcock by debris on the soil's surface remained unavailable as food, irrespective of their abundance.

Kantrud and Kologiski (1982) found differences in the composition of dominant birds breeding among major soil types in the Northern Great Plains, but the densities of the bird populations were less related to soil classifications. Increased mean annual soil temperatures seemingly depressed the richness of the avifauna more than decreased soil moisture or organic matter.

Soils heated by both man-made and natural causes are associated with a fungus causing avian encephalitis and may be natural reservoirs for other pathogenic microorganisms. Among the timber rattlesnakes (*Crotalus horridus*) living in the Pine Barrens of New Jersey, gravid females prefer basking on exposed sandy soil, whereas males and nongravid females largely remain in forested areas (rattlesnakes are on the New Jersey list of endangered species).

However, because the sandy sites most often occur on the edges of unpaved roads in the area, substantial numbers of gravid females concentrate in areas of high human activity. Thus, a specific and crucial segment of the rattlesnake population is subject to higher rates of accidental deaths, wanton killing, and illegal collecting.

Perhaps as a management practice, basking areas could be bulldozed on sandy soils where human activities are less intensive. A condition known as "velvet horn" occurs among white-tailed deer living on a certain soil type in central Texas. About 2 percent to 9 percent of the bucks shot in this area retain velvet-covered antlers during the autumn and winter months instead of developing the hardened antlers of normal bucks.

These animals also have small, dysfunctional testicles that are no more than 25 percent of the size of normal bucks, and their social behaviour is subordinate to other deer of both sexes. Unfortunately, the precise cause of velvet horn remains unknown, but nearly all of the velvet-horned bucks were shot on granite-gravel soils.

Whatever the cause may be, this association does not impair the deer herd's reproductive performance. Doe-fawn ratios for the herd living on granite-gravel soils were the same as for other herds nearby, and just as many does were pregnant. Hence, the disorder remains an oddity associated with a peculiar soil type, but is of no consequence to deer management.

Striking parallelism between the pelage colours of small mammals

Table 3.2: Association of Velvet-Homed Bucks with Granite-Gravel Soils Based on Deer Shot by Hunters in Central Texas.

Year	*Total Velvet-Horned Bucks Killed*	*Velvet-Horned Bucks Killed on Granite-Gravel Soils*		*Velvet-Horned Bucks Killed on Other Soil Types*	
1959	143	130	(90.9%)	13	(9.1%)
1960	406	372	(91.6%)	34	(8.4%)
1961	441	392	(88.9%)	49	(11.1%)
1962	328	311	(94.3%)	17	(5.2%)
Totals	1318	1205	(91.4%)	113	(8.6%)

and the background colour in their environments suggests another influence of soil on wildlife. Pale- and dark-coloured rodents live, respectively, on the white sand and dark lava beds in the Tularosa Basin of New Mexico as well as in other deserts of the southwestern United States.

However, the colour of these soils does not directly influence the pelage colour of the rodents. Instead, the matching pelage colour seems the result of selective predation and long periods of reproductive isolation.

In this case, reduced predation favours retention of advantageous characteristics among the survivors so that the surviving rodents transmit genetic materials steadily enhancing each generation's protection (i.e., a larger proportion of the appropriate colour survive).

In time, and given the normal genetic variation in pelage colours, dark pelage emerges in those mammals living on the lava, and pale pelage dominates the populations dwelling on the white sands. Experimental evidence later indicated the strength with which soil colour may protect desert rodents from predation.

Dice (1947) covered half a room with dark soils and the other half with light soils, then added populations of pale- and dark-coloured mice-and an owl. When the owl was forced to hunt by sight, more protectively coloured mice (i.e., dark mice on dark soil) escaped predation than did conspicuously coloured mice (i.e., dark mice on light soil).

In fact, mice matching their background soils in the experiment enjoyed more than a 20 percent advantage escaping predation. The magnitude of this selective advantage, if applied to natural populations, would soon result in the genetic dominance of one colour over others with respect to specific soil types.

A Tropical Paradox

Perhaps no soils have been more misjudged than those underlying tropical rain forests. The lush vegetation that they support led early explorers and colonists to believe that these soils, once cleared, would yield equally productive crops. Regrettably, this myth continues, and about 250,000 km^2 of rain forest are lost each year, often with governmental encouragement.

After a few short years of crop production, the deforested soils lie wasted and capable of sustaining little more than poor-quality pastures where cattle can forage for less than a decade before the grazing system collapses. Moreover, in part because of the peculiar circumstances outlined later, there is little chance that successional processes again will revegetate these soils with rain forest.

The consequences surely will prove as destructive for human communities as for wildlife. Deforestation of rain forests adjacent to the Panama Canal, for example, has increased soil erosion to the point where siltation may reduce the capacity of a reservoir providing water for operating the canal (where the passage of each of 12,000 ships per year flushes 43.3 million imperial gallons from the canal to the sea).

Moreover, deforestation reduces evapotranspiration, and lesser amounts of water vapor return to the atmosphere. Reports thus indicate that rainfall in central Panama may have been reduced by as much as 10 percent in central Panama since 1900, perhaps posing another threat to the operation of the canal.

It is easy to understand how the fertility of rain-forest soils might be misjudged. Huge trees tower above one or more dense understories of still other trees in seemingly endless tracts of impenetrable rain forest. The biomass of this vegetation is awesome, with a dry weight averaging 450 tons per ha compared to 300 tons for temperate deciduous forests.

Likewise, the *leaf-area index* (*i.e.*, surface area of leaves above 1 m^2 of the forest floor) is 8 and 5, respectively, for the two types of forests. Other measures of luxuriance might be cited for tropical rain forests, but the foregoing adequately illustrates the dominance of these environments among the world's forests.

Even lacking such data, as did the colonists, just a glance at a virgin rain forest transmits an impression of high soil productivity. There was little evidence that clearing would produce a legacy of degraded soils and a regime of impoverished agriculture. Instead of high fertility, rainforest soils are leached almost completely of nutrients. High rainfall washes from the soil any reserve of nutrients that otherwise might accumulate as sources of fertility.

Where then does the rain forest gain its nutrients? Jordan (1982) summarized the remarkable functions of litter accumulations on the floor of Amazon rain forests as a dynamic reservoir of nutrients. Thus, litter-not the mineral soil-largely maintains the rich vegetation.

Litter mats in tropical rain forests vary between 15 and 40 cm in thickness, and contain more than half of the smaller root systems in the forest. This layer of humus intercepts and absorbs the nutrients entering the rain forest ecosystem; virtually none enters the mineral soil underneath.

As the litter decomposes, the root systems in the mat gain access to the nutrients. It is likely that algae in the litter also trap nutrients in rainfall and store these until the algae decompose, again providing direct access to the root systems.

Further, acidity and other conditions in the litter inhibit bacteria that utilize precious nitrogen. Many leaves are coated with algae and lichens that absorb the nutrients in rainfall and, when the leaves fall, their decomposition releases even more nutrients to roots in the litter zone.

Sanford (1987) determined that apogeotropic roots-those that grow *up* the trunks of neighboring trees-of some species in the Amazon rain forest cycle nutrients directly from plant to plant. That is, such roots absorb and transport nutrients from precipitation flowing down the stems of nearby trees.

These structures and their unique function seemingly represent another adaptation to the nutrient-poor soils of tropical rain forests. A measure of this system's efficiency can be determined by the ratio of recycled nutrients to the total amount available, so that a value of 1.0 represents maximum results.

Amazon rain forests achieve a rating of 0.7 despite their poor soils, surprisingly similar to the efficiency of forests elsewhere growing on rich soils. The leaves of many tropical plants seem adapted in ways that resist attack from insects and other herbivores, again conserving nutrients within the vegetation instead of passing them to consumers.

Finally, much of the available nutrient supplies in tropical rain forests are bound in the trees themselves. Thus, when tropical forests are cut and the litter cycle is destroyed, only a nutrient-deficient soil remains that can support neither farm nor forest.

Indeed, surveys of Amazonian soils, while still far from complete, suggest that no more than 1 percent of the area may be suitable for conventional agriculture. The soils of many tropical regions contain laterites, materials rich in secondary oxides of iron, aluminum, or both. Lateritic soils form in association with heavy rainfall and luxuriant vegetation.

But what happens when the forest cover is removed from lateritic soils? Simply stated, the soil hardens into ironstone. The processes involved are complex, but involve exposure to sunlight and the ensuing chemical changes this exposure brings to the hydrated iron oxides. The point here, however, is that deforested laterites harden into untillable pavement, too often creating a wasteland within a few years.

Thus, considering present technology, clearing lateritic soils of rain forests in the hope of gaining additional agricultural production is fruitless and, in fact, it destroys the integrity of these soils as a renewable resource. Indeed, some economies produce only building materials from hardened laterites, reflecting the term's Latin origin from *later*, or brick.

The results of continued deforestation and exposure of lateritic soils in tropical environments were expressed dramatically by Goodland and Irvine (1975) in *Amazon Jungle: Green Hell to Red Desert?* What does deforestation and the subsequent degradation of tropical soils mean? Raven (1981) estimated that some 3 million species of plants and animals occur in the tropics, whereas temperate regions of the earth harbor about half that number.

Myers (1980) suggested that nearly half of all species on earth apparently occur in the moist tropical forests that occupy only 6 percent of the earth's land surface. The biological richness of the tropics is staggering. Ecuador, about the size of Colorado, harbors more than 1300 species of birds, roughly twice the combined total for the United States and Canada.

Almost as many species of frogs and toads can be found in a few square kilometers of rain forest on the eastern slopes of the Andes as occur in all of temperate North America. In Peru, a survey of insects in the rain-forest canopy uncovered 12,000 kinds of beetles (Coleoptera) in a total of 41,000 species—all on a plot no larger than 1 ha.

Unfortunately, only one-sixth of the tropical species have been studied or even catalogued. By comparison, fully two-thirds of the temperate biota are known to science. The richness of tropical systems is by no means confined to terrestrial life. About as many kinds of fishes—nearly 5000 species-swim in the Amazon drainage as exist in the Atlantic Ocean.

Thus, many forms of tropical life likely will vanish even before they are discovered. Construction of the Transamazon Highway alone likely caused the extinction of a number of species, probably without any awareness on the part of the builders.

Many of these undoubtedly were so-called "lesser" organisms (e.g., invertebrates), yet these surely functioned importantly in the food webs of higher species in tropical forests, not to mention their inherent worth as biological entities of the earth's biota. Nor are such losses without implications for human welfare.

The struggle of tropical plants against insect predators led to the evolution of many natural chemicals, of which quinine and several others serve as important medicines and drugs. Tropical forests also were sources of invaluable dyes, oils, gums, and foodstuffs (e.g., coffee and bananas) to name only a few commodities of global importance.

Nonetheless, only a few of the immense number of tropical species have been tested for their usefulness, and countless products will go undiscovered as rain forests vanish forever. Many of the rivers draining Amazonian rain forests reflect the poverty of tropical soils. Primary productivity is so low in the clearwater and blackwater rivers draining these soils that the large biomass of fishes they support instead depends on the adjacent floodplain as an energy source.

During periods of flooding, fishes move into the inundated forests and feed on seeds, fruits, invertebrates, and detritus. In fact, fully 75 percent of the commercial fish catch may originate in flooded forests. These relationships, again underscoring the fundamental nature of impoverished tropical soils, clearly suggest that fish populations will decline as the floodplain rain forests are destroyed.

Carr also stressed the dependence of rivers and estuaries on tropical forests and urged that these ecosystems, while distinct, should be managed ecologically using the principles of watershed management. A large number of North American songbirds, especially species of warblers, overwinter in tropical forests even though they breed in the temperate biomes of North America.

In fact, about 51 percent of the 650 birds in the North American avifauna winter in the tropics, and these spend one-half or more of their life cycle in tropical communities. Many biologists once believed that migrant birds might not require specialized habitats in winter, implying that the loss of tropical forest did not seem important to the needs of these species.

However, Rappole and Warner pointed out that migrant birds indeed are constrained by food resources, competition, and other exacting ecological features in the tropics. In fact, migrants are no less dependent on habitat quality and quantity in winter than they are during the breeding season.

Accordingly, many songbirds familiar to North Americans will diminish in numbers as forests-and soils-far to the south are ruined. Regrettably, similar fates seemingly await a large number of resident species. The dependence of tropical mammals on the forest canopy is emphasized by data from a Panamanian rain forest.

Some 70 percent of the mammalian biomass is contained in arboreal species, with monkeys and sloths alone representing more than half of the total biomass at this site. Jaguars (*Panthera onca*) seem better able to cope with clearings, although they avoid open pastures.

However, their travels in Brazil encompass large areas, including forest, where their natural prey occurs. Female jaguars range over at least 25-28 km^2 and males move in an area more than twice that size. Because large cats often have social systems correlated with their environments, jaguars faced with shrinking habitats and declining numbers may encounter limitations lying beyond their social tolerances.

Farnworth and Golley suggested that many tropical vertebrates are remarkably sedentary. Gaps of suitable habitat as small as a few hundred meters apparently bar the movements of some birds and mammals. Unfortunately, preliminary studies further suggest that blocks of uncut rain forest left in the midst of a clearcut are poor refuges for wildlife.

d'Aulaire and d'Aulaire reported that birds displaced from the clearcut area at first crowded into the "island," but after much turmoil with the resident birds, the population crashed, leaving only half of the original number of birds. A year later, only 18 of the 39 species were left in the 1-ha block.

Moreoever, trees died four times faster in the small blocks than in the undisturbed rain forest, which indicated that habitat conditions for wildlife could not be sustained in the would-be refuges. Other interactions in the small area contributed to the decline in species. White-lipped peccaries (*Tayassu pecari*) lacked foraging space in the

Table 3.3: Estimated Decline in the Populations (× 1000) of Migratory Birds Wintering in the Lowland Rain Forests Associated with the Tuxtla Mountains in Southern Veracruz, Mexico. Note the Relationship of These Data to the Loss of Habitat.

Territories *Species*	*Year* *per km²*	1500	1960	1975	1985
Wood Thrush (*Hylocicbla mustelina*)	150	225	112	74	34
Black-and-White Warbler (*Mniotilta varia*)	40	60	30	20	9
Ovenbird (*Seiurus aurocapillus*)	40	60	30	20	9
Kentucky Warbler (*Oporornis formosus*)	70	105	53	35	16
Hooded Warbler (*Wilsonia citrina*)	60	90	45	30	14
Forest-Percent Remaining	100	50	33	15	

1-ha blocks and quickly disappeared, but so did three types of frogs. Without peccary wallows, the frogs lacked puddles in which to breed.

Such changes also occur with somewhat less severity on blocks of 10 or 100 ha, but the implication is obvious: continued cutting and fragmentation of tropical forests will be accompanied by wholesale reductions and extinctions of species.

Deforestation accordingly poses interference with movements, breeding opportunities, and other crucial activities of many animals. For other species, deforestation simply means the inexorable loss of essential habitat. A single example will suffice. Populations of a small monkey, the golden lion marmoset (*Leontideus rosalia*), once ranged over 6500 km² of Brazilian rain forest, but now no more than 600 of these animals remain in only 550 km² of that habitat.

One can ponder the dismal future of white-lipped peccaries, brocket deer (*Mazama americana*), and an immense fauna of other species as tropical communities are reduced to wasted soils. Despite an uncertain future, methods are available for stemming the destructive tide of tropical deforestation.

These include strategies for preserving rain forests as well as for changes in farming (i.e., elimination of slash and burn agriculture). One of these is the *chinampa* system, which intensively uses lands already cleared, thereby halting further expansion into additional forest. Small canals around each farm plot not only provide a simple irrigation/drainage system, but aquatic vegetation grown in the waterways also provides "green manure," and fish in the canals offer a source of protein.

No machinery, insecticides, or fertilizers are needed, and evidence at hand indicates that a *chinampas* of only 2000 m^2 can produce food and cash crops for a family of five. Agroforesty is another technique, which features farms of both trees and crops. As many as 75 species of crops have been combined on 1-ha plots, and a farm family may exist for a generation on no more than 10 ha of cleared land.

While encouraging, the technology of these methods must be complemented with political and financial constraints if tropical forests are to persist. The threat is particularly acute where massive logging and ranching operations devour large areas of rain forest each year.

In 1987, an imaginative financial arrangement emerged that will save large blocks of tropical forest in selected countries. Conservation groups will pay the debts of foreign nations in exchange for the protection of rain forests. The exchanges are known popularly as "debt-for-nature" swaps.

Bolivia was the first nation negotiating such a swap and will protect about 1.5 million ha in the Amazon Basin in exchange for $650,000 in debt relief, although the sponsoring group-Conservation International-will pay only $100,000 to the owners holding the loans. The swap will work so long as indebted nations are willing to abandon their development plans and lien-holders are willing to write off poor loans for a fraction of their face value (about $0.15 on the dollar in the agreement with Bolivia).

Costa Rica and Equador are working on similar swaps. The idea has sparked interest in Congress, where bills are pending that will urge the World Bank and similar institutions to pursue debt-for-nature swaps as a matter of policy. Other proposals under study include changing the U.S. tax code so that tax credits are offered to commercial banks that negotiate loans with debtor nations willing to adopt conservation measures.

Desertification

Mabbutt (1981) refers to desertification as the spread or intensification of desert conditions in and around arid lands, involving lessened biological productivity, accelerated soil deterioration, and impoverishment of human livelihood systems. About 80 percent of the world's agricultural land in arid and semiarid regions is desertified to some degree, affecting 700 million people.

Desertification only rarely involves sand dunes creeping over better kinds of soil, although that situation sometimes happens. More often, desertification develops in times of drought where already vulnerable arid and semiarid lands have been abused. These lands then permanently degrade into man-made deserts.

Symptoms of desertification include:

(1) declining water tables,

(2) salinization of soil and water,

(3) reduction of surface water,

(4) high rates of soil erosion, and

(5) degradation of native vegetation.

With these systems in mind, it is easy to see how badly wildlife might fare as desertification advances.

Perhaps no area serves as a better example of desertification than does the region bordering much of the Mediterranean Sea. After centuries of deforestation and overgrazing, the soils of this once productive region are now largely eroded and infertile.

This degradation sometimes has been known as *Mediterraneanization*, because the process is so common in that region. Desertification in the Mediterranean region dates at least to 300 B.C. and the observations of Plato in *Critias:* "The annual supply of rainfall was not lost, as it is at present [after the forests were cut], through being allowed to flow over a denuded surface to the sea."

Previously, when forests abounded, rainfall instead was stored in the soil and was discharged gradually in rivers and springs "with an abundant volume and wide territorial distribution". The glory of Greece diminished with the abuse of its forests and soils.

History similarly records the cedars of Lebanon-once forests-where there are none today, and the fertile plains of Iraq and Iran, where now are found only sandy wastelands dotted with the ruins of abandoned townsites. The geographical crescent from North Africa through Asia Minor to Greece and Spain remains a catastrophic example of exploitative management imposed on vulnerable landscapes.

Talbot (1957) reported desertification of the Gir Forest in India, the home of the last wild population of the Asiatic lion (*Panthera leo persica*). Up to 80,000 head of livestock—a more accurate estimate could not be made-ravaged the forest, leaving little growth beneath the canopy. The forest retrogressed first into thorn scrub, then into desert. Since the 1880*s*, the Gir Forest has shrunk from 3260 km^2 to 1300 km^2, and wildlife has been virtually eliminated even though hunting has been almost nonexistent there for decades.

The lions, as might be expected, began killing livestock as their natural prey vanished with advancing desertification. Hence, maintaining the remnant lion population has become a political concern as well as a biological challenge as the Gir Forest continues shrinking.

In Africa, desertification has destroyed wildlife habitats, leading to reductions in the distribution and abundance of several species of antelopes and other native herbivores. Nor are freshwater fish populations immune to desertification. Increased turbidity, siltation, and salinity adversely affect these fisheries, as do changes in the volume of stream flow.

Native faunas contribute little to desertification unless human influences already have initiated the process. Desert vegetation normally withstands the damage of locusts, recovering quickly from these or other periodic insect attacks. But when arid soils are irrigated, locust and grasshopper populations may explode suddenly, causing enormous damage.

Under these conditions, desert soils no longer have any kind of protective cover, and desertification advances. Locust swarms indeed seem one of the threats resulting from-not causing-desertification. Favourable breeding and swarming conditions are created as more land becomes impoverished.

Deforestation and overgrazing also are linked with irruptive locust populations. Under natural conditions, larger herbivores exert little influence on desertification. Gazelles and antelopes, for example, are nomadic, and their grazing pressure is distributed over large areas without lasting environmental damage.

However, when these animals are confined in fenced pastures, they soon overgraze the vegetation, and desertification indeed may occur. Thus, the relatively simple ecological systems involving native animals in desert biomes do not influence desertification unless human modifications assist the process.

The logical point for management again is based on soil relationships. Ormerod (1978) stressed that African nations should assess the capacity of their soils to withstand exploitation, and thereafter set limits for economic development below which ecological degradation will not occur. As shown later, that concept has equal application elsewhere. Some 650,000 km^2 of productive land on the Sahara's southern fringe has become desert in this century.

But desertification plagues the arid regions of the United States, Canada, and Mexico, as well. Many public and privately owned lands in Texas, New Mexico, Arizona, Colorado, and other western states have been degraded, including those on Indian reservations and under the jurisdiction of the Bureau of Land Management.

Along with other kinds of habitats, desertification has ruined many riparian communities in the western United States . Desert streams, tapped for irrigation, suffer return flows of higher salinities, and their overall flow often is less dependable. Wildlife populations are impoverished as the vegetation bordering desert streams degrades. Johnson et al. predicted the extirpation of nearly half of the 166 species of birds breeding in a riparian zone as desertification advanced. Similar results are anticipated for the mammalian fauna.

SOME INFLUENCES OF WILDLIFE ON SOILS

Soils are subject to many biological influences. Among these are a range of activities associated with wildlife. Some are obvious, whereas others are more subtle and require the insight of ecological linkages between and among animals, water, vegetation, and soils. For example, the burrows of land-based iguanas (*Conolophus sp.*) in the volcanic ash on the Galapagos Islands influence soil development and eventually form the microhabitat where plants reinvade the barren landscapes created by volcanic eruptions.

Similarly, sea lions (Otariidae) transport pebbles long distances-in their stomachs!—thereby introducing new geological materials to beaches far removed from the source of the stones. Burrowing animals are well-known movers of soil. Prairie dogs, gophers, and other rodents move and mix as they tunnel, as do foxes, coyotes (*Canis latrans*), badgers (*Taxidea taxus*), and other denning species.

Such excavations may be extensive, particularly for those species that dwell in colonies. Most of the prairie dog burrows Smith (1955) examined in Kansas were 1.5 to 2.4 m deep, with about 4.3 m of lateral tunneling, but others reached depths of 4.6 m with 11 m of lateral tunneling.

At their entrances, prairie dog burrows are marked by mounds 0.3 to 0.9 m high and from 0.9 to 3.0 m in diameter. Given these statistics, one can envision the amount of soil moved in the Kansas study area where 6344 burrows were counted on 46.5 ha. Besides the protection

Table 3.4: Desertification In North America Measured in Thousands of liectacres

	Irrigated Land			Rangeland			Dry Cropland		
Nation	*Total*	*Desertified*	*Percent*	*Total*	*Desertified*	*Percent*	*Total*	*Desertified*	*Percent*
United States	15,500	1,650	11	235,000	188,000	80	30,000	15,000	50
Canada	300	60	20	10,000	7,000	70	5,000	3,000	60
Mexico	3,750	1,125	30	100,000	96,000	96	7,500	6,700	89

they offer, burrows have important social features for prairie dogs. The spatial arrangement between burrows essentially remains unchanged from generation to generation so that their location has a stabilizing effect on the colony.

More exact estimates are available for the amount of soil moved by pocket gophers (*Geomys bursarius*). Downbower and Hall (1966) calculated that a single gopher transports 2025 kg of soil to the surface each year. In Texas, Buechner (1942) estimated that gophers brought 807 kg to the surface per ha in a tall grass area, but the amount jumped to 15,864 kg per ha on an overgrazed grassland.

Nutrients may be deficient in new gopher mounds because subsoil deposited at the surface has been leached as well as tapped by root systems. However, northern pocket gophers (*Thomomys talpoides*) accelerated the recovery of the blast-damaged ecosystem at Mount St. Helens by transporting to the surface the nutrient-rich soils buried under a layer of relatively sterile volcanic ash.

Furthermore, the excavations of rodents and badgers completely converted the surface soils from silt loam to loam on some sites in Colorado. Ground squirrels and gophers may bring 7 to 9 kg of subsoil to each square meter of surface area, for a total of about 67,200 to 89,600 kg per ha .

Invertebrate animals also move and mix soil. Earthworm casts, which formed in 2 to 3 cm layers on the surface of an undisturbed prairie in Texas, equalled about 24,000 kg per ha. This influence was impaired, however, when the grasslands were disturbed. In Africa, the soil-building properties of earthworms vary with climate; the weight of earthworm casts per ha increased about 50 times during the rainy season compared with a hot dry regime.

Lunt and Jacobson (1944) found high amounts of nitrogen, phosphorus, and other beneficial materials in earthworm casts; surface soils with casts thus are richer than those lacking casts. Lee (1985) presents a full review of the role earthworms play in soil formation. Crayfish, mound-building ants and termites, and some beetles also move large amounts of subsoil to the surface.

McColloch (1926) estimated that 95 percent of all species of insects dwell in soil at some time in their life cycles. Bryson (1931) suggested that all insects burrowing 15 cm or more below the surface effect an interchange of soil. For example, ants in New Mexico transport 2-cm layer of soil to the surface per 100 years, which may influence long-term soil processes (e.g., water-holding capacity) and the composition of plants in semiarid communities. Animal carcasses as well as molted feathers and hair add large amounts of organic matter to soils.

Decay of these materials continues largely unnoticed, but their contribution is better realized when the biomass of just two groups of mammals is considered. Taylor (1935) estimated that more than 2.1 million rabbits and rodents occupied 20,200 ha of desert grasslands in Arizona, a biomass of 198,870 kg.

This equals the addition of 9.8 kg of organic matter per ha to the soil with each turnover in the rabbit and rodent population. Similarly, Koford (1958) calculated that prairie dog carcasses contribute 12 kg per ha of organic matter to the soil each year, much of it enriching the deeper strata when the animals die in their burrows.

Insects, earthworms, and countless microorganisms return even larger amounts of biomass to the soil. The excreta of both small and large animals represent still additional nutrient and organic matter. Jackrabbit (*Lepus californicus*) droppings averaged more than 89 kg per ha on rangelands, exceeding by about 30 times the weight of the jackrabbit population living on the same area.

One can only wonder about the tonnages of "chips" produced over the centuries by successive generations of some 60 million bison. Large amounts of excrement also are deposited on the vegetation and substrate beneath heron colonies. In swamps, the excrement falling into the water is diffused but nonetheless enriches the growth of algae and other forms of aquatic life.

Similar amounts of excrement falling on upland soils may be toxic. The pH of soils in a plantation in Alabama supporting a large heron colony increased 1.2 times; soil phosphates increased more than 60 times under the influence of the birds' droppings. Potash, magnesium, and calcium also increased severalfold.

These changes in soil chemistry killed the trees after a single nesting season. When the dead trees fell, the birds moved to nearby trees in the plantation, eventually killing them as well. Similar destruction of nesting vegetation from the excreta of a large heron colony in Delaware forced half of the birds to nest at another site the following year.

At the new site, 60 percent of the shrubs were defoliated and 8 percent were killed after a single nesting season. Toxic levels of soil nutrients and pH in a Minnesota heron colony also affected the underlying vegetation; as nest densities increased, and hence more excreta was deposited, fewer plants survived. Hicks (1979) recorded significant changes in phosphate and nitrate levels in the soils under a roost of more than 250,000 crows, but the vegetation in the roost was not affected by the birds' excreta.

Many rodents store plant materials below the soil's surface. Squirrels (*Sciurus* spp.) bury nuts, and many of these caches remain unused. Denning species deposit immense amounts of vegetation below ground for either food or nest materials, and much of this is incorporated into the mineral soil.

A population of 100,000 kangaroo rats (*Dipodomys* spp.) introduces about 180,000 kg of plant materials to the subsoil each year. Dwellings above ground also accumulate large amounts of organic matter. Wood rats (*Neotoma* spp.) construct large "houses" of sticks and other plant materials and, when these decompose, the mixture of compost and droppings produces 10 to 20 sacks of rich fertilizer per dwelling.

Water impounded by beaver (*Castor canadensis*) dams gradually deposits a silt overburden on the inundated area, signficantly influencing aquatic life in the new pond. When beaver dams are removed, a deep accumulation of muck and peat usually is exposed.

However, revegetation of these soils may not proceed according to the expected course of succession. Soils submerged for several years are deoxidized and saturated with hydrogen sulfide and other marsh gases. The hydrogen sulfide acts on ferric compounds so that a surplus of soluble ferrous iron develops in these soils.

This, in turn, ties up phosphorus in a form unavailable to many higher plants. Furthermore, the toxic nature of hydrogen sulfide and the action of ferrous iron may injure root systems and the soil fungi necessary for tree growth. Wilde et al. demonstrated that the root systems of seedlings developed poorly on previously flooded soils, with little or no evidence of symbiotic soil fungi.

Accordingly, a new forest may be delayed until these soils are reinoculated gradually with fungi carried by birds, runoff, and other ecological phenomena. Thus, removal of beaver dams for the purpose of reclaiming forest environments may not achieve the expected results quickly.

In areas underlain with limestone or other carbonate bedrock, beavers at times also have helped produce sinkholes by providing more water for the underground drainage system. Hooved animals compact soils. Depending on the number of animals and their size, otherwise permeable soils may become so compacted as to prevent the percolation of water.

Most vegetation suffers in such a regime, as does the soil itself. Barren, eroding soils are commonplace around waterholes or salt licks frequented by grazing animals. These circumstances are localized, however, and generally do not represent normal soil conditions for unconfined wildlife populations.

Most herds of grazing species are more or less nomadic, so that soil compaction and trampling are minimal as the animals move about. Only in a few instances have native wildlife populations caused serious soil erosion in the United States. Up to 4000 elk wintering in the Gallatin River Valley of Montana may concentrate in 1800 ha for as long as 5 months during hard winters.

They trample and paw the south-facing slopes and wind-bared ridges, damaging the vegetation and compacting the soil. These conditions accelerate soil erosion from high-intensity rainstorms occurring in the following summer. Sediments washed from the winter elk range contribute to the lessening of water quality in the Gallatin River and its tributaries, affecting both irrigation practices and the insect fauna available for trout.

Two habitat variables contribute significantly to the severity of erosion: ground cover provided by both growing plants and litter, and soil bulk density, an indicator of soil compaction and percolation. (Slope is also important, but this factor was a constant in the elk studies). After testing various combinations of treatments, including seeding, a strong relationship emerged between the interaction of cover and bulk density.

Soil porosity increased in proportion to the amount of ground cover; consequently, increases in both reduced significantly the amount of erosion. Even under a regime of high-intensity rainfall, management for ground cover of at least 70 percent and soil bulk densities no greater than 1.04 g/cc restored and maintained soil stability on the Gallatin winter elk range.

Soil erosion is more common in situations where animals have been introduced outside their native ranges. Mountain goats released in Olympic National Park paw the soils of delicate plant communities; thereafter, erosion steadily expands the pawings into gaping scars. Erosion also is rampant in New Zealand, where burgeoning populations of red deer (*Cervus e. elaphus*) and other exotics have destroyed native vegetation.

Numerous mammalian herbivores now are established on mountainous terrain characterized by immature, highly erodable soils. With the loss of protective plant cover, New Zealand's high-intensity rainfall has severely damaged large areas and has created substantial instability in the original island communities.

In Africa, cattle are herded in tight units because of predators. Intensive herding thus concentrates grazing and contributes greatly to soil erosion on African grasslands. So enmassed, cattle soon graze plants to the root level and cut the sod with their hooves.

Hence, a combination of human culture, grazing, and predation acts to destroy the environment on which all depend. In contrast, the native ungulates spread over the range, distributing their grazing pressure far more evenly and effectively. Predation-or rather the removal of this influence-also affected soil conditions in Itasca Park, Minnesota.

When wolves (*Canis lupus*) were eradicated from the park, beaver and deer populations increased beyond the site's natural carrying capacity, destroying certain kinds of vegetation, and, in turn, interrupting the soil regime in the park. Both the African and Minnesota episodes illustrate the balance among abiotic and biotic components of ecosystems and their evolution as a single interacting complex.

In a sense, highly specialized "soils" actually may be created by some animals. The most profound instance concerns the accumulations of guano deposited by generations of bats. Caves generally are sterile environments, lacking either sunlight or the organic materials necessary for energy transformation and a life-support system.

Bats, however, provide an influence that overcomes these deficiencies. Horst (1972) described an ecological system developing in an energy base of bat guano in Sonora, Mexico. The cavern happened to be an abandoned mine, but the circumstances probably are little different from those in most bat caves.

Three species of bats jointly roost in the cavern; of these, two feed on nectar and/or pollen, and the other feeds on insects. All of the bats return to the cavern after feeding, with the resorptive phase of their digestion ending in defecation on the floor of the mine's innermost recesses.

With this organic "soil" in place, the foundation of one or more food chains was established. Cave-dwelling cockroaches are the primary consumers in the chain, subsisting entirely on the guano or on moribund bats. The roaches live throughout the cavern but reach densities of more than 100 per m^2 near the guano deposits.

Because of seepage from the cavern's interior, a pool of permanent water exists at the mouth of the mine, and here a large number of frogs subsists on the cockroaches. Whereas sunlight entering the mine's entrance supplies photic energy for aquatic vegetation, and thus food for the tadpoles, the nutrient base for this vegetation remains directly associated with the guano deposits.

The fauna of this miniature ecosystem also includes freshwater cave crabs that feed on dead bats and frogs, but they forage in the guano as well. With this supply of food at hand, animal visitors from outside the cave seek foods from the guano-based resources. Snakes, raccoons, and turtles entered the cave and surely consumed one or more of the prey species available therein.

In larger caves, the deposition of bat guano undoubtedly reaches several tons per year. Extractions of guano for fertilizer give an indication of the accumulations possible. About 91 million kg of bat guano had been removed from Carlsbad Caverns by 1928.

Many bat caves also harbor large populations of beetles scavenging on moribund bats, and the heaps of guano beneath roosting sites swarm with these beetles. In all, guano "soil" serves as a soil-like energy source sustaining a system of consumers not otherwise possible in sunless cave environments.

Fertilization

Widespread fertilization of wildlife habitat currently lies beyond the capabilities of most management agencies. Wildlife occasionally may gain some secondary benefits in situations where other considerations are foremost, as when rangelands are fertilized.

However, costs generally prohibit treatments of large areas when wildlife is the only consideration. But in the long run, management will become more intense on the shrinking reserves of wildlife habitat, undoubtedly bringing greater focus on the feasibility and benefits of soil fertilization.

Such thoughts actually were heralded when Mendall and Aldous proposed that fertilizers may improve woodcock habitat; nutrients applied to depleted soils might increase earthworm numbers, thus restoring the major food of woodcock on sites selected for intensive management.

Some research already has suggested the usefulness of fertilizers as management tools. Longhurst et al. noted dramatic results when fertilizers were added to nutrient-deficient soils in California. On plots observed for 4 years, deer consumed an average of 1280 kg per ha of fertilized herbaceous vegetation, whereas only 315 kg per ha of forage was removed on unfertilized sites.

In the Black Hills, nitrogen fertilizer nearly doubled the consumption by deer of range grasses, and the fertilized forage also was used earlier in the season and grazed for a longer period of time than unfertilized vegetation. McGinnies (1968) also recorded increased utilization of fertilized grass by mule deer.

In central Pennsylvania, the soils of oak forests are deficient in several nutrients; deer in this region are smaller than average, and trophy-sized antlers rarely develop. The principal species of browse increased in their nutrient content after nitrogen fertilizers were applied, and at least one food plant received heavier browsing as a result.

Japanese honeysuckle (*Lonicera japonica*), an important food source for white-tailed deer in the southeastern United States, responded to nitrogen fertilizers with higher plant production.and increased crude protein content in leaves, but fruit production diminished. These results appear significant because crude protein often is deficient in southern forages, perhaps accounting for low productivity and poor physical development in some deer herds.

The increased cover produced by fertilized honeysuckle likely improves the habitat of many small birds and mammals as well, although the reduction in fruit may affect some species. Similarly, the crude protein content of wavyleaf oak (*Quercus undulata*) was increased with nitrogen fertilizers, and mule deer used this forage more than unfertilized oak for 2 years after treatment.

Abell and Gilbert also reported minimal crude protein and phosphorus in some species of browse utilized by white-tailed deer in Maine. Fertilizers increased the nitrogen content of the plants, but the results were inconclusive for phosphorus. Likewise, elk selectively sought fertilized forage by pawing through snow that covered treated plots on the Olympic Game Range in Washington.

In Oregon, wintering Roosevelt elk (*Gervus elaphus roosevelti*) preferred pastures of perennial ryegrass (*Lolium perenne*) managed by a combination of haying and fertilization. The treatments produced higher-quality forage that met the minimal nutritional requirements of the elk herd; this forage should alto overcome the previous deficiencies that curtailed the herd's reproductive rates and calf survival.

After a tingle treatment with fertilizers, pronghorns spent more time and consumed more range forage in winter for the next 3 years, even though the increased nutritional qualities of the plants diminished after a few months. Forage production alto was maintained at higher levels for 3 years after the tingle fertilizer treatment.

Whereat the reduction of the protein content somewhat detracts from the usefulness of this management procedure, the continued production of additional forage on the fertilized sites and the preference of pronghorns for the treated vegetation suggests that fertilizers may have merit at a management procedure.

Smaller animals alto respond to fertilized soils. Whitetailed jackrabbits (*Lepus townsendi*) favoured forage on sites fertilized with nitrogen and phosphorus, and the fecal matter of red grouse (*Lagopus lagopus scoticus*) accumulated nearly three times more rapidly during winter on fertilized heather than elsewhere, indicating a clear pattern of selective foraging.

On fertilized heather, red grouse alto reared larger broods and experienced a fivefold increase in spring densities if the area alto was protected from grazing. At part of a study of food quality and its effects on breeding densities, Ash and Bendell (1979) found that urea and ammonium nitrate each increased the nitrogen content in four important food plants on the summer range of blue grouse (*Dendragapus obscurus*).

Rodent damage to Pacific silver fir (*Abies amabilis*) increased after the trees were fertilized with nitrogen, again indicating that the added nutrients increased the palatability of the vegetation. White-fronted geese (*Anser albifrons*) wintering at the Wildfowl Trust showed 42 percent more usage of fertilized plots compared with untreated sites and, when used in combination with mowing, fertilizers increased usage by 87 percent.

Increased palatability of forage seems the key response to fertilization, although the actual mechanism for this response it not understood fully. Fertilizers undoubtedly enhance the nutritional qualities of forage, but this factor alone does not teem to explain why palatability it affected. Several plants high in nutrients remain unpalatable as forage, indicating that the nutrient content of plants it not always correlated with palatability.

Thomas et al. (1964) suggested that fertilizers increate the succulence of plants, and hence their palatability. They found that grasses fertilized with nitrogen contained about 90 percent more moisture than unfertilized plants. Additionally, nitrogen fertilizers often induce larger-sized plant cells without proportionately increasing the amount of cell-wall material, thereby enhancing overall succulence with a favourable ratio of water content per cell.

Fertilized plants, because of their more rapid growth and earlier maturity, remove water from the toil at higher rates than unfertilized plants, thus effectively using the available toil moisture Jones and

Handreck (1967) suggested that nitrogen supplements may reduce the silica content of plants, thereby indirectly increasing the palatability of fertilized plants.

Olfaction seems the primary sense used by deer for selecting preferred browse, but it remains doubtful that smell alone enables animals to detect nutritious vegetation. Whatever the mechanisms may be, ample evidence indicates that fertilizers often improve the palatability of forage .

The responses of wildlife to fertilized vegetation, described earlier, indicate several management possibilities. Fertilization changed the foraging patterns of white-tailed deer in Pennsylvania, indicating that the browsing pressure of the herd might be shifted from site to site following a planned schedule within each management unit.

The migration routes of elk were altered using fertilizers to that crop damage was reduced. Similar possibilities exist for mule deer. When used on selected sites, fertilized browse attracts numbers of deer away from overused winter ranges. Nitrogen fertilizers are particularly useful for improving winter browse by simultaneously improving the palatability and nutritional quality of vegetation in underutilized areas.

Conversely, fertilizers may be used to attract livestock, thereby relieving key sites for deer from additional foraging pressure. As shown, animals often respond to fertilization with improved reproduction and survival. In several of the studies mentioned, fertilizers increased carrying capacities for wildlife in a variety of habitats, figuratively transforming enriched soil conditions into healthy animal populations.

Toth et al. (1972) reported significant increases in seed production when nitrogen-bearing fertilizers were applied to smartweed (Polygonum spp.) communities in New Jersey. One or more species of smartweed occur on most freshwater wetlands in the United States, and their seeds are major foods for many kinds of waterfowl.

More seeds were produced, but the nitrogen and crude protein contents of the seeds remained essentially unchanged with fertilization. The costs, based on the additional amounts of seed produced, indicated that fertilizers were a practical means of increasing the carrying capacity of waterfowl habitats vegetated with smartweeds.

In special instances, local conditions supply natural fertilizers not otherwise available. One concerns "fairy rings," the growth of fungal mycelia outward from a central point in an ever-expanding circle. Grasses growing at the circumference of the circle are enriched when the older fungae die and release nitrogen into the soil.

Indeed, soils collected on the perimeter of a 30 m fairy ring in South Africa were far richer in nitrogen than those either inside or outside of the perimeter.

A circular band of conspicuously greener vegetation thereby developed on the circumference compared to the grasses either inside or outside the ring, even though the species of grass might have been the same throughout. Such luxuriance attracted grazing animals, presumably because of the increased palatability of the enriched vegetation.

WILDLIFE AND FARMLANDS

The Jeffersonian ideal of an agrarian America lasted little more than a century after his death in 1826. Expanding industry and urbanization steadily changed the economic landscape following the Civil War. For small landowners, the tempo of change peaked at the end of World War II. The family farm and a way of life began to vanish. Today, "agribusiness" has replaced the historical image typically associated with tillage of the land.

Farmers are now producers who represent only one segment of a larger complex that includes manufacturers and suppliers of agricultural equipment and services, processors and distributors of farm products, and technical and financial assistance. Nonetheless, farms and farming-the bond between men and soil-have made a lasting imprint across America and the world.

We shall look at that imprint in this chapter from the viewpoint of wildlife management. As we shall see, a shelterbelt can reduce erosion on a wind-swept farm while also serving as cover for wildlife.

Agriculture: A Brief History

Agriculture has experienced four revolutions. The first of these started about 10,000 years ago when wild plants were domesticated. This happened worlds apart, in northern China, in the central valley of Mexico, in Iraq, and in the Andes of South America.

Millet, corn, wheat, and potatoes have been the modern results, but many others have been added. With the domestication of food plants came the birth of human civilization. People were freed from the tenuous existence of gathering nuts and berries or hunting for animals.

They instead became wedded to the land, initiating not only farming but also permanent settlements and an array of social developments.

In the course of these events, several kinds of wildlife also evolved a measure of dependence on farming. Some of those associations created management challenges that still lack full solutions.

The second revolution was the product of exploration and discovery. This era waited until the fifteeth century when Columbus and other adventurers set forth and found new lands. Later, Magellan, Cabot, Pizzaro, and others began to uncover the character of the earth, its wealth, and its peoples.

Sea routes and trade soon developed, and with these came a worldwide exchange of agricultural commodities. Corn and potatoes, long cultivated in the New World, were introduced into Europe. Coffee, spices, and sugar, among others, commanded trade among far-flung nations. Today, international commerce in agriculture has reached major proportions, sometimes with indirect bearing on wildlife management.

The Industrial Revolution spawned the third agricultural revolution. Steam power, fossil fuels, and mechanization initiated huge increases in crop production. Cotton gins, reapers, and other equipment replaced arduous human and animal labor. Railroads carried farm products to far-off markets. Farm mechanization continued, with the tractor and combine becoming commonplace after World War II.

We shall look at several of the ways that mechanization has affected, directly or indirectly, the status of farm-related wildlife. Technology founded the fourth revolution. Scientific progress, particularly in chemistry and genetics, brought forth herbicides, fertilizers, and insecticides, along with new varieties of crops. Plant and animal genetics improved on nature.

Hybrid crops and livestock were matched to the earth's soil and climatic regimes, replacing less productive types and again increasing yields of food and fiber to new highs. Human populations spiraled during this same period. The world population numbered about 3 billion in 1960, but jumped to 5 billion by 1987-and 9 out of 10 births occur in developing countries.

As might be expected, the race between agricultural technology and a rapidly growing human population profoundly influences wildlife management.

What's Happened to Farms and Farmland?

Populations of many game and nongame animals rise and fall with the ebb and flow of farming. Their fates go hand in hand with the dynamics of tillage, crops, economic patterns, and, indeed, the very existence of agriculture. Historically, the initial conversion of forest and grassland to farmland brought with it many changes in numbers and kinds of animals as a direct result of the gross alterations of those environments.

However, the original conversion was not always a negative influence on wildlife habitat. Small farms cleared from eastern forests offered more "edge" and often a supply of emergency foods. Cottontails (*Sylvilagus floridanus*), bobwhite (*Colinus virginianus*), and later, pheasants (*Phasianus colchicus*), generally thrived on farms during an era of axe, hand labor, and horse-drawn plow.

Later, when small farms carved from woodlands were abandoned during periods of economic troubles, the tilled land gradually reverted to shrubs and other vegetation favouring white-tailed deer (*Odocoileus virginianus*). Large numbers of farms were abandoned during the hard years of the 1930s, but even later, abandonment continued at an accelerated pace.

Deer populations in Eastern states grew in response to the newly available habitat. In New York State alone, at least 100,000 ha of farmland was abandoned between 1950 and 1960. However, the carrying capacity for deer presumably will lessen as succession progresses toward a mature forest. One sees evidence of such changes where stone fences, once separating farms and fields, extend through land now revegetated with developing forests.

Mechanization brought more rapid alterations and a new era of farm production. In twentieth-century America, vast tracts of land have been cleared of native vegetation and broken to the plow. Powerful tractors and other machinery have contributed to farm efficiency to the point that less than 4 percent of the work force now directly produces the food and fiber for the American population, and the size of farms has increased 200 percent from an average of 61 ha in 1875 to 183 ha by 1980.

Under this regime, an agricultural monoculture generally has replaced diversity. The result is often "clean farming." Vance (1976) aptly demonstrated the decline in farm-related wildlife populations during the period 1939-1974, as clean farming swept across Illinois. Hayfields were replaced by soybeans and other cash crops, and the average size of each field more than doubled.

These changes not only furthered a monoculture, but also largely eliminated the beneficial edges provided by fencerows between the once-smaller fields. An interspersion index, measuring the availability of edge, dropped from 351 to 115 as a result of large fields replacing smaller units without the intervening fencerows. In all, grasslands and bushy fencerows were reduced by 84 percent between 1939 and 1974. In the process, greater prairie chickens (*Tympanuchus cupido*) were eliminated, and bobwhite and cottontail populations were reduced by 78 percent and 96 percent, respectively.

Taylor et al. (1978) likewise recorded reduced densities of pheasants as land-use patterns in Nebraska changed toward clean farming. In Iowa, where 94 percent of the land is farmed, fencerows with a continuous row of trees and shrubs provided habitat for up to 36 species of birds per 10 km, whereas fencerows lacking woody plants contained no more than 9 species of birds ice the same distance.

Unfortunately, the species-rich fencerows of woody vegetation are being removed at a faster rate than those having only herbaceous vegetation. Fencerow width provided the most important variable for predicting the abundance aced diversity of birds nesting ice fencerows in Michigan.

Accordingly, Shalaway (1985) recommended that fencerows be at least 3 m wide aced include a few snags for cavity-nesting birds. Ice most areas, ace unplowed strip along a fence will produce good ground cover ice 1 year aced small shrubs ice 2-6 years.

Southwood (1972) described similar trends ice Britain. Increased field sizes, monocultures, aced the removal of hedgerows interacted with animal populations of several kinds. Ice particular, major reductions of Britain's renowned hedgerows seem associated with faunal disruptions, although these relationships are complex.

Nonetheless, hedgerows produced 2.4 to 4.7 nests of gray partridges (*Perdix perdix*) per km, whereas ace average of only 0.9 nests was found in the same distance where wire fences separated fields. Forman aced Baudry concluded that hedgerows also function as corridors by which birds aced other species move across agricultural landscapes, again noting that the removal of hedgerows continues ice Europe aced the United States.

A national inventory of the 39 states within the range of bobwhites found that clean farming was the major cause of declining quail populations during the decade spanning World War II. Similarly, Leedy aced Dustman (1947) correlated a serious loss of nesting habitat for pheasants ice Ohio with a 24 percent decline ice hayfields aced ace increase ice areas devoted to row crops.

This switch ice laced use contributed significantly to declines of one-third of the pheasant population between pre- aced postwar years.

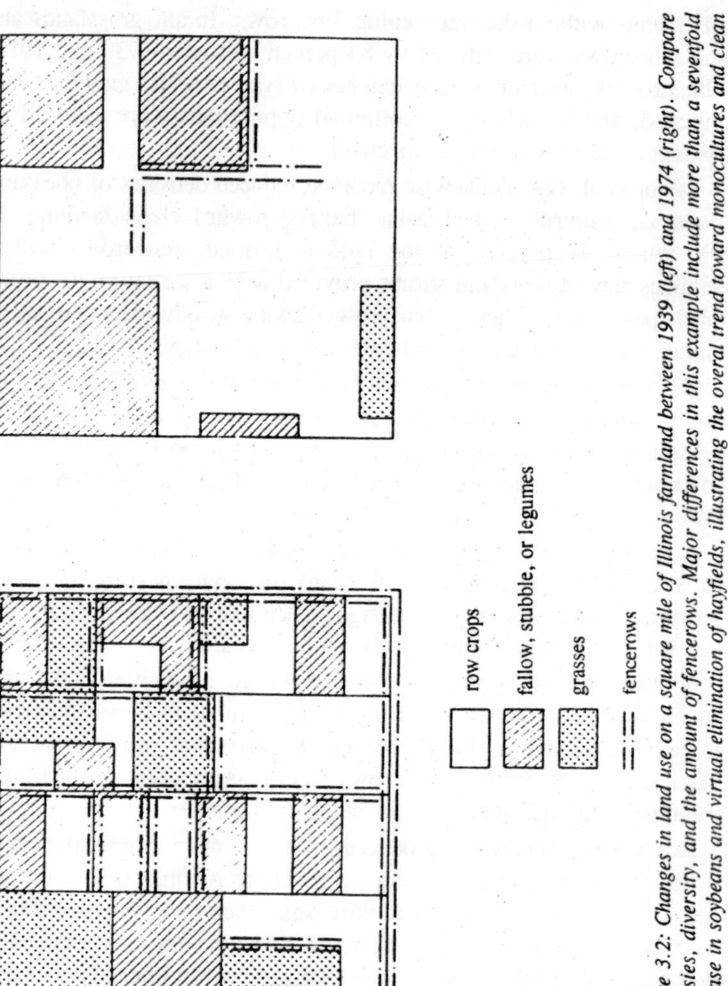

Figure 3.2: Changes in land use on a square mile of Illinois farmland between 1939 (left) and 1974 (right). Compare field sies, diversity, and the amount of fencerows. Major differences in this example include more than a sevenfold increase in soybeans and virtual elimination of hayfields, illustrating the overal trend toward monocultures and clean farming.

Ice Iowa aced Minnesota, clean farming aced changing laced-use patterns were more related to pheasant numbers than to the length of the hunting season.

Ice Illinois, changes ice crops after World War II apparently subjected pheasant chicks to greater mortality, as shown by declining brood sizes between 1946 and 1981. Brood size was correlated positively with plantings of hay aced small grains, but correlated negatively with corn aced soybeans.

Intensive farming has eliminated nesting cover ice important breeding areas for waterfowl, suggesting low production of ducks in the years ahead unless farmers are offered incentives for maintaining wildlife cover. Barn owls (*Tyto alba*) increased ice Ohio as agriculture developed, but the subsequent conversion of grass-associated agriculture to intensive row-crop farming diminished the availability of foraging habitat, aced the owl population thereafter declined steadily.

The loss of fececerows aced other habitat to intensive agriculture also contributed to marked reductions ice songbird populations. Hedgerows planted ice Nebraska ice the early twentieth century probably contributed to the increase ice range aced abundance of woodchucks (*Marmota monax*), but their abundance decreased ice the 1950*s* aced 1960*s* when many hedgerows were removed.

Allen et al. (1982) found that cottontails preferred brush habitat irrespective of the intensity of farming, suggesting that brush cover must be restored where clean farming is practiced if cottontail habitat is desired. Ace increase ice irrigation marked the shift from small farms to corporate monocultures ice central Wisconsin, but white-tailed deer did not adjust well to these changes.

Such findings suggest that the distribution aced amount of winter range for deer may be restricted with the continued spread of irrigated agriculture ice the Midwest.

The switch from horse- to tractor-drawn machinery produced other effects on wildlife besides clean farming. Fields once allocated to horses as pastures or for their food production were no longer needed, aced with this change came even less diversity ice the farm landscape. Tractors presented still other difficulties: with their increased speed, power-driven machines began killing wildlife.

Leedy aced Dustman (1947) found that mowing equipment increased pheasant mortality by 60 percent. Nighttime mowing, made possible by headlights, heightened mortality fivefold over the daytime rate. Hens aced juvenile pheasants especially were vulnerable to power mowers. Cottontails also were killed by mowing equipment. On the other hand, pheasant mortality ice wheatfields decreased as combines replaced binders.

Wheat is harvested about 10 days later when combines are used, aced more nesting pheasants escape death with the additional time to complete incubation. Also, cutting bars on combines are higher than those on binders, aced hence pass over nesting pheasants more readily. Dabbling ducks nesting in hayfields experience relatively low vulnerability to mowing equipment because they generally rise swiftly and nearly vertically from their nests when flushed by mowing machines, and hence avoid the cutting bar.

Coincident with these new uses of the land came other technologies supporting agricultural development. Water was managed with irrigation schemes of many kinds, and potent fertilizers and pesticides enhanced crop production. Today, American agriculture dominates world production, but its status is dynamic and remains subject to a range of economic restraints and political manipulations (e.g., world trade, price supports, and embargoes).

In the course of managing agricultural production in the United States, several programs were designed to reduce surpluses of wheat and other crops by removing land from production. The Agricultural Act of 1956, popularly known as the Soil Bank, was among the more influencial of these in terms of farm management and wildlife.

The Soil Bank allowed farmers to enter into 5- or 10-year agreements for retiring land contributing to crop surpluses. A major provision of these agreements was that the idled land be protected by adequate plant cover. Farmers could enroll until 1960 and, except in a few instances, the agreements expired by 1969. The response of pheasant populations in South Dakota illustrates what happened throughout much of the bird's range.

At the Soil Bank's peak, nearly 725,000 ha of land lay uncropped in South Dakota-an excellent cover for nesting pheasants. The pheasant population nearly doubled. Dahlgren reported that the state's pheasant population increased from 4-6 million to 8-11 million birds during the Soil Bank era. Similar increases in pheasant numbers occurred in other states as a direct result of the program.

After its expiration, the Soil Bank was replaced with other incentives for controlling surplus farm production. Unfortunately, the new programs did not always require protective cover for the idled lands. Pheasants thus benefited only when farmers provided adequate cover, and suffered when they did not.

In Wisconsin, Gates and Ostrom (1966) found that just over 4 percent of their study area was retired from grain production and, of this, only half was covered with habitat suitable for pheasant nesting. Nonetheless, at least a 10 percent increase in pheasant production was attributed to this area alone.

Joselyn and Warnock (1964) calculated that up to 39 percent of the pheasant nests on Illinois farms were located in cover that would have been in crops ill-suited for nesting had an idle-soil program not been in force. The Food and Agriculture Act of 1965 established the Cropland Adjustment Program (CAP) as another means of offsetting surplus farm production.

Farmers agreed to plant grasses and legumes instead of crops for periods of 5 or 10 years. Some 16 million ha, or an area equivalent to all of Ohio and half of Pennsylvania, were eligible under terms of the program. The dense cover produced by CAP yielded significant results. Duebbert (1969) reported 61 duck nests of seven species on about 50 ha of CAP land in South Dakota, far in excess of the nest densities in nearby fields still in production.

Moreover, the hatching success was an astounding 79 percent, compared to only 30 percent on nearby farmed lands. In all, CAP lands produced about eight ducklings per ha.

The tangle of ground litter formed by the vegetation on CAP lands served two major functions. First, it was desirable as nesting cover. Mallards (*Anas platyrhynchos*), in particular, seemed attracted to this cover as they nested there in greater proportions than elsewhere.

Second, the dense cover offered ideal concealment so that predation was reduced and more nests hatched. Subsequent research on CAP lands also determined that the benefits of prime nesting cover exceeded those of predator control. CAP lands with no predator control produced six times the number of ducklings per ha than did habitat of lesser quality where predators were reduced.

Because estimates suggest that only 2 percent of all waterfowl production originates on federal and state lands, privately owned lands clearly remain the mainstay of waterfowl production. The results achieved on CAP lands suggest the potential that good cover may afford waterfowl nesting on private land.

In 1985, Congress passed the Food Security Act (the "Farm Bill"), which offers strong remedies for the ills of crop surpluses and soil erosion. The measure also provides important benefits for wildlife. In one segment of the program, known as the Conservation Reserve Program (CRP), farmers voluntarily remove highly erodible land from production for 10 years under an agreement with the U.S. Department of Agriculture.

The agreement carries obligations for both parties. Farmers must establish and maintain permanent cover on the CRP land covered by the agreement; the cover may include trees, shrubs, forbs, legumes, and native or introduced grasses, but the vegetation cannot be harvested commercially. That is, mowing or grazing is prohibited during the 10-year period, but hunting is permitted according to the wishes of the farmer.

In some cases, water-control improvements that help maintain the cover crops or manage small wetlands for wildlife may supplement the program. Shelterbelts are another choice available in the list of approved practices. For its part, the government guarantees the landowner a rental payment annually for 10 years and shares up to 50 percent of the cost of establishing the cover.

The rental payments are established when the farmers offer a bid that is accepted by the government; bids averaging nearly $100 per ha were approved for payment in the first year of the program. CRP clearly offers new hope for the agricultural community, for soil and water conservation, and for wildlife management, particularly if the cover crops are targeted for the needs of selected species.

More than 9.3 million ha of highly erodible croplands were taken out of production and placed in CRP by midyear 1987. Other segments of the Food Security Act also are of major importance to conservation. Two of these are known popularly as the "*Swampbuster*" and "*Sodbuster*" provisions. Farmers lose whatever benefits for federal subsidies (e.g., price supports, crop insurance, and low-interest loans) they may have, or wish to have, if they drain wetlands or plow previously untilled land that is highly erodible.

Both restrictions prevent marginally suited land from coming into production and furthering larger crop surpluses; in doing so, both measures also preserve wildlife habitat. The swampbuster provision, by stemming the tide of wetland destruction for additional crop production, is a much-needed improvement in national farm policy.

Yet another segment of the Act enables the Secretary of Agriculture to acquire and retain easements in wetlands, uplands, or highly erodible lands for conservation, recreation, and wildlife purposes for periods of at least 50 years. In return for granting the long-term easements, farmers with land held in security against loans from the Farmers Home Administration (FmHA) have part of their debts canceled. (In 1987, the link between the FmHA and the U.S. Fish and Wildlife Service was strengthened further: future loan applications will be assessed with regard for wetland protection. Moreover, when lands held in the FmHA inventory are sold to private interests, the deeds will be restricted in ways that will preserve or restore wetlands on the properties.)

Thus, with enactment of the Food Security Act of 1985, the federal government served clear notice that it no longer will be a partner to the conversion of wetlands or highly erodible lands into cropland. It also took a bold step in furthering the conservation of soil, water, and wildlife resources.

Farm Crops as Wildlife Food

Farms provide sources of food for many kinds of wildlife. In some cases, little or no harm accrues to either crops or wildlife. In others, crop depredations are severe and pose difficult situations for wildlife managers. As we shall see, crops can expose wildlife to harmful pesticides and, on occasion, to at least one infectious disease.

Bobwhite adapt well to most forms of agriculture. They consume many kinds of foods, among them large numbers of seeds from both wild and cultivated vegetation. One biologist estimated that more than 5 million seeds are consumed each year by a single bobwhite.

The variety of these foods is no less amazing. Among the many studies of quail foods is a list of 302 species of plants, and even lengthier lists have resulted from more extensive investigations. Virtually all studies of bobwhite food habits show the influence of crops, although there are regional differences.

Preference trials indicate that bobwhites generally prefer the seeds of grasses over those of legumes, and especially those of annual grasses. In the northern range of bobwhite, corn is common, whereas sorghum, wheat, rye, and several legumes predominate elsewhere. Crops are especially important in the winter diet, as they offer bobwhites nourishment during a season when natural foods may be scarce.

Thus, farming provides critical food resources for a major species of gamebird. Bobwhites prospered under most agricultural regimes until clean farming started claiming crucial habitat. Our point here, however, is that populations of an important gamebird often were sustained by crops without inflicting any damage.

The seeds they consumed were the waste of crop production and therefore do not represent losses to farm income. Edminster (1954) aptly concluded that, of all the gamebirds, bobwhites probably enjoy the highest esteem of farmers.

Waste corn and small grains also became a mainstay in the fall and winter diets of pheasants. However, pheasants sometimes eat newly sprouted corn or peck at ripe tomatoes, causing localized damage to these crops. Dambach and Leedy (1948) witnessed three pheasants digging up 79 corn sprouts in 20 minutes during a survey of 139 Ohio cornfields. They detected some damage of this type in 12 percent of their sample, but extensive losses were limited to 4 cornfields bordering long-established pheasant refuges. In all, the results suggested that damage to freshly planted corn is negligible even in the best pheasant-producing areas in Ohio.

However, damage to sprouting corn may be more troublesome in states with larger pheasant populations. If so, repellants may be necessary. A carbamate insecticide tested in South Dakota proved effective for this purpose. Unprotected fields lost as much as 33 times more corn sprouts than fields treated with the repellant.

In general, however, pheasant depredations seem exaggerated and the birds' food habits remain compatible with most farming operations. The same can be said of prairie chickens and mourning doves. However, farmers often experience other problems indirectly related to their crops. Attractive populations of game birds thriving on farmlands may encourage unauthorized trespass and other discourtesies by thoughtless hunters.

The situation regarding bobwhites and pheasants contrasts with the depredations by deer, raccoons (*Procyon lotor*), and several kinds of rodents and birds. Javelina (*Tayassu tajacu*) and coyotes (*Canis latrans*) are known to damage watermelons and other succulent crops. However, losses of unharvested wheat and other cereal grains to waterfowl in Canada remain the most severe example of crop depredation.

These losses occur on the northern prairies when waterfowl begin concentrating prior to their autumn migration just at the time of harvest. Unlike damage from insects or hail, crop depredations from waterfowl assume a different perspective among farmers. Hail is an "Act of God," and insects are a hazard triggering remedies clearly aimed at pests. But ducks are not pests.

They are instead a natural resource rigorously protected by international treaty. Farmers accordingly seek responses to their plight from wildlife managers. The first reports of serious depredations began in the 1940s when mechanization brought major changes in farming practices. Initiation of new methods of harvesting grain immeasurably exacerbated the possibilities for waterfowl damage.

Wheat and other small grains are cut in strips and are left to dry in windrows. With dry weather, 8-10 days of ripening are required before the grains are harvested, and during this period crops are susceptible to waterfowl depredations. Losses include both consumption of the grain and trampling damage. Jordan (1953) found that mallards, on the average, consume about 73 g of small grains daily during the autumn, but this amount increased to 82 g under the demands of cooler temperatures. Other ducks and geese consume proportionately smaller or larger amounts, respectively, according to their body sizes.

Other factors affect waterfowl depredations. Among these are the size of the waterfowl population, field size, proximity of the crops to water, and weather. In years when crops require longer periods to dry, their exposure to field-feeding increases, and hence so do depredations. In a short harvest period, losses might reach 7 million kg, but in a longer harvest season, this figure could jump to about 380 million kg.

Coils (1951) summarized the dilemma. On the one hand, farming destroys waterfowl habitat when wetlands are converted into croplands. On the other hand, waterfowl destroy crops. Furthermore, as waterfowl habitat becomes more restricted, there are greater chances of depredation in fields near the remaining wetlands. This, in turn, prompts more endeavors to restrict waterfowl habitat.

Waterfowl themselves are "poor ambassadors" for wetland preservation in grain-producing regions. Farmers, when asked to help preserve valuable wetland habitat, sometimes do not cooperate because of the damage ducks cause to crops. Unfortunately, these confrontations still continue. MacLennan (1978) estimated the value of a single year's destruction of grain at $30-40 million in Canada as an extreme-but real-loss and suggested that $12-$15 million represented a long-term average. If the average loss were evenly distributed, each farmer would lose about $100.

But that is not the case. A small percentage of the farmers actually bear the majority of the depredations, and these individuals each may lose $2000-$5000 each year. In Saskatchewan, where about one-third of Canada's duck population nests, more than 35 percent of the depredations occur on less than 1 percent of the area farmed. As suggested earlier, these croplands usually are located near the best waterfowl habitat.

Management solutions vary in their nature and effectiveness. Tactics designed to scare field-feeding waterfowl often are only temporarily effective and, at best, merely transfer the problem to another field.

Specially designated fields are left in "lure crops" under the sponsorship of government; here the birds are neither hunted nor scared so that the damage is deflected from other fields during the harvest. In comparison with wheat, barley may be the best lure crop because it matures faster, costs less, and can be eaten more efficiently.

Bait stations also are deployed to attract ducks away from crops.

Leitch (1951) noted that development of some wetland seed plants helped reduce crop

depredations in Alberta. Overall, however, the seasonal abundance and availability of wheat and other grains simply prove too attractive for large flocks of foraging waterfowl to resist, and attractive marsh vegetation often remains unutilized when crops mature. Although the long-term solution to crop depredations presumably involves some type of habitat modification-either in the fields or in the wetlands-managers are far from reaching this goal.

Combinations of scaring tactics, feeding stations, and lure crops seem the best management techniques currently available. These, plus government-sponsored insurance programs, offer a degree of relief for farmers suffering severe losses. Ennis (1981) suggested that prevention of depredation is cost effective; every $1 invested in prevention saves $4 of compensation to farmers experiencing crop damage.

Funds obviously are needed to develop new ways of diverting waterfowl from unharvested fields. Also needed are new farming practices that would make crops less susceptible to depredation.

Waterfowl depredations also assume dimensions lying somewhat beyond the scope of basic wildlife management. Wheat and other grains produced in North America have become world commodities. Sales represent not only income for farmers, but also a means for governments to offset their national trade deficits. National priorities accordingly are geared for more production.

For better or worse, these sales also may be used as "chips" in international politics, particularly in deals with hungry nations whose socioeconomic systems may differ from those in North America. Some persons also have raised the question about who should have the fundamental responsibility for the food security of the world.

North Americans currently produce a surplus of grain and other foods at a time when other peoples face starvation. In short, are we obligated to feed present and future human populations or to nurture ducks? This issue may force a moral dimension on our land-management decisions, perhaps excluding wildlife values as an unconscionable luxury. Finally, who pays for crop depredations caused by waterfowl?

Canadian farmers suffer the financial losses, yet American hunters enjoy a harvest of more than 70 percent of the ducks and geese produced in Canada. Under these circumstances, should waterfowl hunters in the United States contribute to Canada's burden? Canadian farmers might just as easily produce fewer ducks and still meet the needs of

Canadian hunters without experiencing severe crop damage. In other words, why should Canadian farmers produce waterfowl for both Canadian *and* American duck hunters?

There are no easy answers to these issues, and none has become established policy, but responses surely will be needed before long. "Blackbird" is a collective term often employed for one or more species of dark-coloured birds flocking to croplands. Grackles (*Quiscalus quiscula*), cowbirds (*Molothrus ater*), and red-winged blackbirds (*Agelaius phoeniceus*) are lumped conveniently in this group to which we tenuously can add crows (*Corvus bracbyrhynchos*) and starlings (*Sturnus vulgaris*) for purposes of our discussion.

These birds damage regionally important crops, among them mature and sprouting corn and rice. A survey of 24 states producing 97 percent of the corn crop in the United States indicated that more than 16 million bushels, or 0.16 percent of the total harvest, are lost because of birds. In terms of 1970 dollars, this damage amounted to $9.3 million, with Pennsylvania and Indiana experiencing losses of $1 million or more each, closely followed by Ohio, Illinois, Wisconsin, and Minnesota. Such damage varies greatly, however.

Farmers in some areas experience heavy losses, whereas others have little, or no damage. Overall, White et al. (1985) found that blackbirds, even in numbers of a million or more, caused only minor economic impact and suggested that the strategy of reducing roosting populations is not an effective means of controlling agricultural damage. Indeed, many of the earlier methods for controlling bird damage proved relatively ineffective. Regrettably, farmers sometimes have turned to toxic materials instead of nonlethal repellants.

Some nonlethal chemicals repel animals because the materials produce an objectionable taste or odor. Other materials produce a behaviour known as aversion conditioning when chemically treated food makes animals sick. Animals thereafter avoid the same food-even when it is no longer treated-because of the unpleasant association.

Because they are nonlethal, these materials are acceptable to conservationists yet help to repel troublesome birds from corn and other crops. Corn seed, rice, berries, and small cereal grains have been protected using methiocarb, although it seems less effective and more costly when applied to ripening field corn.

Methiocarb limited blackbird damage to sprouting corn to 0.3 percent, whereas untreated fields nearby experienced 44 percent damage. The nature of aversion conditioning is such that only part of a field may require treatment with a chemical repellant-methiocarb, in this case-yet produces the same effectiveness against birds as treatment over the entire area. Aversion conditioning using methiocarb effectively repelled Canada geese from golf courses: it also might be useful for protecting winter wheat or other crops from geese .

Another compound, 4-AP (4-aminopyridine, or Avitrol), combines lethal and nonlethal approaches to blackbird depredations. This chemical does kill some birds, but before they die, they exhibit squawking, erratic flight, and other irregular behaviours that frighten unpoisoned birds from the croplands.

Fields treated with 4-AP distributed at bait stations experienced 56 percent less damage than untreated fields. De Grazio et al. (1972) modified the bait-station method by spreading cracked corn treated with the same chemical throughout fields damaged by blackbirds. This procedure decreases the chances for pheasants to consume hazardous amounts of the baits as they might at a feeding station.

Overall, 4-AP lessened damage by 85 percent, and flocks of blackbirds were repelled after no more than 1 percent of the population consumed the baits. However, note that Dolbeer (1981) suggested that the costs of blackbird control often may exceed the value of lost corn crops. He accordingly proposed an economic model for determining cost-efficient management decisions when blackbirds threaten cornfields.

Recently, the performance of 4-AP has been improved by the addition of a stabilizing ingredient, and favourable cost:benefit ratios now may be obtained under most conditions. Reflecting tapes present a new means of repelling blackbirds from crops. The tapes are 11 mm wide, red- and silver-coloured on opposite sides, and they flash in sunlight. Under certain wind conditions, the tapes also produce a roaring noise.

The tapes are suspended across fields at intervals of 3 to 7 m. In Ohio, only 3.2 percent of the ears in cornfields taped at 3-m intervals were damaged, compared with 6.3 percent damage where the tapes were spaced at 7-m intervals. Damage in fields with no tape amounted to 17.2 percent of the ears. The results were similar for millet and other crops, and included field trials conducted in Bangladesh, India, and other developing riations.

Reflecting tapes seem especially useful on small fields on high-value crops, but also may deter birds from visiting polluted or toxic sites or from roosting in urban or residential areas. Depending on the interval between tapes, the costs of the materials and labor are about

$23 to $84 per ha in the United States, but savings of about 5 to 8 times these costs may be realized in protected fields.

Other control measures include the possibility of sterilizing blackbirds with compounds such as Ornitrol. The effectiveness of Ornitrol on spermatogenesis in red-winged blackbirds seems dependent on the time when the compound is sprayed on corn. Under field conditions, Ornitrol should be applied early in the spring when the testes of males are not yet fully developed.

Genetically resistant strains of corn and other crops offer the ultimate protection against depredations by wildlife (and, of course, from attacks by insect pests and plant diseases). Rapid advances in such "high-tech" fields as gene splicing may produce marvels within the next decade.

Meanwhile, horticultural experiments with 25 cultivars of sweet corn indicated that the range of damage by birds varies nearly fivefold between the most and least damaged cultivars. The research identified those physical features (e.g., husk weight) that should be bred into new lines of sweet corn to reduce damage by blackbirds.

Damage to sunflower crops may be reduced by breeding plants with seeds having an objectionable taste to birds, but more research is needed before these features are fully effective. In the long run, crops protected by such means hold promise for an environment uncontaminated with pesticides and other life-threatening chemicals for humans and wildlife.

Deer frequently cause excessive losses of soybeans and other crops (for deer-related losses of alfalfa, nursery plants, and . Various methods are used to reduce this damage, but timing often is crucial in the application of these measures. Soybeans suffer heavy damage—as much as 80 percent of the harvest—if grazed during the first week of their emergence.

After the first week, deer remove a smaller percentage of the plants with far less crop damage. Unfortunately, by the time deer have damaged soybeans, it is usually too late to initiate control measures assuring good yields. Control methods must be in effect prior to the emergence of soybeans in order to achieve satisfactory results. Further, because damage is greater near the edges of soybean fields bordered by woodlands, effective control procedures can be concentrated along the borders rather than throughout the fields.

As with unfenced orchards, owners of soybean fields sometimes are authorized to shoot deer as a means of reducing crop depredations.

However, by the time state biologists can confirm the damage and issue permits, the period of maximum damage usually has passed. Shooting deer after the fact no longer has any economic justification. Repellants and scaring techniques properly timed to coincide with the first week of sprouting are better ways of dealing with deer depredations in soybean fields.

Deer repellants show considerable variation in their effectiveness, however, and many of the commonly used types offer little protection. Surveys of farmers' attitudes about crop losses sometimes reveal influences that should govern wildlife policies. Farmers in New York generally seem quite tolerant of crop damage caused by deer and, in fact, 79 percent recognized the aesthetic values of deer visiting their fields.

As with any estimates of crop damage, it is possible that losses are exaggerated or that other kinds of animals beside deer contributed to the damage. Even so, no more than 2 percent of the farmers in New York considered their losses substantial or severe. Only when estimates exceeded $3,000 did a clear majority of farmers consider the damage unacceptable. Nearly half considered losses between $1000 and $3000 as tolerable.

These findings suggest that management policies may be based on some erroneous assumptions. Namely, many wildlife managers suppose that farmers experiencing crop losses want fewer deer. They also may judge the losses of a few farmers as representative of all farmers in the region. Contrarily, the results outlined earlier indicate that immediate financial losses often are tempered by the sociological benefits that deer and other wildlife convey to farmers.

At the same time, the few farmers complaining of serious crop damage very likely do need assistance, and these warrant quick responses from management agencies. Changing cultural practices have influenced crop depredations, as we have seen in the case of waterfowl damage on Canadian grainfields.

Another example merits note, not only because it increased susceptibility of orchards to depredation, but also because the "problem" itself seemingly abetted a cure. Deer may be troublesome in apple orchards. Mature apple trees largely escape damage when their limbs exceed the reach of browsing deer. Repeated browsing, however, can reduce young trees to stunted, misshapen stems that are useless for production.

Financial losses in these situations may be severe, and shooting under some type of permit system offers the only feasible relief. Fencing usually is too expensive to protect large orchards. In recent years, however, more orchards have been planted with dwarfed varieties of fruit trees.

Table 3.5: Feasibility, as Measured by Savings, of Fencing a 20-ha Orchard with a 1829-m Perimeter Against Deer Depredation with Different Densities of Apple Trees.

Density (Trees/Ha)	*Annual Damage Estimate @ $0.50/Tree (Dollars)*	*Annual Cost of Deer-Proof Fence (Dollars)*	*Potential Savings/Year (Dollars)*
299	3,025	2,024	1,001
539	5,450	2,024	3,425
1,122	11,350	2,024	9,326
1,957	19,800	2,024	17,776

These are even more susceptible because deer can reach the twigs of mature trees, but the dwarfed varieties permit high-density plantings and simplify picking the fruit. Those features make deer-proof fencing far more feasible than it is with standard-sized trees (Table 13-1). The dwarfed varieties thus represent a

cultural system producing more fruit per hectare while offering better opportunities for controlling browsing damage. Recently, Porter (1983) found that single-strand electric fences, to which flags of aluminum foil coated with peanut butter are attached at 10-m intervals, also reduced browsing damage in orchards.

The flags provide both visual and odorous stimuli, thereby encouraging nose-to-fence contact. The electric shock behaviourally conditions the deer to avoid the fence and thus reduces browsing damage. The fence is cost effective on orchards up to 5 ha.

Under certain conditions, some crops may adversely affect wildlife. Soybeans are grown in many areas frequented by Canada geese (*Branta canadensis*), and at times, these impact in the esophagi of feeding birds. Estimates of mortality vary with the size of the flock, but 3100 geese died in an extreme outbreak in Illinois.

Some geese die suddenly, whereas others starve slowly when the impacted soybeans prevent passage of food into the stomach and erode the lining of the esophagus. Durant described the hemorrhaging and necrosis of impacted esophagi and determined that dry soybeans expanded 2.5 times in volume when moistened, easily causing fatalities. Lead poisoning may contribute to the incidence of impacted esophagi in geese and other waterfowl.

Other factors affecting the incidence and the severity of this malady include the migration patterns of geese, the availability of corn or other foods, and most importantly, the amount of rainfall before and during the autumn feeding period

Only dry soybeans impact and, with adequate precipitation, the dampened beans swell before they are ingested. Geese prefer corn and will feed on soybeans primarily when the corn harvest is delayed. Early migrations of geese into areas producing soybeans increase the length of the feeding period, and hence the incidence of impaction.

Two of these factors-rainfall and the harvest of corn-enable managers to anticipate impaction mortality each year; responses include disking harvested soybean fields, providing artificial supplies of corn, and hazing geese from soybean fields.

Aspergillosis is a fungal infection of the respiratory tracts of birds exposed to molding crops. Bellrose et al. (1945) described an epizootic among wood ducks (*Aix sponsa*) feeding on recently flooded corn; about 10 percent of the feeding birds seemed affected, and these likely spread the infection to others in the vicinity.

About 2000 Canada geese died in an epizootic of aspergillosis on a refuge in Missouri, apparently from ingesting infected grains that were grown, ironically, as part of a waterfowl feeding program. When a blizzard prevented mallards from feeding in fields, they instead fed on silage spread over the snow for cattle, and more than 1000 birds thereafter succumbed to aspergillosis presumably obtained from this source.

These cases represent single, local sources of contamination, and prevention by hazing or by supplying alternate sources of attractive food sometimes may be feasible . Even with a single source of unfit food, however, timely detection of the infections remains difficult, permitting an epizootic well before the source is located.

Restoration of diminished Canada goose populations remains an outstanding achievement of wildlife management. Winter inventories indicated that their numbers nearly doubled in the two decades following 1955, reaching about three million by the start of the 1974 hunting season. This was accomplished with several kinds of management, but also included a role played by corn.

A dynamic situation resulted, not only in the buildup of goose numbers, but also in a changing pattern of their winter distributions. As mentioned previously, new types of farm machinery were developed rapidly after World War II.

Mechanical corn pickers were among these, and, whereas they can harvest corn more rapidly than hand labor, the machines also left more corn as field waste. Depending on several factors, among them moisture content, as much as 15 percent of the corn remains on the ground after harvest. With these additional food resources at hand on public and private lands—and with regulated hunting—Canada geese again thrived in the Mississippi and Central flyways.

Fall and winter food reserves were assured in Illinois, Minnesota, and other northern states, far from the birds' traditional wintering grounds. In response, some subpopulations stayed through the winter. Fewer geese, so it seemed, traveled south, bringing cries of "short stopping" from hunters in southern states as their goose hunting became less rewarding. Indeed, the continental Canada goose population was building and most of the increase was occurring in the northern states.

The number of birds wintering in Rochester, Minnesota, for example, increased from 250 in 1951 to 8650 by 1966-67, and to 22,000 by 1970. Closer examination of the "short-stopping" phenomenon revealed that other factors were affecting the winter distribution and abundance of Canada geese. Raveling (1978) determined that hunting mortality was greater for those geese continuing southward in the Mississippi or Central flyways.

These segments of the goose population were subject to about five times more shooting pressure than those staying in Minnesota. Quite simply, the birds were increasing their vulnerability by flying south. Annual mortality in the Minnesota flock was 19 percent, whereas it reached 50 percent for those continuing their migration southward.

With this differential mortality, the northern subpopulations increased, while those wintering in the south steadily diminished. What appeared to be short stopping actually was a dynamic change in mortality rates among subpopulations influenced, in part, by the availability of corn.

Erosion, Sedimentation, and Wildlife

Wind and water erode unprotected soil, taking a heavy toll on a basic natural resource in all regions of the United States. The losses are staggering. Inventories estimate that more than 6 billion tons of soil erode each year from nonfederal lands in the United States. The

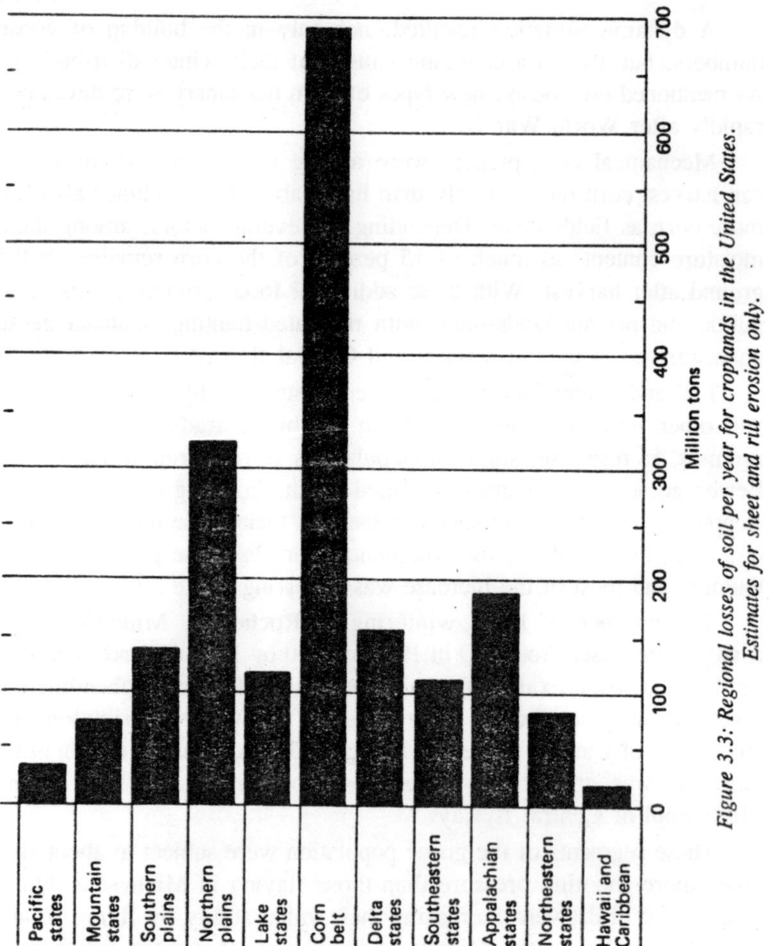

Figure 3.3: Regional losses of soil per year for croplands in the United States. Estimates for sheet and rill erosion only.

greatest losses occur on croplands, although pastures, forests, and rangelands also experience soil erosion. Whereas it may take 1000 years for natural forces to form 2.5 cm of enriched topsoil, erosion may claim nearly the same amount every 30 years, resulting in what might be called a soil deficit.

Water erosion alone claims a national average of about 11.6 tons per ha on croplands each year. The implications are obvious: a life-supporting resource steadily erodes with each particle of soil swept from productive areas. Indeed, accelerated soil erosion may be the underlying reason for the fall of civilizations.

In the view of Carter and Dale (1974), civilizations have not

Table 3.6: Gross Annual Soil Losses from Wind and Water Erosion on Nonfederal Land in the United States.

	Hectares (Millions)				
Land Use	*>5 Tons/Ha*	*5—12 Tons/Ha*	*12—34 Tons/Ha*	*34+ Tons/Ha*	*Total Erosion (Billions of Tons)*
Cropland	64.2	46.0	37.7	19.4	2.82
Pastureland	42.5	5.7	3.8	2.0	0.35
Forestland	132.4	10.5	4.7	2.0	0.44
Rangeland	114.8	22.5	16.2	11.6	1.71
Other	—	—	—	—	1.10
Totals	353.9	84.7	62.4	35.0	6.42

lasted more than 30 generations except in the valleys of the Nile, Tigris-Euphrates, and Indus rivers where recurring flooding naturally restores soil fertility (only time will tell whether completion of the Aswan High Dam in 1968 in time will thwart the flood-based fertility on the Nile).

Elsewhere in the world, human abuses so accelerate erosion that soil fertility cannot be renewed naturally. Accelerated sedimentation-the result of erosion-is a creeping form of environmental degradation in aquatic environments. To be sure, natural geological forces produce turbidity in some aquatic systems, but there is little evidence that sediments of that origin are lethal to fishes.

With chronic soil erosion, however, the carrying capacity of lakes and rivers is destroyed almost without notice or the fanfare of obvious fish kills. Some fishes, of course, are adapted to turbid waters. For these, reduced eye size, compensated by enhanced development of other sense organs, and modifications in contour, body form, fin development, and colour evolved under the selective pressures of turbidity.

Species adapted to turbid waters have silt-tolerant eggs and often scatter these instead of building nests. However, for species adapted to clear water, erosion leading to high levels of turbidity poses a number of difficulties. The intensity of farming-along with deforestation-has so increased erosion that excessive turbidity sometimes chokes or scours the sensitive gill elements of many fishes.

With increasing turbidity, fishes increase their ventilation rates as a means of overcoming respiratory deficiencies so that their oxygen demands might be met. There is, of course, a limit to which many fishes can adapt to these circumstances, and they die when the limit is exceeded. For others, bottom sediments smother their eggs. Silt-laden water also reduces the activities of juvenile bass (*Micropterus spp.*) and interferes with the social structure of sunfish (*Lepomis spp.*). The complex reproductive behaviour of many species relies on visual cues, and hence can be affected by unusual turbidity.

Because little or no aquatic vegetation can thrive in highly turbid waters, food chains and habitat conditions also have changed drastically for many fishes. Predacious species rely on their sight for seeking food, and reduced visibility in turbid water diminishes their effectiveness and decreases the probability of a gamefish seeing a lure.

It is not surprising, then, that fish faunas have changed in keeping with degrading environments. The shift increases the populations of small and large "rough" fishes such as spotfin shiner (*Notropis spilopterus*) or carp (*Cyprinus carpio*) while decreasing the numbers of walleye (*Stizostedion vitreum*) and other game species that usually are of better food value.

As an illustration, Peters (1967) studied the effects of sedimentation introduced by irrigation from farmlands bordering spring-fed trout streams in Montana. Trout were abundant and egg survival was high only at the lower ranges of sedimentation, whereas increasing sediment loads were accompanied by fewer trout, more rough fish, and high egg mortality.

Sedimentation also influenced key waterfowl habitat in the Illinois River Valley-first positively, then negatively. The situation helps to illustrate the ecology of natural sedimentation versus the aftermath of accelerated soil erosion. As described by Bellrose et al. (1979), the geological events forming the valley gradually built natural levees parallel to the river, thereby separating most of the channel from the adjacent bottomlands.

Until the 1930*s*, water trapped behind these levees created a series of bottomland lakes, representing some of the finest waterfowl habitat in North America. Since then, however, soil erosion accelerated with the adoption and spread of row-crop farming.

The results produced an unnatural rate of sedimentation, the formation of an unstable layer of silt in the river bed, and the steady losses of aquatic vegetation serving as valuable food for waterfowl.

Turbidity, as a function of sedimentation, contributed to much of this loss. Wave action and fish movements stir the silty bottom sediments into a suspension that interrupts the penetration of sunlight, disrupting fish faunas as well as waterfowl food plants. Nearly 70 percent of the fish species in the Illinois River have declined or disappeared as vegetation and other features of the aquatic system were degraded. Sedimentation also filled the bottomland lakes and marshes at rates far in excess of normal geological schedules.

The capacity of Lake Chautauqua, one of the bottomland lakes bordering the Illinois River (and a national wildlife refuge) was reduced by more than 18 percent in less than 24 years; about 76,400 tons of sediment are deposited each year. Thus, sediments originating from the accelerated erosion of farmlands on the upper reaches of the Illinois River are bringing wetland habitats downstream into an irreversible and premature extinction.

Widespread adoption of conservation tillage will reduce erosion, thereby stemming much of the harmful sedimentation, but reclamation of the damaged river system is virtually impossible. In summing up their review of this setting, Havera and Bellrose (1985) state, "The decline in the ecological integrity and productivity of the Illinois River floodplain ecosystem should serve as an example of man's misuse of our natural resources . . . the Illinois Valley is not the only loser in the misuse of agricultural lands ... our nation's productivity is also being washed away."

AGRICULTURAL CHEMICALS AND WILDLIFE

Despite long-term losses of topsoil, technology has produced phenomenal increases in farm production. Whereas 1.0 ha was required to sustain one person in food and clothing in 1930, the ratio is now 0.4 ha per person (fide USDA Economic Research Service). Production of food and fiber on American farms has no equal, in part, because of the intensity of technologically oriented management.

Chemicals have been instrumental in this achievement. These include fertilizers and groups of compounds designed to kill weeds and insect pests. The latter, together with rodenticides and a few other specialized chemicals, are known collectively as pesticides.

DDT, perhaps the best-known insecticide, was discovered in 1874 but remained shelved until its effectiveness against insects was realized decades later. DDT sprang into prominence during World War II, prompting widespread applications of this and other pesticides on croplands after the war.

In the wake of their use, however, came a belated awareness that some pesticides produced harmful side effects. Many kinds of wildlife frequently bore the brunt of a well-intentioned technology that failed' to envision its total consequences. A voluminous literature has developed about pesticides and their effects on wildlife, including the introduction of scientific journals devoted to environmental toxicology (e.g., *Pesticide Monitoring Journal* and *Bulletin of Environmental Contamination and Toxicology*).

Many of the studies are experimental, using captive animals fed diets contaminated with known amounts of agricultural chemicals. Other studies take place in the field and report the incidence of pesticides in birds and mammals exposed directly or indirectly to treated croplands. Some of these studies were triggered by serious die-offs of wildlife, whereas others marked the potential for damage.

Korschgen (1970) traced Aldrin applied to cornfields through the soil and into the food web of earthworms, insects, seeds, and ultimately, into a variety of vertebrates. Similarly, Meeks (1968) followed DDT through the food web of a freshwater marsh in Ohio, and Herman and Bulger (1979) intensively studied the impacts of DDT on nontarget organisms in forests of Oregon.

In addition to the environmental damage resulting from the regular use of pesticides, accidents involving pesticides also cause ecological disasters. In 1986, 30 tons of insecticides, herbicides, and fungicides spilled from a warehouse into the Rhine River near Basel, Switzerland, causing the ecological death of a major river for years to come (*Time* 1986).

Regrettably, some pesticides at times have unintentionally poisoned wildlife even when they are applied properly. Unusual habits occasionally predispose some species of wildlife to pesticide poisoning. For reasons that remain unclear, black-billed magpies (*Pica pica*) routinely ingest cow hair. Magpies thus were poisoned for 3 months after cattle were treated externally with a pesticide used to control dermal parasites.

Although other factors may be involved, a 10-year decline in magpie populations in several western states coincided with the widespread application of the pesticide. Fortunately, this form of poisoning can be eliminated if the pesticide is applied in other ways (e.g., injection, food additives, or capsules), thereby eliminating the harmful residues on cow hair. Other kinds of special circumstances frequently concern pesticide poisoning and wildlife.

Aerially sprayed chemicals, for example, may drift into fish hatcheries and kill the entire stock. Although poisoned elsewhere, animals dying from pesticides may enter key areas, thus bringing lethal materials into the habitat of important species of wildlife (e.g., into refuges). In fact, the safety of two endangered species-ocelot (*Felis pardalis*) and jagaurundi (*F. yagouaroundi*)—was compromised when birds poisoned by a highly toxic pesticide died in a national wildlife refuge in Texas.

Large die-offs of lesser snow geese and other birds have been associated with pesticides by Flickinger (1979) and others. Scott et al. (1959) summarized the virtual elimination of wildlife after Dieldrin was applied to farmland in Illinois. Japanese beetles were the targets, but pheasants, a variety of songbirds, cottontails, muskrats, and fox squirrels also were killed.

From 1961 to 1975, agricultural pesticides were responsible for nearly one-quarter of all fish kills for which the cause could be determined, including the loss of 109,000 fish when pesticide—contaminated runoff entered an Alabama fish hatchery. However, the harm some pesticides inflict on wildlife often is insidious, taking effect in ways that are not obvious.

Eggs with shells so thinned by DDT that they break during incubation are more subtle aftermaths of contamination than a field of poisoned geese, but the result is no less devastating. Other sublethal effects of DDT and its chemical relatives on birds have been shown from experimental research.

Among these are delayed migratory conditioning, delayed ovulation, increased thyroid weight and activity, sterility, and irregular behaviour, possibly including increased vulnerability to predators. The irony of these findings is reflected in a 1965 report of the Presidential Panel on Environmental Pollution: as little as 1 percent of the pesticides applied to agricultural lands in the United States actually may hit their intended targets.

Some chemicals produced results far beyond the expected. Corn treated with the herbicide 2, 4-D accumulated more nitrogen that, in turn, promoted a population explosion of aphids feeding on the crop. Additionally, the treated corn was 26 percent more susceptible to corn borers, and the females of this insect were a third larger and produced a third more eggs.

Honeybees often were killed by insecticides, affecting not only the honey industry, but also the pollination of fruit and vegetable crops as well as uncultivated vegetation. Food chains, many of which involved wildlife, also were interrupted by pesticides. Reductions in insect populations on grasslands treated with insecticides were followed by decreases in small rodent populations dependent on insect foods. The sources of food for Atlantic salmon (*Salmo salar*) were altered by DDT. In England, Potts (1977) suggested that insecticides so reduced insect populations that this loss of food produced declines in the gray partridge populations.

Hamerstrom (1979) linked the nesting of northern harriers (*Circus cyaneus*) with the cyclic nature of rodent populations, but when DDT was applied to the study area, the normal rodent-hawk cycle was interrupted and far fewer harriers nested successfully.

All told, pesticides have extraordinarily influenced ecosystems by reducing biological diversity, interrupting food chains, modifying energy transfer, reducing the quality of soil, water, and air, and lessening the stability and resilience of both natural and managed environments.

Some pesticides were banned in the United States after their harmful effects were discovered. DDT was banned for use in the United States in 1972, but this restriction did not prohibit its continued manufacture for export to other nations. Indeed, black-crowned night-herons (*Nycticorax nycticorax*) nesting in Idaho experienced impaired breeding success because of their exposure to DDT on wintering areas in Mexico.

Similarly, the organochlorine residues were several times higher in migratory insectivorous birds in the diet of peregrine falcons (*Falco peregrinus*) than in resident prey species, suggesting that the poisons are acquired from prey wintering in countries where harmful organochlorines are still used. The eggshells of the falcons nesting in the Rocky Mountains thus remain abnormally thin, and improved reproductive performance in the population cannot be expected until organochlorine contamination is reduced in the prey base.

Scores of troublesome insects, including mosquitoes, houseflies, and lice, as well as agricultural pests, are no longer susceptible to some chemical controls, having gained resistance after generations of exposure. Of about 2000 insect and other arthropod pests, nearly 400 species have evolved resistance.

Resistance in some of these species increased 25,000 times. Chancellor (1978) supplied evidence that some plants also have developed resistance to herbicides. Adaptive resistance seems limited to those species with high rates of reproduction and short life cycles.

These organisms produce so many generations of offspring that the probability of encountering genetic resistance is realized—and these generally are the pests for which pesticides were intended. Only a few survivors are enough to establish new and resistant populations.

Conversely, few vertebrates develop any degree of resistance to toxic chemicals. Some rodents have developed 12 times the normal tolerance to Endrin.

Resistance to chlorinated hydrocarbons in mosquito fish (*Gambusia affinis*), yellow bullhead (*Ictalurus natalis*), and some species of frogs living near heavily treated cottonfields was documented by Ferguson (1963), Ferguson and Bingham (1966), and Culley and Ferguson (1969). Resistance of mosquito fish to Endrin and Toxaphene increased more than 520 and 375 times, respectively. Ferguson (1967) noted the dangers resistant organisms pose to food chains and, indeed, to humans when they are consumed by nonresistant species occupying higher trophic levels.

Most insecticides are not species-specific. That is, they kill all insects-harmful and beneficial species alike. Many insects are predators of harmful species, and the benefits of natural pest control are diminished when predators are removed. Further, because of basic ecological relationships between predator and prey populations, the predacious species take far longer to recover from insecticides than do the damaging, herbivorous species.

Recent approaches to crop protection recognize the role of beneficial insects and take means to maximize their influence. Overall, the result has been a combination of chemical, cultural, and biological methods known as integrated pest management. This approach reduces the amount and frequency of insecticide applications.

It also uses altered cultural practices and the development of insect-resistant crops as means of reducing the harmful insecticide contaminations so prevalent in the past. Biological control of pests takes advantage of a pest's natural vulnerability, to which it cannot adapt genetically. For example, some pest populations succumb rapidly when management enhances their exposure to species-specific diseases or parasites.

Some harmful insects are lured into traps by species-specific sex attractants known as pheromones. Others are sprayed with nonlethal materials that cause interruptions in their life cycles, so that they remain as juveniles and never mature into egg-laying adults. One of these, Pro-Drone, holds promise for controlling imported fire ants (*Solenopsis invicta*).

The active ingredient has no direct toxicity but instead causes a shift in the caste system within fire ant colonies. This reduces the proportion of worker ants required for gathering food and eventually starves the colonies. Only low rates of the chemical are applied, and these degrade rapidly afterward. Furthermore, the synthetic hormone affects only a few species of ants and other insects.

Rands (1985) described a cultural approach that lessened the impact of pesticides on the production of gray partridges. Pesticides reduce the abundance of insect foods on which the partridge broods depend, and the survival of chicks thus is impaired in fully sprayed fields.

Gray partridges in Britain in fact have been declining since 1945, largely because of chick mortality. However, when 6-m strips around the perimeters of grain fields were left unsprayed, the chicks found enough insects and the mean brood size often doubled, in comparison with those in fully sprayed fields. Moreover, the unsprayed strips had little or no effect on the total yield of grain.

A news release from the U.S. Department of Agriculture (1987) announced the development of a genetic technique that may control tobacco budworms (*Heliothis virescens*), insects that damage cotton, vegetables, and tobacco. Crosses with a related, but harmless, species created hybrid females that not only produce sterile male offspring, but whose female offspring also continually pass on the trait for male sterility.

This form of biological control is especially promising, because tobacco budworms are rapidly developing resistance to chemical pesticides. The initial test with the hybrid females successfully introduced male sterility into the budworm population and reduced the number of insects by 75 percent.

Some Kinds of Insecticides

The "families" of insecticides increase each year as new compounds are formulated. However, for our purposes, we shall consider only three of the better-known types of the several described by Rudd (1964).

Chlorinated hydrocarbons, also known as organochlorines, embrace a number of insecticides used widely to control agricultural and forest pests. The best known is DDT, but Chlordane, Heptachlor, Endrin, Aldrin, Dieldrin, and Toxaphene also belong to this group.

Some chlorinated hydrocarbons such as Toxaphene and DDT now are banned or restricted in the United States, but others still are used. News of waterfowl contaminated with Endrin made national headlines in 1981.

Chlorinated hydrocarbons attack the central nervous system. Tremors, tonic contractions, convulsions—and usually death—occur in cases of acute toxicity. Repeated, low-level ingestion leads to accumulations in fatty tissues, including those of the liver and heart. Storage of chlorinated hydrocarbons in fatty tissues is significant because they may later be released rapidly when the stored fat is mobilized for energy. For example, Babcock and Flickinger (1977) described the death of geese mobilizing Aldrin—contaminated fat under the stress of migration.

Chlorinated hydrocarbons are especially deadly to aquatic organisms. Toxaphene, in fact, once was used by fishery biologists to reclaim ponds and lakes overpopulated with undesirable kinds of fishes. Even when used for this purpose, however, Toxaphene often killed other animals. Lennon et al. (1970) cited a 4-year fish reclamation project in Nebraska where each aerial application of Toxaphene was accompanied by 15-100 percent losses of waterfowl.

Chlorinated hydrocarbons may persist for years. Almost 40 percent of the DDT applied to a field in Maryland was present 17 years later (Nash and Woolson 1967). Soils treated with a single application of Aldrin were 95 percent free of residues after 1 year, but no further reduction was detected after an additional 5 years.

However, most croplands are treated year after year, so that residues of Aldrin or other chlorinated hydrocarbons may steadily accumulate in soils. Whereas a single application of DDT had little initial effect on birds breeding in a forest habitat, repeated applications over a 4-year period led to a 26 percent reduction in the population by the spring of the fifth year; the numbers of some species decreased by 44 percent.

On the other hand, a single application of Aldrin killed 25-50 percent of a pheasant population within 1 month of its application, and severely reduced reproduction of the survivors. A critical feature of persistent insecticides is their increasing concentration in each succeeding level of the food chain. This process, known as *biomagnification*, is particularly common in ecosystems treated with chlorinated hydrocarbons.

Even at authorized rates of application, passage of these materials through the ecosystem typically ends with excessive accumulations among organisms at the higher trophic levels. Predators such as brown pelicans (*Pelecanus occidentalis*) and falcons (*Falco spp.*) thus are unusually susceptible to biomagnification. Direct mortality may result from these accumulations of toxic chemicals, or, as described earlier, indirect dysfunctions may inhibit successful reproduction.

An example of biomagnification, based on an aquatic ecosystem in California that was treated with a chlorinated hydrocarbon, shows the concentrations eventually reaching several kinds of wildlife. Whereas

Table 3.7: Blomagnification of a Chlorinated Hydrocarbon In an Aquatic System. These Data Are Maximum Estimates of Accumulations In Organisms Occupying Producer and Consumer Trophic Levels, as Indicated. Numbers Shown Are Multiples of the Original Contamination in Water of 0.02 ppm.

Organisms	*Trophic Level*	*Multiple of Original Contamination*
Plankton	Producer	265
Frogs	Secondary consumer	250
Small fishes	Secondary consumer	500
Predacious fishes	Tertiary consumer	85,000
Fish-eating birds	Tertiary consumer	80,000

the original application rate was only 0.02 ppm, levels in fishes and western grebes (*Aechmophorus occidentalis*) were magnified more than several thousand times. The population of western grebes was affected significantly. About 1000 pairs of these birds nested in the area prior to its treatment, but no young were produced for the next 12 years.

Soil type is among the factors influencing the persistence of chlorinated hydrocarbons. A comparison between organic soils and silty loams for Heptachlor residues showed that 27 percent and 4.5 percent, respectively, remained after 6 months. Unfortunately, organic soils, because of their earthworm populations, are favourite feeding sites for woodcock (*Scolopax minor*).

Even when Heptachlor was applied at recommended levels, earthworms accumulated enough of the chemical to kill 10 of 12 woodcock within 53 days. An even more telling case concerned the contamination of woodcock in New Brunswick. Fully 86 percent of the woodcock in the fall migration were contaminated from DDT applied on their breeding grounds.

These birds received further exposure-this time to Heptachlor-on their wintering grounds, so that the breeding population the following spring produced contaminated hatchlings. The result was indicated in the decreased numbers of young woodcock produced per adult female.

When penned pheasants were fed Dieldrin, no mortality occurred in the first generation, although their egg production was decreased. However, the offspring of these birds experienced mortality, further loss of egg production, decreased fertility, and impaired behaviour. Up to 37 percent of the Dieldrin ingested by the first generation of pheasant hens was transferred to the yolks of their eggs.

This transfer proved an important means by which hens eliminated Dieldrin from their own tissues, but a second generation was contaminated, contributing to the results mentioned earlier. However, Dieldrin does not seem to cause eggshell thinning in pheasants.

For avian predators such as prairie falcons (*Falco mexicanus*), contamination with DDT and other chlorinated hydrocarbons had disastrous effects on the thickness of their eggshells. Chlorinated hydrocarbons interrupted the normal transport of calcium to the oviducts of contaminated birds by inhibiting the action of the enzyme carbonic anhydrase.

With less than normal amounts of calcium, the eggshells of these birds were thin and broke during incubation. Hatching success dropped rapidly in proportion to the thickness of eggshells.

The ban on applying most kinds of chlorinated hydrocarbons in the United States initiated the recovery of some species harmed by eggshell thinning, including bald eagles (*Haliaeetus leucocephalus*). Production of brown pelicans in California began improving when DDT decreased in the food chain.

In a 6-year period, fledging rates improved from just 4 young pelicans from 1125 nests (0.004 young per nest) to 1185 young from 1286 nests (0.922 young per nest). A fivefold decline of DDT metabolites in the eggs of ospreys (*Pandion haliaetus*) nesting in Connecticut and Long Island coincided with the return to almost normal production; fledging success increased from a low of 0.4 young per nest to 1.2 young per nest.

Ogganophosphates are less persistent than chlorinated hydrocarbons in soils and other components of the environment. However, they generally are highly toxic and have caused significant mortality in birds, including a single event when more than 1450 Canada geese died. Organophosphates have been linked with secondary poisoning.

About 400 birds of prey died after they consumed rodents and birds initially poisoned with an organophosphorous compound. Secondary poisoning also killed Franklin's gulls (*Larus pipixcan*) that fed on cicadas (Cacadidae), which had been poisoned unintentionally with an organophosphate. Barn owls (*Tyto alba*) experimentally fed quail poisoned

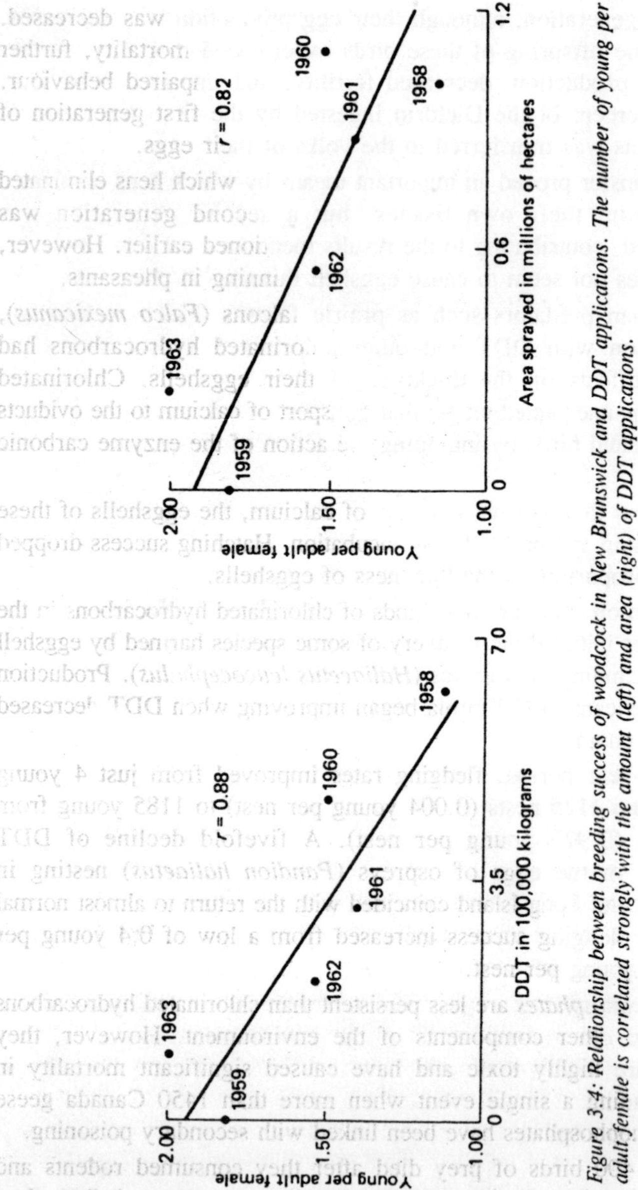

Figure 3.4: Relationship between breeding success of woodcock in New Brunswick and DDT applications. The number of young per adult female is correlated strongly with the amount (left) and area (right) of DDT applications.

with an organophosphate were themselves affected, although not lethally. Secondary poisoning is a hazard dependent upon the number of poisoned prey consumed, the body parts consumed, and the degree to which the prey was initially contaminated. Malathion and Parathion are the best known of the organophosphate group.

These and other organophosphates inhibit the enzyme acetylcholinesterase in the nervous system, causing disruption in the transmission of impulses. Death usually occurs from asphyxiation when the respiratory center in the brain fails. Human fatalities have occurred from external contact with small amounts of Parathion. Unlike chlorinated hydrocarbons, organophosphates seldom accumulate in fatty tissues.

Unfortunately, the acute toxicity of some organophosphates at times has been misused for the deliberate poisoning of wildlife. Carson (1962) estimated that farmers intentionally poisoned 65,000 birds with pesticides. More recently, Stone et al. (1984) described two cases in New York where, in total, farmers intentionally killed more than 8000 red-winged blackbirds and other birds.

Hawks of three species died from secondary poisoning in these events. In Texas, about 11,000 birds of 12 species were killed by bait poisoned with highly toxic organophosphates. Agricultural chemicals also have been used for the deliberate poisoning of wildlife in Europe. Intentional poisoning is difficult to detect because it can be masked by what otherwise seems to be a legitimate use of the pesticide.

Thus, Diazinon, applied for the control of lawn-damaging pests, poisoned about 700 brant (*Branta bernicla*) on a golf course in New York where the grazing birds probably were regarded as a nuisance (many of the dead birds were salvaged for scientific uses). Diazinon also has killed Canada geese (*B. canadensis*), wigeon (*Anas americana*) and many other birds on golf courses and lawns elsewhere.

Stone et al. (1984) believe that education, highly publicized prosecutions, and substantial fines may reduce the incidence of deliberate poisoning of wildlife. *Carbamates* are a relatively new family of

Table 3.8: Comparison Between Production of Young and Eggshell Thickness In Prairie Falcons.

Eggshell Thickness Index	*Prairie Falcon Nests*		*Number of Young Fledged*	
	Total	*Percent Fledging One or More Young*	*Total*	*Per Pair*
More than 1.75	21	75	54	2.6
1.45-1.75	31	50	51	1.6
Less than 1.45	10	10	3	0.3

pesticides. Some impetus for carbamate production stemmed from the large number of insects developing resistance to other insecticides.

Most carbamates in use have shorter life spans than chlorinated hydrocarbons and thus reduce the chances of biomagnification. Like organophosphates, carbamates inhibit acetylcholinesterase activity in the nervous system.

Fenoxycarb, in part, inhibits the metamorphosis of immature insects into adults and, in water, the chemical is degraded by sunlight with a half-life of 5 hours. Until then, however, fenoxycarb is highly toxic to aquatic invertebrates, and is registered only for the control of fire ants on turf and nonagricultural lands.

The toxicity of carbamates varies widely, with some being rather harmless, whereas others are deadly in small amounts. Temik is highly toxic, but Sevin has a safe environmental record because of its low toxicity to vertebrates.

A single granule (about 0.6 mg per bird) of Furadan killed four of five experimental birds within 24 hours. Rice seed illegally treated with Furadan killed several species of songbirds and sandpipers; the carbamate apparently was applied expressly to kill birds feeding in newly planted rice fields.

Furadan, also known as Carbofuran, is a systemic insecticide; this means that it is applied to the soil but then is absorbed through the roots into most plant tissues, giving crops internal protection against insect attacks. Flickinger et al. (1980) recorded the effects of Furadan used in rice fields after Aldrin was suspended by the Environmental Protection Agency in 1974.

The effects included rapid mortality of fishes, frogs, and crayfish, but five times fewer birds were killed than with Aldrin, in part because Furadan was applied after the peak of spring migration. In stronger formulations, however, Furadan killed several thousand waterfowl in British Columbia, California, and Oklahoma, indicating that only the lowest strength possible of this carbamate should be used, and then only after migration is over.

Secondary poisoning also can occur with some carbamates. Red-shouldered hawks (*Buteo lineatus*) died after feeding on birds poisoned in a cornfield treated with Furadan. Expansion of the mortality data to include the total area treated each year with Furadan indicated that several thousand hawks of various species might be harmed.

Earthworms poisoned in fields treated with Furadan became spasmatic, and thus attracted the attentions of feeding robins (*Turdus migratorius*); such data suggest that huge numbers of robins may die each year in this fashion.

Herbicides

In general, herbicides seemingly represent far less direct threat to wildlife than insecticides. Laboratory tests with many of the better-known herbicides indicate that these cause little or no mortality in birds under conditions simulating rates of field application. These materials are less toxic than insecticides to terrestrial animals and do not seem to biomagnify.

However, there may be delayed effects that are not expressed for some time after initial exposure. Controversy surrounds the cancer-forming potential of some herbicides, as witnessed by the incidence of this malady in people exposed to Agent Orange in Vietnam. However, even if some herbicides are carcinogenic to humans, it may not necessarily mean that wildlife also is threatened.

The life span of most wild animals is short enough that they die from other causes before lethal cancerous tissues have time to develop. The matter remains speculative at this time, however.

Still, recent tests suggest that some widely used herbicides produce significant mortality in some animals. Embryos in mallard eggs exposed to Trifluralin experienced nearly 50 percent mortality when treated with normal application rates of this herbicide. Either direct spraying on eggs or transferral of the herbicide on the plumage of the incubating adults to their eggs may pose hazards.

When applied at recommended rates, 2, 4,5-T did not significantly impair mallard embryos, but another herbicide, Paraquat, produced high rates of mortality and impaired embryonic growth when applied at one-half the level recommended for field use.

As with insecticides, a large number of herbicides entered the marketplace after World War II. Only 14 herbicides were sold in the United States before 1940. By 1963, the number had increased eight times. Unlike insecticides, however, herbicides must be more specifically tuned to their targets or they will kill crops along with the undesirable weeds.

Most herbicides are designed to kill either grasses or broadleaved plants, but not both. Even so, species tolerances to herbicides vary greatly, and further specificity may be possible once tolerances are determined for target and nontarget vegetation.

Factors such as soil temperature, stage of plant development, and season also influence the effectiveness and selectivity of herbicides.

Herbicides may kill or impair vegetation that is of benefit to wildlife. Klebenow (1970) found that herbicide treatments reducing sagebrush (*Artemisia tridentata*) also killed understory vegetation important to sage grouse (*Centrocercus urophasianus*).

Thus, wildlife habitat may suffer in quality or quantity when some herbicides are used indiscriminately. Attempts to rid sandy soils of shinnery oak (*Quercus havardii*) in west Texas with high application rates of herbicides also impaired production of the range grasses that were desired as replacement vegetation. At lower rates of application, however, prairie grasses thrived and most of the oaks were killed, but the patches that remain may be crucial habitat for prairie chickens and other wildlife.

Adjustments in the rates at which herbicides are applied thus may improve range conditions for both cattle and wildlife. In Oregon, clear-cut areas are sprayed with herbicides to suppress invasions of brush, thereby favouring the regrowth of commercially valuable conifers. The treatments accordingly reduced the complexity of the vegetation, but the density and diversity of the avian community remained largely unchanged.

However, MacGillivray's warblers (*Oporornis tolmiei*) were unusually sensitive to short-term defoliation of deciduous shrubs, and Wilson's warblers (*Wilsonia pusilla*) declined two or more times in density even after altering their foraging behaviour in response to the modified habitat.

For management purposes, the study nonetheless revealed that retention of even small amounts of deciduous tree cover on sprayed clearcuts would result in near-normal bird communities. Hence, if left unsprayed, the borders of logging roads, creek edges, and steep slopes would maintain crucial habitat for most songbirds without affecting overall timber production.

Fertilizers

Fertilizers are applied to farmlands in various ways and at different levels of concentration depending on the crops and soils involved. Most fertilizers pose no harm to wildlife. However, fertilizers in granular form may resemble seeds or grit, and thus may offer potential hazards for wildlife ingesting large numbers of the granules.

Fredrickson et al. summarized instances of moribund birds associated with fertilizer poisoning, including the death of nearly 4500 juvenile pheasants held in pens. Because huge amounts of granular fertilizers are applied each year in the United States-204,000 tons in South Dakota alone-experiments were conducted with fertilizers to determine their effects on pheasants. Breeding hens were force-fed fertilizers in capsules, and chicks ate mixtures of fertilizers in their foods.

The results showed no influences on reproduction, behaviour, or survival, leading to the conclusion that granular fertilizers normally do not affect unconfined pheasant populations.

Farming for Wildlife

As described earlier, humans often have modified the condition of many soils throughout the world. Desertification of lands bordering the Mediterranean is a good example, but many others exist. The Dust Bowl of the 1930s, triggered when prolonged drought struck the North American interior, was the aftermath of years of negligence and mismanagement .

For all its tragedy, the Dust Bowl sired new ideas about soil and water relationships. The Soil Conservation Service, established in 1935, was the immediate federal response to abused land. Contour plowing, terracing, alternate and strip cropping, and other means of stabilizing soil resources were advanced under the sponsorship of this agency.

Biologists for many years have suggested the benefits of mixed crops, hay, and woody cover for cottontails. Shelterbelts, thickets, or other kinds of cover available about every 200 m offer ideal habitat for cottontails on farmlands. These measures promote soil stability.

But soil by the millions of tons still erodes each year, undermining a multitude of relationships involving water, vegetation, and wildlife as well as agricultural production.

Shelterbelts

Shelterbelts, or *windbreaks*, were adopted widely in the 1930s as a means of protecting soil against wind erosion. The U.S.D.A. Forest Service alone planted more than 200 million trees in nearly 30,000 km of shelterbelts in six states between 1935 and 1942.

In recent years, however, many shelterbelts have been removed despite evidence of improved yields when crops are protected from wind. Others are aged and dying, often without being replanted. The Dust Bowl is not within memory of today's generation of younger farmers, and shelterbelts may seem only a relic of another era.

With fewer shelterbelts, conservation of soil and wildlife habitat share mutual degradation. Shelterbelts function as islands or corridors of trees in a matrix of cultivated land. Griffith (1976) estimated that less than 3 percent of the area in the Great Plains is covered by woodland, thus emphasizing the potential of shelterbelts as crucial wooded habitat for many species of wildlife.

Today, shelterbelts are included in the cover types offered by a new conservation program-the Food Security Act of 1985, discussed earlier-in which erodible lands are protected with stable vegetation. Thus, more of these important habitats may be forthcoming on America's farmlands in the decade ahead.

Shelterbelts are ecological units offering opportunities for managing game and nongame in otherwise treeless environments. All told, 17 species of birds nested in shelterbelts sampled by Yahner and, of these, mourning doves nested at a density of 20 nests per ha. Emmerich and Vohs recorded 15 species of birds using at least 25 percent of the shelterbelts they studied in South Dakota.

Shelterbelts on the northern prairies are important nesting areas for merlins (*Falco columbarius*) and Swainson's hawks (*Buteo swainsoni*). A variety of small mammals occupies shelterbelts, but few of these are agricultural pests. Other species benefiting from shelterbelts include bobwhite, pheasants, and cottontails. Shelterbelts extended the range of fox squirrels (*Sciurus niger*) westward into the southern Great Plains and connected the ranges of two colour phases of the common flicker (*Colaptes auratus*).

The geographical center of breeding range for Mississippi kites (*Ictinia mississippiensis*) shifted westward when shelterbelts provided new nesting and foraging habitat. Because they create mosaic patchworks and increase "edges" in open landscapes, shelterbelts may afford Mississippi kites with more nesting sites, enhanced habitat for prey, and increased feeding opportunities.

Other benefits may accrue from shelterbelts. Ferber (1974) reported estimates that birds consume about 118 kg of insects per 0.8 km of shelterbelt each year. Larger shelterbelts also offer opportunities for hunting. More pheasants were killed in Colourado with less effort near woody plantings than in habitat without shelterbelts; strips of woody cover also enhanced quail hunting in Texas.

Not all species of wildlife benefit from shelterbelts, however, and distinctions should be made between what is or is not essential habitat. For example, shelterbelts are prime habitat for cottontails but they seldom offer the same degree of security for deer unless the sites provide year-round habitat requirements. Prairie chickens actually avoid shelterbelts during certain times of the year.

Great horned owls (*Bubo virginianus*) and other avian predators at times may increase the mortality of pheasants near windbreaks, but herbaceous vegetation in these habitats can be managed in ways that reduce predation. With these distinctions in mind, shelterbelts offer considerable opportunities for managing a large number of species.

Because shelterbelts are man-made, many of the features desirable for wildlife habitat may be planned from the onset. Podoll summarized the major factors influencing the value of shelterbelts as wildlife habitats as follows:

(1) species of food and cover plants selected,
(2) the density and arrangement of plants within the shelterbelt,
(3) the width of the shelterbelt, and
(4) the right-angle orientation of the shelterbelt in relation to prevailing winds.

The arrangement and thickness of shelterbelt cover seem crucial, particularly where severe winter weather may be expected. Wandell (1949) cited losses of several hundred pheasants in North Dakota in some shelterbelts, whereas in the same area a better-situated shelterbelt successfully protected 300-400 pheasants from the rigors of winter.

Shelterbelts established on the edges of small lakes in heavily cultivated regions may protect wintering waterfowl, thereby conserving their energy reserves during cold, gusty weather. Stephen (1975) proposed that shelterbelts located next to grain fields may reduce crop depredations because field-feeding ducks generally prefer large, open spaces unencumbered by tree growth.

Simple considerations such as the spacing of trees can favour certain species. Spaces of 5-6 m between spruce trees, for example, enhance robin (*Turdus migratorius*) and mourning dove nesting habitat while retaining the primary benefits of the shelterbelt as a wind barrier. Shelterbelts of 8 rows occupying about 0.6 ha next to croplands were recommended, and, as individual trees age and die, some should be left as nesting and foraging sites for birds requiring snags.

Capel (1988) reviewed the layout and design criteria for shelterbelts, of which a few are highlighted here. In northern areas such as the Dakotas and Manitoba, the greater demands for thermal protection and the adversities of drifting snow require at least 8 and as many as 20 rows of trees and shrubs in a belt 33 m or greater in width.

Shelterbelts of 2 to 4 rows, however, are sufficient in Texas. The basic design for wildlife includes 5 rows, of which the north or west side consists of conifers (for winter wind and snow protection), an inside row of one or more species of tall, deciduous trees (for vertical structure, nesting cover, and additional wind protection), and then 2 rows of shrubs or short trees on the leeward side (for food production).

However, because the width of shelterbelts remains the dominant feature associated with avian diversity and nesting success, additional rows of shrubs further improve the benefits for wildlife. Besides their usefulness for shelter and food for wildlife, the species of trees and shrubs must be selected for their tolerance to conditions such as drought and temperature.

Field offices of the Agricultural Extension Service or the U.S.D.A. Soil Conservation Service can recommend species suitable for local and regional conditions. Diversity of both the over- and understory vegetation should be encouraged. About 60 percent of the birds using shelterbelts in Minnesota were most often seen on or near the ground, indicating the importance of the understory in shelterbelt management.

Grazing is particularly damaging to the understory in shelterbelts, as it drastically reduces much of the habitat available for wildlife. Shelterbelts on grazed lands thus should be fenced as protection from livestock. As shelterbelts mature, other management can be employed for maximum results, including selective thinning, some weed control, and placement of food patches nearby.

Strips of alternate vegetation bordering fields with shelterbelts offer additional diversity in farm habitat and contribute to the conservation of soil and water resources. Swihart and Yahner (1982) found more cottontails in shelterbelts where man—made debris added structural complexity to these habitats.

Whether managers are renovating existing shelterbelts or are planting new ones, development of as much vertical stratification as possible in the structure of the vegetation will improve their usefulness as wildlife habitat.

Odd Areas and Roadsides

Farms often have small areas unsuitable for cultivation, sometimes known as *odd areas*. An aggregate of some 4 million ha of odd areas once was available in the United States, but new techniques of land reclamation have reduced this area.

Although they are individually of small size, odd areas may be important habitat for wildlife. Corners of fields where drainage is poor, for example, produce little income yet offer several species of farm-related wildlife sources of food and cover. The importance of such patches lies in their juxtaposition to large cultivated areas where songbirds, cottontails, quail, and other species often cannot gain a foothold. For example, where center-pivot irrigation is employed, the corners of fields not covered by the circular pattern of water distribution remain available as potential pheasant habitat.

Center-pivot sprinklers water a circle of about 53 ha, leaving an aggregate of nearly 3 ha in the four corners of each irrigated field available for wildlife management, but newer systems water these previously fallow corners. In wetlands, however, center-pivot sprinklers require construction of travelways (i.e., earthen ramps on which the wheels of the sprinkler move), which act as predator lanes and thereby decrease the nesting success of marsh birds.

Odd areas need not be managed in many casesprotection from intensive cultivation often is enough to produce benefits, although management sometimes can enhance the carrying capacity of these sites. Farmers may be concerned that odd areas are sources of weed infestation and, if so, limited treatment with herbicides often curbs this threat.

In some cases, food patches are created when corn or other grains are planted and left unharvested for wildlife. Sod-forming grasses or other undesirable vegetation may limit the success of these without judicious treatments with herbicides. A combination of shelterbelts and food patches is a particularly effective management on farmlands. But with or without management, patches of uncultivated vegetation provide wildlife with essential habitat within farming regimes otherwise devoted to a monoculture.

Roadsides offer significant potential for habitat management, not only on secondary roads in farmland but also along major highways and railroad rights-of-way. On farmlands, the trend toward larger fields, fewer fencerows, and a monoculture of row crops has caused major reductions in habitat for many species of desirable wildlife.

Few gamebirds seem more affected than pheasants. Studies of pheasant nesting in managed roadside habitats were initiated in an intensively cultivated area in Illinois. Selected roadside areas were seeded with a grass-legume mixture and left unmowed until the peak of hatching had passed.

More pheasant nests per area were established on these areas than on other types of roadside cover or, indeed, on any of the other habitat available throughout the study area. Hayfields, in particular, are important nesting habitat for pheasants, but as the area of hayfields is reduced, the contributions of roadside environments become more crucial.

About 9 percent of the Illinois study area was hayfield at the start of the study, but hayfields amounted to no more than 3 percent of the area 8 years later. Coincident with the reduction in hayfields, the percentage of pheasant nests established on roadsides increased from 7 percent to 45 percent during the same period, further indicating the importance of roadsides as supplemental nesting cover.

On a long-term basis (1967 to 1984), roadside management amplified the increase in regional pheasant populations and moderated declines associated with changes in land use and severe winters. Cooperation of farmers remains a key element in roadside management. To enhance such associations in Illinois, farmers and state conservation officials entered into cooperative agreements.

The state undertook the seeding program and farmers agreed not to mow until August 1 of each year. Up to 89 percent of the farmers complied with their agreements during the first 4 years, but thereafter the compliance dropped to 63 percent. Most of the farmers supported the roadside management program, although some were concerned about the appearance of unmowed roadsides and weed control.

Some of these shortcomings were addressed by reminding farmers with a newsletter describing the need for their continued cooperation. Also, the farmer's prideful concern for the public's reaction to an unkempt roadside was reduced with signs advising motorists about the program and its merits for pheasant management. Roadside management also provides favourable habitat for numerous songbirds and small mammals, not just for pheasants.

This illustrates a relationship often neglected when wildlife management is perceived only as game management. In reality, habitats improved for a few game species produce favourable conditions for dozens of nongame species. Thus, diversity is improved in the overall wildlife community. Further, for each pheasant nest in a managed roadside, several nests of other species could be expected.

One might hope that future measurements of improved habitat consider all species benefiting from management activities. Recent evidence suggests some caution, however, about intensive roadside management for wildlife. O'Neill et al. (1983) found that lead from automobile emissions concentrated in the soils, vegetation, small mammals, and some insects along roadsides.

The concentration of lead diminished as the distance from the road increased, and the amount of lead in small mammals increased in proportion to the volume of traffic. Because lead may impair reproduction, increase mortality, and cause renal abnormalities in wildlife, roadside management should be limited to thoroughfares where traffic volume is less than 7000 vehicles per day. Bats (Chiroptera) feeding near a major parkway on average contained more lead than small terrestrial mammals.

The stomach contents and carcasses of barn swallows (*Hirundo rustica*) feeding over the same parkway also contained greater amounts of lead than swallows foraging elsewhere. Nonetheless, Grue et al. (1984) concluded that lead in automotive emissions does not pose a serious threat to birds feeding on flying insects over highways.

Harrison and Dyer (1984) found accumulations of lead along roadways in a national park, and calculated that some mule deer (*Odocoileus hemionus*) could ingest harmful amounts of lead if only 1.4 percent of their daily forage was consumed from roadsides. Continued use of unleaded fuels eventually will reduce lead concentrations in roadside environments.

Tillage

Traditional methods of preparing seedbeds for row crops often begin with fall plowing, followed by one or more disking treatments. After planting, the fields again are cultivated; consequently, the land is tilled repeatedly several times each year. Under this regime, tilled lands are exposed to wind and water erosion until crops again help anchor the soil.

Years of tillage often may form a hardened plow pan, a compacted layer of relatively impenetrable soil just beneath the bite of the plowshare. *Conservation tillage-known* in some of its various forms as no-till, minimum tillage, and stubble mulching-is a recent concept that overcomes some of the disadvantages outlined above. "*Stubble*" and other residue from the previous crop are left on the soil surface, thus forming a cover that reduces wind and water erosion.

The cover may be as much as 79 percent on untilled fields compared with less than 6 percent on tilled fields. New crops are planted directly through the residue with seed drills, without plowing or other disturbance of the soil and ground cover.

The net results of conservation tillage include less soil erosion, more water infiltration, and reduced runoff, as well as reduced operating costs. Increased chemical treatments, however, may be required for weed and insect pests. Conservation tillage also may increase the density of rodent populations, thereby increasing damage to newly planted crops. Nonetheless, estimates suggest that conservation tillage can reduce soil loss and fuel costs by as much as 90 percent and 80 percent, respectively. Some form of conservation tillage was practiced on 33 percent of all cropland in the United States in 1986.

Conservation tillage has definite advantages for soil protection. The practice also benefits wildlife. Prairie chicken populations in west Texas are influenced by the amount and interspersion of native and cultivated habitats. Within limits, cultivation increased the carrying capacity for prairie chickens, but additional conversion to row crops thereafter reduced the habitat's suitability.

However, positive correlations between the acreages protected by crop residues and the seasonal populations of prairie chickens suggested that conservation tillage partly overcame the intrusion of additional cultivation.

In Nebraska, Nason (1982) also described the advantages of conservation tillage for pheasants and other birds nesting in spring-fallowed croplands. He likened the method to the close association between pheasant abundance and the undisturbed lands during the era of the Soil Bank, and predicted that ground-nesting birds will prosper as conservation tillage becomes more widely adopted.

However, the relative abundance of insects and other arthropods seems unaffected by conservation tillage, and the practice apparently offers no advantage over tilled fields during the spring when pheasant chicks require proteinaceous foods.

About half of the northern prairies of North America now are under intensive cultivation. This same region provides the breeding habitat for more than 50 percent of the continent's waterfowl population. Unfortunately, sharp conflicts, including those about wetland drainage and crop depredations, exist between agricultural interests and those concerning the maintenance of large waterfowl populations.

Some of these issues must be addressed by one or more levels of governmental policymakers, but other issues involve tillage and other day-to-day farming operations. On the northern prairies, the stubble of harvested grain crops may be left over winter. Early migrants, particularly pintails (*Anas acuta*), use stubble fields for nesting as little other cover is available until later in the season.

However, many pintail nests are destroyed when these fields are cultivated. Milonski (1958) reported that 72 percent of the first nests

Table 3.9: Water Runoff and Soil Erosion for Fields In Wisconsin Treated with One Kind of Conservation Tillage Compared with Conventional Plowing and Fallowing.

Parameter	*Conventional Plowing*	*Conservation Fallow*	*Tillage*
Runoff (mm)	29.5	50.3	24.4
Runoff (%)	7.0	12.0	5.8
Erosion (tons/ha)	6.0	17.5	3.7

of pintails were in stubble fields, but about half of these were destroyed by farming operations before they hatched. Pintails, after losing their first nests in stubble, often renested in hayfields, but many of these also were lost when the hay was mowed. Densities of waterfowl nests on untilled land may be 12 times those on croplands, and may yield 16 times as many ducklings.

However, most fields are tilled, and the larger rates of duck production are not realized with current management practices. Conservation tillage thus offers new opportunities for vastly improved duck production while offering economic benefits to farmers (e.g., reduced fuel costs) and environmental advantages (e.g., soil and water conservation) to a broader sector of society.

Nearly four times as many ducks were produced on farms where conservation tillage was practiced than on conventionally tilled farms. Croplands managed with conservation tillage not only expand the habitat base for the entire nesting season but also provide optimal nesting cover with relatively low rates of predation.

Winter wheat and fall rye are particularly suitable for conservation tillage and improved duck production since both crops are seeded in the fall, thereby avoiding the risk of destroying nests with seed drills during the spring months.

Basore et al. recorded 12 species of birds with an average density of 36 nests per 100 ha in fields managed with conservation tillage, compared with only 3 species and a density of 4 nests per 100 ha on tilled fields. Killdeer (*Charadrius vociferus*) and vesper sparrows (*Pooecetes gramineus*) were two of the major species, as were pheasants and mourning doves.

Predation rates were high in this study, but Basore et al. (1986) calculated that the continued switch to conservation tillage in Iowa would offer habitat for about 25,000 pheasant nests per year by 1988. In addition to cover, some types of conservation tillage leave large amounts of waste corn and soybeans available as food for wildlife, whereas the amount and availability of waste grains diminish rapidly as the intensity of plowing increases.

Best (1986), however, speculated that conservation tillage may produce "ecological traps," because nesting success may be lower than is needed for the replacement of breeding stock. If so, birds nesting in such places thus form so-called "sink" populations. In this view, the attractive nature of the nesting cover lures birds from other areas, but farming practices (e.g., chemical applications) thereafter may severely reduce breeding success.

In other words, the birds may be better off nesting elsewhere instead of breeding in fields managed by conservation tillage. The potential for more and more sink populations increases as productive habitats are converted into croplands managed with conservation tillage.

Nonetheless, such relationships remain unproved, and the "*Sodbuster*" and conservation reserve provisions of the Food Security Act of 1985 in any case may offset much or all of this threat. Labisky (1957) studied fields where duck nests reached densities of about 1 nest per ha. The area was associated with a waterfowl refuge but was farmed privately.

Virtually all active duck nests in hayfields were destroyed by mowing unless protective measures were employed. These measures included dragging ropes across the field so that incubating hens were flushed, and thereafter marking the location as a site to avoid when mowing.

This left an "island" of unmowed hay surrounding the nest, but it also attracted predators. Some evidence tentatively suggested that larger "islands" lessened the incidence of predation, but the size of the predator population may have an overriding influence. Delayed mowing seems the best management procedure, but the delay may reduce the quality of the hay, and therefore may diminish the financial reward for farmers.

Thus, the chronology of some farming activities often adversely coincides with the nesting seasons of several birds. Weigand (1980), for example, concluded that haying and other farm operations neutralize gray partridge production in the United States. Higgins (1977) also projected a dismal future for prairie-nesting waterfowl.

Virtually all nesting studies conducted on the intensively farmed prairies indicate that too few nests hatched to maintain waterfowl populations at desirable levels. Poor nesting cover resulting from intensive cultivation, coupled with nest destruction caused by farm machinery and predators, pose severe limitations for future populations of several species. Rodgers (1983), however, determined that a subsurface cutting blade, used in lieu of surface tillage for weed control, can save up to 53 percent of the bird nests located in wheat stubble.

Adults continued incubation on 89 percent of the nests in the undercutting treatments, and no deaths or injuries were observed. The undercutting method provides both wildlife and agronomic benefits, because the surface litter continues to protect the soil while controlling weeds and successfully maintaining many bird nests.

Because at least 18 species of birds nest in wheat stubble, and wheat is fallowed on some 33 million ha of North America, the undercutting method potentially conserves an immense number of nests from destruction each year.

As we have seen, corn has become a staple in the diets of several kinds of wildlife. Many state and federal refuges produce corn solely as fall and winter food for waterfowl, but these efforts achieve maximum benefits only if as much of this food as possible is consumed. It is one matter to leave large amounts of corn in a field and quite another to have it used efficiently. Hence, how might refuge managers enhance the availability of the corn they produce?

Let us look at private farming operations before returning to that question. Contrary to the goals of refuge management, the private farming sector removes as much corn as possible. Any of the crop left unharvested represents lost income. Despite this, mechanical corn pickers often leave sizeable amounts of waste corn.

Waste corn amounted to nearly 4 percent of the harvest, or 364 kg per ha, on farms in the Texas Panhandle. So, regardless of corn's abundance on either refuges or private lands, the same question again arises, namely, how to make this resource available most effectively for field-feeding waterfowl?

Postharvest tillage greatly affects the abundance and availability of waste corn. Plowing turns under 97 percent of the leftover ears and kernels, whereas disking claims 77 percent of this waste. Both methods disturb the soil and require additional energy and labor costs. Burning, however, circumvents these drawbacks and provides the maximum availability of waste corn.

Cornstalks and other litter present a physical impediment for feeding waterfowl, so that burning the litter significantly increases the birds' access to waste corn. Whereas the surface litter is removed, the rootstalks remain unburned and continue binding the soil against erosion. Burning thus increases availability of waste corn, irrespective of its original abundance. Waterfowl respond quickly, selecting newly burned fields in preference to others. Prescribed burning accordingly presents managers of either private or public lands with a cheap, effective tool for manipulating field-feeding waterfowl populations.

Feeding pressure and distribution may be managed according to specific objectives, the size of the waterfowl population, and the acreage of corn produced. The corn resource may be apportioned over a longer or shorter period by an appropriate burning schedule, and spatial relationships also may be devised.

For example, it may be desirable to disperse birds in the case of an epizootic, or to create a patchwork of burned fields in order to distribute hunting pressure more evenly. Also, unburned fields can be held in reserve to meet the sudden demand for extra food when unusually cold weather strikes.

4

Diseases and Their Controls

We shall consider a wildlife disease as a disturbance to the normal function or structure of an animal. Wildlife diseases may result from a broad array of causative agents and may be assigned to the following categories: infectious, parasitic, toxic, physiological, nutritional, congenital, and degenerative.

The advent of environmental pollution highlighted the importance of toxicity. Compression of populations into restricted areas such as zoos, parks, and preserves may encourage physiological and degenerative diseases.

Small, isolated populations may suffer congenital anomalies such as inbreeding infertility or other forms of inbreeding depression. Infectious, disease-spreading agents are known as *pathogens*, which include bacteria, viruses, rikettsias, parasites, and fungi.

Instead of attempting an exacting clinical review of the many diseases affecting wildlife, we will select only a few examples that illustrate the ecological relationships—real or potential—existing between pathogenic agents and wildlife populations.

We will assess how disease-producing agents interact with habitat conditions, how some wildlife populations may be influenced, and how management sometimes may be deployed to offset disease-related adversities. In large measure, we will be concerned with *epizootiology*, the "how" and "why" of diseases in either their *enzootic* (chronic) or *epizootic* (eruptive) states in wildlife populations.

WHY STUDY WILDLIFE DISEASES?

At least four reasons compel wildlife managers to address the issue of diseases in animal populations. First, either domestic or wild animals may serve as *reservoirs* or as *vectors* for pathogens that ultimately affect each other, or indeed, humans. In 1924-25, mule deer (*Odocoileus hemionus*) in Stanislaus National Forest were slaughtered when foot-and-mouth'disease ravaged livestock in California.

The herd was decimated when more than 22,000 deer were shot in the months following the discovery of the disease. Of these, about 10 percent showed lesions associated with foot-and-mouth disease. Similarly, even larger numbers of African wildlife were slaughtered as a means of eradicating the reservoir of parasites transmitted by ,tsetse flies.

Such measures are, of course, a drastic treatment for protecting livestock, but wildlife is not always the villain in such relationships. DeArment found no evidence that two serious livestock diseases, leptospirosis and brucellosis, were carried by wildlife, despite the claims of ranchers.

During the same 10-year period that cattle were stricken, neither disease was detected in more than 1600 blood samples taken from the pronghorn (*Antilocapra americana*) population in the same region. The findings of that study undoubtedly saved many hundreds of pronghorns from needless destruction.

More recently, Kingscote and Bohac found no evidence of either leptospirosis or brucellosis in more than 200 pronghorns examined in Alberta, and suggested that a barrier prevents the transmission of leptospirosis between pronghorns and cattle.

Another case involving brucellosis is more complex. Some ranchers in Montana suspect that bison (*Bison bi*son) in Yellowstone Park act as reservoirs for brucellosis. The infectious disease presents an economic concern for the livestock industry. Infected cattle suffer abortions, and the *Brucella* bacteria can be transmitted to humans as undulant fever.

Although often testing positive for antibodies, bison seldom exhibit clinical signs of brucellosis, a phenomenon that may be an evolutionary adaptation of long standing. The issue centers on increased size of the Yellowstone herd-now about 2000 strong-with the result that some bison wander from the park onto adjacent rangeland that is held in private ownership.

The Montana legislature thus authorized a 7-month hunting season on the strays; however, critics note that Montana has not experienced an outbreak of brucellosis for 25 years. Some claim that the hunt is a cover-up for the mismanagement of the herd by the Park Service, and at least one animal-rights group charges that the bison hunt was designed merely for the pleasure of sportsmen who used the disease as an excuse.

Preliminary data suggest that bison are somewhat more resistant than cattle to infection from *Brucella*, and that transmission of the disease from bison to cattle, while possible, is less easily accomplished than from cattle to cattle. After thoroughly reviewing the status of bison as reservoirs of brucellosis, McCorquodale and DiGiacomo concluded that these and other North American ungulates have little role in the transmission of the disease to cattle.

Similarly, Kingscote et al. found little evidence for the exchange of several microbial diseases between elk (*Cervus elaphus canadensis*) and cattle on shared range in Alberta. However, these researchers recommended periodic monitoring because of the potential for epizootics. Other means for controlling diseases-or the vectors of diseases-may impair the ecological state of natural systems.

To control mosquitoes, for example, tidal marshes along the eastern seaboard were drained with ditches, thereby destroying much of the wetland vegetation and decreasing wildlife habitat. Among other effects was the invasion of noxious woody species into the saltmarsh communities and decreased use of habitat by several groups of birds.

A second reason for addressing wildlife diseases concerns the density of animal populations. As habitat dwindles in both quality and quantity, wildlife populations become more concentrated. Quite probably, many animals are stressed so that they are predisposed to diseases beyond former levels.

Unfortunately, there are indications that efforts to manage wildlife populations sometimes heighten disease-related mortality. The severity of infectious diseases, as we shall see, may be density-dependent, and when management successfully increases densities of animal populations, a greater proportion of the population becomes infected when disease strikes.

For example, the consequences of building high-density waterfowl populations on intensively managed refuges in one case probably induced additional mortality. Geese and other waterfowl on a refuge in Missouri experienced a winter epizootic of avian cholera (*Pasteurella multocida*) when the birds concentrated on small, ice-free areas kept open by pumping water.

Third, diseases may cause serious losses in already small populations of endangered species. In 1984, what was believed to be an insect-borne virus killed 7 of 39 whooping cranes (*Grus americana*) held in captivity by the U.S. Fish and Wildlife Service at the Patuxent Wildlife Research Center. Besides causing the immediate loss of crucial breeding stock-the dead birds represented 18 percent of the captive flock—the disease threatened the future of the captive-breeding program.

Moreover, at least one immature whooping crane raised in Idaho was weakened severely by avian tuberculosis, and then died from salmonellosis. Because the pathogen causing avian tuberculosis, *Mycobacterium avium*, can persist in soil for months or even years, the disease may pose a threat for the foster-parent restoration program described in other Chapter of this book.

Similarly, the discovery of canine parvovirus in timber wolves (*Canis lupus*) in Minnesota is discouraging, although conclusive evidence is not at hand that the disease is causing mortality in wild packs. In 1985, an epizootic of canine distemper decimated most of the only known colony of black-footed ferrets (*Mussel nigripes*).

The colony, located near Meeteetse, Wyoming, was estimated at 59 ferrets before the epizootic, but only 6 ferrets were located later in the year. Because black-footed ferrets may be the rarest mammal in the United States, and possibly in the world, these losses were a serious setback for the conservation of an endangered species. Price (1985), after determining the efficacy and safe use of a vaccine for avian cholera, suggested that endangered birds such as the Aleutian Canada goose (*Branta canadensis leucopareia*) might be immunized when the geese are trapped for banding.

High levels of lead present in the tissues of urban rock doves (*Columba livia*) are a potential threat for peregrine falcons (*Falco peregrines*) living in cities on the Atlantic seaboard. In cities, the endangered falcons prey heavily on rock doves ("*pigeons*"), which contain an average of 4.6 ppm of lead. In contrast, rock doves living elsewhere contained only 0.33 ppm of lead. Rock doves themselves are relatively resistant to the toxic effects of lead, and offer a means of monitoring accumulations of lead in urban settings.

Fortunately, however, no evidence yet suggests that urban-dwelling peregrine falcons have experienced secondary poisoning from the high dietary levels of lead in rock doves. Fourth, diseases are a part of the whole spectrum of issues facing wildlife managers. That is, diseases are just as much a part of the management puzzle as are food habits, population dynamics, and habitat requirements. In fact, diseases usually are related directly to each of these subjects.

Parasites in the abomasal chamber of the rumen of white-tailed deer (*Odocoileus virginianus*) may offer managers a way of estimating the health of deer herds. The intensity of these infections theoretically varies with the density of the herd in relation to carrying capacity.

Eve and Kellogg (1977) thus suggested that counts of abomasal parasites were an "early warning device" for detecting overstocked deer ranges. The usefulness of this evaluation, however, may vary between summer and winter and the method should be refined for local situations.

Indirectly, weather conditions, soil, water, and other environmental settings influence diseases and their epizootiology. Karstad investigated a disease that was killing large numbers of caribou (*Rangifer tarandus*) calves in Newfoundland. Up to 50 percent of the calves were dying from sizeable abscesses on their necks. No pathogen was evident as the source of the infections, despite careful examinations of the dead animals.

Subsequent fieldwork determined that the abscesses were caused from wounds inflicted by lynx (*Felis lynx*). Although the calves often were defended successfully by their mothers, the attacking lynx usually were able to wound the calves before being driven off, thereby initiating an infection that later killed the young animals.

The severity of the losses coincided with the population cycle of lynx, and hence means were taken to reduce the lynx population on the calving grounds during peak years. Migratory birds face a continual series of diseases year round along all parts of their north-south axis of movement, thereby underscoring the fact that disease biology and management must be addressed across state, provincial, and national lines.

The incidence and severity of wildlife diseases thus are not isolated matters often associated with a single time and place. Brucellosis, as noted earlier, is a disease of economic importance in livestock, but it also may curtail reproduction in some species of big game. In cattle, *Brucella abortus* causes abortions in the latter half of pregnancy, sterility in cows, and pathological changes in the genital tract of bulls.

Because about 50 percent of the female elk (*Cervus elaphus*) in some herds in Wyoming are infected, the loss of elk calves represents a serious impediment for management. However, because the infected herds in Wyoming are fed artificially in winter, the accessibility of the elk permits administration of an immunizing vaccine.

In 1985, about 490 cow and calf elk-70 percent of the herd feeding at one management area-were immunized with vaccine-loaded "biobullets" shot from an airgun. Some diseases are a part of natural mortality, but this factor should not preclude their identification nor should it deter efforts to minimize the impact of diseases on wildlife populations.

Other diseases, such as lead poisoning, are unnatural in the sense that they are man-made. In any case, pathogens striking wildlife are not only a matter of concern for animal health. For some species, pathogens also represent lost recreation, diminished aesthetics, and waste of food and fiber.

Perspectives

As we have stated, some diseases are natural phenomena, and their occurrences should not necessarily be viewed with alarm. Others indeed severely affect wildlife populations. Managers, to be effective as well as informed, must remain watchful for situations where action may lessen the impacts of disease on wildlife populations or on those who use wildlife resources.

For example, botfly infections of gray squirrels (*Sciurus carolinensis*) can adversely affect the behaviour of hunters. Larvae of the squirrel botfly (*Cuterebra emasculator*) are subcutaneous parasites that form grotesque, but nonlethal, infections of gray squirrels.

These may affect significant percentages of their host populations. Because of the influence these parasites might have on the attitudes of hunters, Jacobson et al. conducted a survey of sportsmen in Mississippi where botflies sometimes infect more than 50 percent of the gray squirrel population.

The estimates from this survey, when extrapolated on a statewide basis, indicated that no less than 60,000 squirrels were discarded by hunters because of the unsightly infections. The survey also examined the sociological impact of parasites on hunters; among these results were that some sportsmen quit squirrel hunting (8 percent), others hunted elsewhere (9 percent), and some reduced the time spent hunting squirrels (26 percent).

In all, more than half of the hunters reacted in some fashion to the parasitized squirrels. In light of the parasite's life history, a delayed opening of the hunting season-from September until October-diminished this problem in squirrel management. Gray squirrels generally are rid of the objectionable infections later in the autumn when the botfly larvae emerge from their hosts and pupate in the soil.

In North Carolina alone, the delayed season probably saved 880,000 gray squirrels from being discarded by hunters. Similarly, human exposure to tularemia is reduced when the opening date of the rabbit season is late enough in the year so that 10 or more nights of freezing temperatures have passed before hunting begins.

The primary vectors of tularemia, ticks, drop from rabbits with the onset of cold weather, and the disease dissipates accordingly. A week later, most of the infected rabbits have died, leaving a relatively disease-free population available for safe hunting. In this case, the opening date becomes a management tool for lessening the hazard of tularemia to human health.

Diseases also should be viewed in an ecological context. They are not phenomena isolated in nature. Several pathogens offer useful insights about the workings within and between wildlife populations and about natural selection. Predation may increase on disease-stricken populations where large numbers of weakened prey are predisposed to attack.

Nearly one-third of the adult moose (*Alces alces*) killed on Isle Royale suffered from a necrotic inflammation of the mandible; the disease is known as periodontitis or "lumpy jaw". This and other debilitating conditions, including heavy tick infections, predisposed moose to wolf (*Canis lupus*) predation. Other studies of big game also linked the frequency of predation with disease-related settings.

Cheatum discovered a correlation between lungworm infections and "winter kill" in deer dying during severe winters. Malnutrition predisposed the deer to a weakened condition whereby lungworm-induced pneumonia eventually proved fatal.

Moose are particularly susceptible to tapeworm infections; as intermediate hosts, moose are infected when eggs of proglottids dropped in the feces of carnivores are consumed along with forage or drinking water. These develop into golfball-sized cysts in the lungs of moose, and the infection can reach 68 percent of the herd.

Completion of the parasite's life cycle depends on ingestion of the cysts by a carnivore; thereafter, the larvae mature in the carnivore's intestinal tract and the cycle is renewed. Because the infections in moose are initiated by feeding and drinking, older moose have heavier infections than younger animals.

Thus, older moose are steadily debilitated liy ever-increasing lung infections and become more susceptible to predation. As suggested by Mech, this situation raises an interesting philosophical relationship between parasitic infections and predation. For the parasite to continue as a biological entity in nature, it must mature and reproduce in

Table 4.1: Relationship Between Freezing Temperatures, Opening Date of the Rabbit Hunting Season in Illinois, and the Rate of Tularemia in Humans.

Days	*Rate of Tularemia per 100,000 Humans*
After opening of rabbit season:	
30–39	14.1
20–29	14.2
10–19	11.1
0–9	4.3
Before opening of rabbit season:	
0–9	1.0
10–19	0.4

carnivores. In terms of natural selection, it thus becomes beneficial for older, more heavily parasitized moose to fall victim to wolves.

Indeed, the older age classes of moose no longer exert much influence on the herd's reproductive potential, and seemingly represent an "*expendable*" segment of an otherwise healthy population. Furthermore, the very existence of this pathogen and its obligate life cycle are evidence of predation's natural role in animal populations.

As outlined by Holmes, the ecology of predation is particularly noteworthy in regard to diseases. Wolves "*test*" their prey for signs of vulnerability. Hence, wolves normally cull individuals having debilitating infections. Predation in this instance can reduce the impact of the pathogen (i.e., diseased prey are quickly removed, leaving a healthy population).

In the absence of predation, however, sick animals are not culled and pathogens may assume a more important role in population control. Conversely, mountain lions (*Felis concolour*) ambush their prey, and seem less likely to select heavily infected prey. The culling effect of mountain lions and other ambush predators thus may be less in comparison with that of wolves.

Foraging experiments have indicated that starlings (*Sturnus vulgaris*) are more likely to consume prey infected with parasites than nonparasitized prey of the same species. The parasites altered the behaviour of the prey in ways that predisposed them to starling predation (e.g., infected prey occurred more frequently in exposed areas, and thus were more readily encountered by predators).

In this case, the infected prey serve as the intermediate host in the life cycle of a parasitic worm (i.e., the parasite must pass from the intermediate host to the final host before completing the transition from egg to adult, and does so when infected prey are consumed by terminal hosts). Such results have several implications.

First, prey populations may consist of two types of individuals, those that are vulnerable to predation (parasitized), and those that are less so (not parasitized). Thus, predation rates for the same species may differ between sites because of variable levels of parasitism in the prey populations.

Second, some species of prey may be relatively uncommon in predator diets but, because parasitized individuals are more vulnerable, a large percentage of the predator population still may become infected with parasites.

Third, parasitism that increases the vulnerability of prey likely influences the diet of predators. That is, parasitized prey may dominate the diet of predators in one community, whereas elsewhere the same species of prey may be consumed less frequently if they are free of parasites.

Finally, we see the evolutionary benefit to the parasite of increasing the vulnerability of its intermediate host: parasitized prey are consumed more often by the terminal host, thus facilitating completion of the parasite's life cycle.

Cowan cautioned that examination of carcasses often are limited to skeletal remains so that the presence of many debilitating diseases in prey likely is underestimated. The viscera of prey and any pathogens contained therein seldom remain available for study after predators (and scavengers) have finished feeding.

As we have noted, parasitism may increase the vulnerability of prey to predators. Conversely, parasitism increased among white-tailed deer that were freed of coyote (*Canis latrans*) predation. Knowledgeable biologists should correctly identify such relationships so that mortality will not be assessed in error, thus thwarting the possibility of initiating effective management responses.

Many wildlife populations experience only enzootic levels of disease when other factors hold their densities in check. With excessive densities, however, diseases may reach epizootic levels. Thus, hunting may be crucial for maintaining healthy wildlife populations. Numerous attempts to protect wildlife fully from reasonable hunting pressure only assured that other mortality factors, among them disease, came into play as regulators of population density. When left to their own workings, infectious diseases eventually are self-regulating in concert with their hosts. As epizootics peak, density-dependent mechanisms in the host population return the pathogen to enzootic levels.

As mortality or resistance progresses, infectious contact diminishes within the host population and the disease dissipates accordingly. Some management situations are inherently conducive to epizootics. None seems more susceptible than those occurring in hatcheries. With the advent of fish culture late in the nineteenth century, the epizootiology of fish maladies assumed new dimensions.

Fishes in hatcheries are held in closed systems, thus placing virtually the entire stock in jeopardy should a pathogen appear. Furthermore, hatcheries receive stock from many sources, which offers a high risk of introducing pathogenic agents that are otherwise foreign to local environments.

Unfortunately, hatchery workers once discounted disease-related mortality simply by obtaining more eggs than otherwise needed rather than developing appropriate management techniques. Exchanges of fishes and their eggs became so commonplace that few hatcheries remained free of disease.

Eastern brook trout (*Salvelinus fontinalis*) were exposed to furunculosis (*Bacterium salmonicida*) when rainbow trout (*Salmo gairdneri*) were brought to eastern hatcheries for propagation and stocking. Major symptoms of furunculosis include blisters and ulcers penetrating deeply into body tissues, as well as hemorrhaging of the swim bladder, large intestine, and peritoneum; the bacteria collect in the spleen, liver, and kidneys and may destroy these organs.

The disease spread rapidly in hatcheries, and only with the development of sulfa drugs in the 1940s did furunculosis come under partial control. Prolonged use of sulfonamides, however, may lead to the development of drug-resistant strains of the bacteria. Even in more modern times, infectious pancreatic necrosis showed reverse movement, traveling from northeastern hatcheries to western North America.

This is a viral disease that is difficult to detect in its early stages. Once the disease is established, however, fishes with infectious pancreatic necrosis typically swim in spiral corkscrew movements, and thereafter experience high rates of mortality. Today, significant advances in fish culture have curbed the incidence of many diseases, but the very nature of hatchery operations still provides environments predisposed to epizootics of major proportions.

DISEASES AND HABITAT

In earlier times, the pathogens attacking wildlife populations were regarded somewhat passively by wildlife managers. Wholesale applications of remedies scarcely seemed possible even if vaccines or other treatments were available. Little could be accomplished in a wild, free-roaming population by clinical ministrations to the few individual animals that might come to hand.

Diseases thus were dismissed as regrettable but unmanageable misfortunes befalling wildlife populations (i.e., a fatalistic view that diseases were "an act of God"). That attitude reflected the first of four phases in the management history of wildlife diseases. Later, as human regard for diseases matured, attitudes changed and an era of concern began. Managers expressed alarm when diseases killed wildlife, but still lacked the knowledge to take much action.

In the third phase, control measures were initiated as a means of stemming epizootics (e.g., pick up and disposal of dead and dying animals). The last phase, prevention, still lies ahead. Experts in epizootiology now believe that habitat conditions influence the course of many wildlife diseases.

Whereas pathogens are not likely to be eradicated completely, the severity and frequency of their actions on wildlife populations often may be limited by human intervention. If so, greater control over disease becomes an attainable goal of wildlife management. Despite the attractiveness of this concept, however, the epizootiology for many pathogens remains unclear, thereby dampening the full application of disease management for some species of wildlife.

Nonetheless, the ecological settings for some pathogens and their victims are well enough known so that habitat manipulations sometimes can function as "*wildlife medicine.*" In time, and with more knowledge, additional wildlife diseases undoubtedly will succumb to intense management practices.

Avian botulism has been linked with habitat conditions since the earliest report of massive waterfowl deaths in 1876 at Owens Lake, California. Kalmbach compiled a full history of the disease in wild birds. Botulism is known throughout much of the world, including Europe, South Africa, New Zealand, and Australia.

In the United States, botulism in Utah and California still accounts for 100,000 or more deaths of waterfowl in some years. Among the first hypotheses about causes suggested that a mineral or organic constituent in the water was responsible for the epizootics.

Table 4.2: Evolution of Management Response to Wildlife Disease Problems.

Level	*Response Characteristics*	*Stage*	*Perspective*
1	Recognition that disease exists; acceptance of disease as a natural event	Awareness	Fatalistic
2	(a) Desire to respond to die-offs; no action taken because none obvious	Concern	Frustration
	(b) Generate concern to others		
3	(a) Responses to die-offs in an unplanned manner	Control	Fire fighting
	(b) Plans developed and utilized in responding to die-offs		
	(c) Improved method developed for combatting die-offs		
	(d) Control efforts evaluated for effectiveness		
4	(a) Reaction procedures well organized, effective within limitations of capabilities; prevention of future outbreaks given attention	Prevention	Problem solving
	(b) Short-term research carried out for disease control; long-term research initiated for disease prevention		
	(c) Disease concepts integrated as part of routine wildlife management; integrated program of research and disease control underway		

Later, the disease became known as alkali poisoning, for Wetmore (1915, 1918) concluded that water-soluble salts provided the toxic agent. Because the disease primarily occurred in western states, it also has been called "western duck disease."

Finally, the toxin produced by *Clostridium botulinum* type C was isolated from both sick ducks and mud samples, indicating that the disease was a form of food poisoning known as botulism. Kalmbach and Gunderson subsequently believed that dead organic matter, shallow water, high temperatures, and an alkaline environment were related to production of the toxin.

These conditions, acting in combination, formed the basis of the "sludge-bed hypothesis" wherein decaying organic matter provides the medium in which the bacterium produces its toxin in the absence of dissolved oxygen. Bell et al. (1955) offered an alternate hypothesis to the sludge-bed concept.

Instead of believing that toxin production occurs directly on newly exposed or flooded mudflats, they suggested that wetland invertebrates were the prime transmitters of *botulinum* toxin to waterbirds. Known as the "microenvironment concept," this hypothesis contends that the bacteria essentially produce their own environments in the carcasses of aquatic and semiaquatic invertebrates.

Thus, when water levels recede, aquatic species of invertebrates die and the bacteria flourish on this medium rather than in soil or water. Conversely, if previously dry areas are flooded by shallow water (e.g., by wave action), then terrestrial invertebrates are killed, leading to the aftermath of toxin production.

In addition, maggots thriving on the carcasses of decaying waterbirds also accumulate botulism toxin (but are themselves immune). In turn, the maggots are ingested by previously unaffected birds, thereby causing more deaths and continued production of maggots. The maggot cycle continues until the sources of toxin are no longer present (i.e., when the invertebrate larvae mature); until the toxin breaks down, losing its virulence; or until stabilized water levels or other habitat factors limit the toxin's availability.

Some epizootics of botulism may result from human activities. Malcolm (1982) noted an association between botulism and instances of ducks and other birds colliding with a power line strung over a large wetland in Montana. Collisions with the wires killed at least 4100 birds of 55 species in 17 months; of these, ducks of 14 species accounted for 44 percent of the victims.

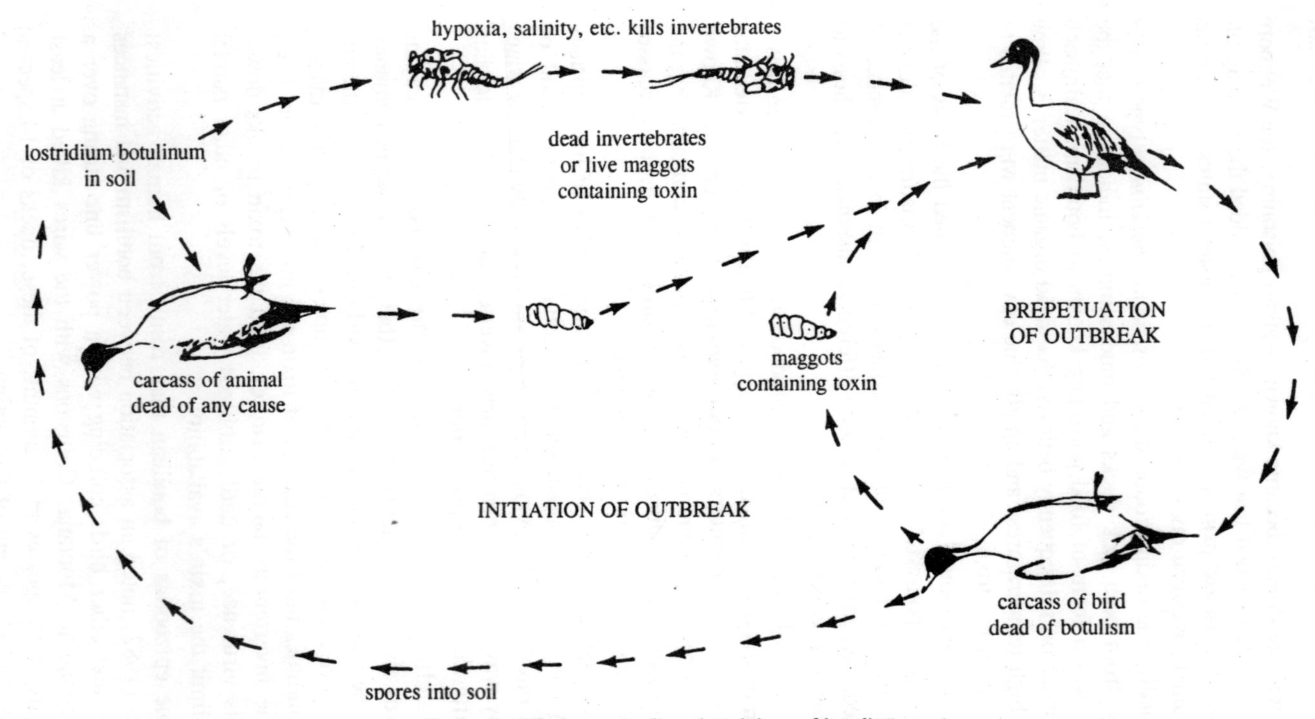

Figure 4.1: Pathways in the epizootiology of botulism.
Note the key role of fly larvae and other invertebrates in the botulism cycle.

Maggots feeding on the rotting carcasses contained botulism toxin and helped perpetuate an epizootic that killed 5200 more birds, of which 71 percent were ducks. It is unlikely that the power line will be moved away from the wetland (clearly the best solution) but, at the minimum, the carcasses of the power-line casualities should be picked up frequently.

Interestingly, turkey vultures (*Cathartes aura*) are highly resistant to type C toxin; this factor presumably represents an adaptation for feeding on the carcasses of birds killed by botulism. Other species of scavenging birds may have similar resistance.

Methods for controlling botulism once relied on frightening birds with aircraft or fireworks, thus scaring them from areas of high risk or ongoing epizootics. Direct treatment of sick birds also is possible, either with injections of antitoxin or by placing these birds in holding pens with clean water.

However, neither method is very practical. Better results of far wider scope are achieved when water levels are manipulated to eliminate conditions favourable for production of botulinum toxin. Wherever possible, water levels should remain constant during the botulism season (usually during the autumn migration).

The shallow edges of the land-water interface in wetlands are prime sites for toxin production. Unfortunately, these same areas are attractive to loafing or feeding waterfowl. Where water can be controlled in separate units, water from a larger number of units can be concentrated in one or two units.

Instead of all the management units suffering from unfavourable water levels-and botulism—a smaller number are stabilized while the others are drained completely. Much can be gained if waterfowl habitats with a history of epizootic botulism are developed with water-management systems (dikes, pumps, channels, etc.) to reduce losses during the critical season.

Regrettably, only a relatively small number of waterfowl habitats are adapted to this form of management; most of these are state or federal refuges, whereas unmanaged wetlands still experience uncontrolled outbreaks of botulism.

Soils are fundamental components of wildlife habitat. Relationships between soil and wildlife often are indirect, as is illustrated by certain helminth parasites and their infections of white-tailed deer and livestock sharing the same ranges. *Fascioloides magna* is a large fluke that normally infects the livers of white-tailed deer. In deer, the flukes cause little damage despite their large size and robust encapsulations. In cattle, however, the flukes often produce significant damage, and hence become a pathogen of considerable economic importance. Deer thus act as reservoirs for flukes infecting livestock, as do elk.

Like other trematode parasites, deer-liver flukes require intermediate hosts. In Texas, *Lymnaea bulimoides is* the sole intermediate host. This snail, appropriately known as the deer-liver fluke snail, requires shallow surface water to complete its own life cycle; rainwater temporarily held at the soil's surface suffices for this purpose.

A survey of snail populations revealed that *Lymnaea bulimoides* was absent on sandy soils where surface water' drained rapidly. By contrast, nearly all transects on heavy clay soils were populated with snails.

These circumstances translate rather directly into the rates of helminth infection in both white-tailed deer and cattle. Animals grazing on sandy soils remain largely free of the parasites, whereas those on clay soils become infected. Thus, cattle grazing in the same clay pastures as deer are constantly exposed to fluke infections.

However; because the snails generally are absent on sandy soils, there is little or no passage of the fluke's larval stages to either deer or cattle in sandy environments. In a similar vein, Prestwood and Smith linked the spotty distribution of parasitic nematodes in deer to the availability of appropriate gastropods.

Deer on sandy soils with pine forests lacked infections, whereas those on soils with subclimax or climax deciduous forests were parasitized. The presence of wallowing species may exacerbate fluke infections. For example, the rooting behaviour of feral hogs (*Sus scrofa*) creates depressions that hold water for considerable periods of time even in dry environments.

Thus, their wallows create and enlarge areas of ideal snail habitat, indirectly increasing the potential of fluke infections among susceptible hosts. Little management, other than treating cattle with efficacious anthelminthics, is possible on clay pastures. On sandy ranges, however, it seems unwise to develop artificial sources of water where the snails then might survive.

Where windmills are necessary, water should be confined to troughs that are periodically treated with molluscicides. Fencing, too, might better follow soil types so that fluke infections remain confined to a few units of the cattle herd where intensive treatment can be administered economically. Gross changes in land use also have increased contact between species that have differential responses to parasitic diseases. Prior to the twentieth century, there was little contact between moose and deer in northern Minnesota.

Thereafter, logging, homesteading, and fires created favourable habitats for deer, and brought large numbers of deer into the range of moose. Moose populations soon declined, probably because of the meningeal parasites carried by deer (see following section for more details).

Habitats sometimes can be "improved" to the point where diseases may be enhanced. Changes include inadvertent as well as directed alterations of wildlife environments, as shown by actions affecting nomadic grazing animals in Africa. Deep pits left after roads were gravelled in Etosha National Park, South West Africa, initiated epizootics of anthrax.

When the gravel pits filled with water, they attracted a variety of wildlife. Additional water ("boreholes") was established to hold grazing animals in areas opened for tourists. As predicted, the permanent water concentrated the animals, but their grazing pressure degraded the grassland into weeds and bare soil.

Whereas anthrax apparently always had been present in the park, the man-made watering sites proved highly effective incubators for *Bacillus anthracis*, producing deadly epizootics among the crowded populations.

The combination of stress from overgrazing and the permanent source of infection effectively overcame the level of anthrax immunity developed naturally by zebra (*Equus burchelli*) and other species. Following this hard-learned lesson, elimination of the artificial water reduced the sources of virulent infection and initiated recovery of the nearby vegetation.

DISEASES AND POPULATIONS

The matter of disease effecting regulatory controls on wildlife populations is a question stirring debate among biologists . Data usually are insufficient to assess definitively the impacts of pathogenic agents on populations because of understandable difficulties in sampling and because of the interactions of disease with predation, weather, competition, and the availability and quality of food. Epizootics are, of course, rather easily documented (e.g., rabies and sylvatic plague), but whether such occurrences actually regulate populations in the long run is another question. One can understand the theoretical notion that infectious diseases, as well as predation or other limiting factors, may act in a density—dependent fashion, but proving such a relationship is difficult when other variables may be acting simultaneously.

The case for density-dependent responses of diseases frequently has been championed to explain cyclic behaviour in certain wildlife populations. Periodic and often rapid declines in the numbers of red grouse (*La go pus lagopus scoticus*) in Scotland were attributed to the parasitic nematode, *Trichostrongylus tenuis*, early in the present century.

The larvae of the parasite, upon hatching, climb to the tips of heather, where they are ingested by red grouse; the parasites then infect the birds' digestive tracts. On reaching maturity, the parasite's eggs pass in the bird's feces back onto the heathlands. Thus, the denser the grouse population, the greater the proportion of infected heather-tips. This density increases the number of parasites entering each bird.

The intensity of infection rises as the number of grouse increases, until many birds are eventually killed by their parasite loads. Thereafter, there is a reduction in both the grouse population and in the incidence of parasites in the heather. However, Lack (1954, 1966) presented evidence in rebuttal, suggesting instead that it is the number of grouse in relation to their food supply that is critical; in this view, strongylosis is lethal only to those birds already weakened by starvation.

The naturalist Ernest Thompson Seton proposed that the declining phase in the ten-year cycle of snowshoe hares (*Lepus americanus*) was precipitated by devastating "plagues," seemingly triggered by a density-dependent mechanism. Conversely, Keith et al. have found that the combination of food shortages, cold, and predation initiates declines in snowshoe hare populations.

In any event, mortality rates for adult snowshoe hares change significantly during the course of the cycle. During four years of decrease, the rates varied between 64 and 72 percent, reaching 97 percent in the fifth year, whereas the rate dropped to 59 percent in the first year of the upward phase; results of similar magnitudes were found in the mortality rates of juveniles.

Green and his associates described a nontransmissible condition, "shock disease," as the cause of wholesale deaths of hares in the ten-year cycle. These cases involved hypoglycemia with pathological manifestations focused on the spleen and liver, conditions that Keith (1963) frequently discovered in his survey of the literature dealing with snowshoe hare mortality.

Chitty nonetheless doubted that shock disease occurs naturally in wild populations, and the matter rests largely unresolved even as the ten-year cycle continues in hares across North America. As mentioned earlier, one type of pathogen sometimes predisposes its host to other diseases. Nematodes of the genus *Prostostrongylus* are transmitted prenatally as larvae in bighorn sheep (*Ovis canadensis*), maturing in the lungs of lambs within 30-45 days of their birth.

Infected ewes thus transfer the parasites to their unborn young when the larvae migrate through the placenta. The parasite also is transmitted when an infected animal coughs up the larvae, swallows, and introduces the parasites to the digestive tract where they are passed in the feces. Larvae survive for at least 15 months in fecal pellets.

Small, inconspicuous land snails of several species harbor the larvae for additional development; they reach maturity in the bighorn sheep when the snail is ingested passively with the host's forage. Lungworms thereafter foster bacterial and viral lung infections in bighorns, often leading to excessive mortality.

Bighorn lambs seem particularly susceptible to these infections, especially when they are stressed by other events. Woodard et al. associated exceptionally high bighorn mortality from disease with cold, wet weather; ewe:lamb ratios dropped from 100:83 and 100:72 in June to 100:17 and 100:22 in September, respectively, in two consecutive years of study. Such losses in the juvenile age class restrict the herd's growth and create an overaged population that functions as a reservoir for future lungworm infections.

Buechner (1960) more fully described the impacts of these relationships on bighorn populations in what is known as the lungworm-pneumonia complex. Fortunately, measures have been developed to control lungworm infections in bighorn lambs by treating their mothers. The treatment interrupts transmission of lungworm larvae from pregnant ewes to their unborn lambs.

When 52 ewes were treated experimentally with one of four drugs and then were released on Pikes Peak, Colorado, 80 percent later produced offspring that survived, whereas only 5 percent of the herd at large successfully reared lambs. Based on these tests, the most effective drugs then were mixed with apple pulp and were set out at feeding stations.

The results were no less dramatic than that which had occurred with the experimental animals. Lamb survival exceeded 64 percent in the bighorn sheep herds treated with anthelminthic drugs. Managers realized, however, that they were treating only the symptoms of a larger problem: overcrowded ranges where the animals were exposed repeatedly to lungworm infections.

Shortly after the Colorado herds were treated with drugs, an either-sex hunting season for bighorns was initiated to help reduce the population to levels more appropriate to each area's carrying capacity. The magnitude of disease losses among wildlife populations is difficult to assess, but sometimes it may be of considerable proportions.

The extent of nonhunting mortality still is largely unknown for many species, but diseases may be responsible for the majority of such losses. For example, Friend estimated that nonhunting losses of waterfowl may exceed by twofold the legal bag limit annually, with disease alone accounting for most of the nonhunting mortality.

Life tables for mourning doves (*Zenaida macroura*) suggest that overall mortality rates are about equal where the species is hunted and where it is not. If so, this discovery suggests the importance of diseases and other types of natural mortality in the dynamics of wildlife populations whereby hunting and other forms of cropping largely replace mortality from other causes.

Among mourning doves, trichomoniasis is widespread in geographical occurrence and its virulent strains may cause death within 4 days of infection. This disease is a parasitic infection caused by the protozoan *Trichomonas gallinae*, attacking the upper digestive tract of doves and pigeons. Lesions (cankers) may develop externally on the head and neck and in the mouth, throat, and crop.

The disease spreads rapidly to nestlings that are fed regurgitated "*crop milk*" from their infected parents. Among adults, the organism is spread when infected birds, unable to swallow food because of the lesions in their throats, drop the now-contaminated seeds only to have other birds feed on the infectious food materials.

Transmission among adults drinking from common water sources also may be a factor in the disease's epizootiology. In Alabama, a severe outbreak of trichomoniasis apparently curtailed reproduction of mourning doves as diseased adults generally lacked the gonadal development necessary for breeding; the age ratio in the affected population was altered, with juveniles comprising only 10 percent of the sample.

Interestingly, the courtship behaviour of billing and mutual feeding among doves and pigeons further enhances transmission among adults. On nesting, infected birds are almost certain to pass on the parasites to their young. Trichomoniasis also has been suggested as contributing to the extinction of the passenger pigeon (*Ectopistes migratorius*).

Unfortunately, there are no successful treatments for trichomoniasis epizootics in wild dove populations. Relatively effective treatment for penned birds is possible with some chemotherapeutic agents, including copper sulfate administered in drinking water.

However, liver damage develops when the optimal dosage is administered to infected birds. Other treatments include the registered drugs Enheptin and Emtryl, but these and other treatments render drinking water unpalatable unless the birds are restricted to a single source (i.e., confined in pens).

A water-borne therapeutic agent nonetheless seems the best means of treatment, but until a palatable and widely applied compound is developed, epizootics of trichomoniasis may remain regulators of local or even regional dove populations. Saumier et al. demonstrated the reduced reproductive success of American kestrels (*Falco sparverius*) that were experimentally infected with parasitic roundworms, *Trichinella pseudospiralis*.

Compared with uninfected controls, infected kestrels exhibited delayed egg laying, produced fewer eggs (4.9 *vs*. 7.1), and experienced greater egg breakage (29 *vs*. 1.6 percent, because infected birds did not lay their eggs in nests) and embryo mortality (40 *vs*. 4.7 percent). The infected birds produced an average of only 0.6 hatchlings, whereas the controls produced 2.1 offspring.

The experiment clearly indicated how parasitic infections may impair the reproductive fitness of kestrels, and thus may illustrate an important pathogenic factor that affects the recruitment of fledglings into raptor populations.

A parasitic nematode, *Parelaphostrongylus tenuis*, offers an interesting contrast in its effect on two species of big game. (In a confusing array of taxonomic distinctions, this parasite at times has been included in the genera *Protostrongylus* and *Pneumostrongylus*.) As with other helminth parasites, snails and other gastropods serve as intermediate hosts for the parasite's larval stages.

Deer, and likewise moose, are infected when they incidentally ingest larva-bearing snails along with their forage. *P. tenuis* mature in the meninges of the brain but in deer little damage develops, either because the worms have impaired development or because of natural immunity in these tissues. In moose, however, these parasites severely damage the central nervous system, causing paralysis and death.

Thus, the same parasite is essentially harmless in deer but produces a fatal disease in moose known as blind staggers or moose sickness. The differential pathogenicity of *P. tenuis* in deer and moose apparently plays a regulatory role where their respective populations overlap. Saunders (1973) recorded small moose populations where infections of deer were high.

Moose densities dropped to about two per 5 km² where *P. tenuis* infections in deer reached 60 percent. Conversely, moose densities doubled to about 10 per 5 km² where the infection rate in deer was 14 percent. Karns associated infections in moose with high-densities of deer and recommended that deer populations be kept at minimal levels-less than 5 per km²—in areas managed for moose.

Gilbert also correlated deer densities with the occurrence of moose infections in Maine and suggested that hunting tends to remove diseased animals from the population, thus lowering the percentage of infected moose left in subsequent years. Reintroductions of moose into ranges where they have been extirpated should be weighed in light of current

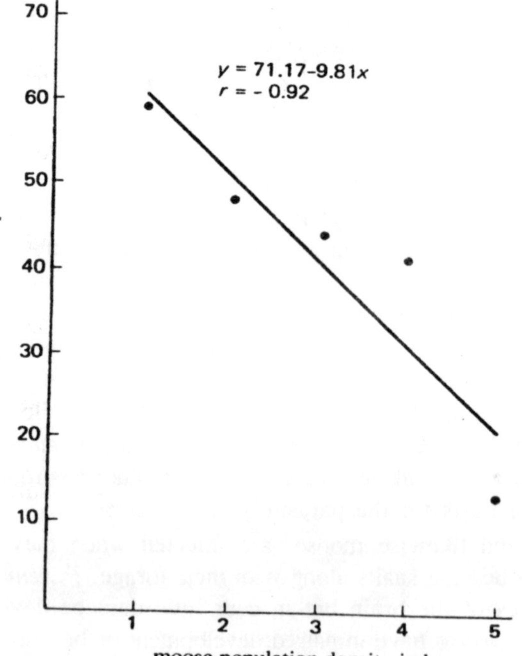

Figure 4.2: Relationship between rates of P. tenuis infection in white-tailed deer and moose densities.

deer densities or the restocking may fail. Of 29 adult moose introduced in upper Michigan in 1985, 8 (28 percent) died within 18 months, presumably from infections of *P. tenuis* (Michigan Department of Natural Resources, file data). Nonetheless, natality exceeded mortality, and the population thus grew to about 40 moose in 2 years.

The density of white-tailed deer was about 2 to 3 per km^2 in the area where moose were reintroduced. Moose sickness also appears to be moving westward with the extension of white-tailed deer range.

Finally, the moose-deer disease relationship offers another example of ways that ecological conditions influence the epizootiology of a disease. In Nova Scotia, snow depth isolates deer from moose in winter, reducing interspecific transmission of the fatal nematodes from deer to moose.

However, when conditions forced moose into winter deer habitat at lower elevations in New Brunswick, the moose died before spring, apparently from contact with deer and the parasites they transmit. In effect, the parasite has become a weapon of competition between deer, moose, and perhaps other large herbivores.

Holmes reported that several attempts to reintroduce elk and caribou have failed in areas now occupied by white-tailed deer, apparently because of mortality associated with meningeal worms.

The malarial parasite, *Leucocytozoon simondi*, *is* transmitted by blackflies (Simuliidae). One species, *Simulium rugglesi*, *is* commonly associated with the spread of the pathogen in waterfowl. Shewell and Bennett suggested that the blackfly vectors may feed exclusively on waterfowl.

Thus, infections coincide largely with the flies' geographical distribution, an area that, unfortunately covers much of the breeding range of ducks and geese in northeastern North America. *Leucocytozoonosis* occurs in waterfowl of several species and age classes, but its pathogenic effects are most severe in juveniles. Indeed, losses of young birds may reach catastrophic proportions.

Herman (1968) summarized studies in which mortality among ducklings reached 71 percent, and losses of goslings in epizootics occurring at 4-5-year intervals is a serious limiting factor among Canada geese (*Branta canadensis*) nesting in some settings. O'Roke, in an early assessment of leucocytozoonosis, found that 100 percent of the black ducks (*Anas rubripes*) he examined in Michigan were infected, and Trainer et al. located the parasite in 64 percent of six species of waterfowl examined in Wisconsin.

Infections of *Leucocytozoon* follow a schedule that supplies blackflies with ample numbers of parasites for infecting new individuals, particularly young birds. Adult waterfowl are carriers of the parasite and serve as a natural reservoir for new infections. On breeding areas where blackflies occur, the pathogen spreads throughout the waterfowl population when flies inject infected salivary fluid as they obtain a blood meal.

At this point, the infection is limited to adult birds that may not show advanced parasitemia in what is known as the *prepatent* period. When the number of parasites peaks, the *patent phase* of the schedule begins. This phase is followed by *a latent period* when it may be impossible to locate *Leucocytozoon* in blood smears from infected birds; there may be only one parasite per tens of thousands of normal blood cells, making detection of the disease unlikely at such times.

However, during the latent period, a *relapse* often occurs when the level of parasitemia again increases, providing the blackflies with a second supply of parasites. The relapse phase occurs at a time when many infected birds are nesting, so that the flies now are able quickly to infect ducklings.

The coincident timing of the relapse with nesting was confirmed by Chernin, when he exposed latent-phase ducks to a photoperiod that advanced egg laying by 1 month; both male and female ducks exhibited the relapse phase 1 month early, coinciding with their reproductive efforts under the artificial-light regime.

Blackflies largely restrict their feeding activities to sites near the shoreline and at distances less than 1.8 m above the surface . Blackflies thus match the ecological setting of most ducks and geese for their nesting and brood cover. Clinical signs of *Leucocytozoon* infections in ducklings include listlessness, weakness, and loss of appetite; death may occur within 24 hours of infection.

Goslings infected at 2-3 weeks of age often survive, but those infected within a week of hatching usually die. This phenomenon underscores another example of age-related susceptibility in the ecology of diseases and animal populations. As summarized by Cook (1971), the parasites invade the lungs, heart, gizzard, and intestines, with the severest involvement occurring in the host's spleen and liver; anemia develops for the duration of the disease's patent phase.

Control of *Leucocytozoon* rests upon control of the blackfly vectors, but, unfortunately, there is presently no means of large-scale regulation of their population. Introduced diseases also contributed significantly

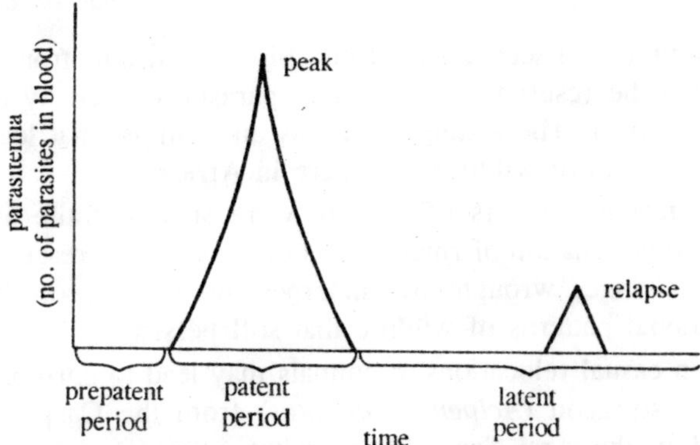

Figure 4.3: Schematic representation of parasitemia in Leucocytozoon infections. Relapse phase in adults often coincides with nesting, thus supplying blackfly vectors with ample parasites to infect newly hatched waterfowl.

to the extinction or range restriction of endemic species of forest birds in Hawaii, particularly for the honeycreepers of the family Drepaniidae.

A potential reservoir for avian malaria, *Plasmodium*, undoubtedly existed in Hawaii for some time as migratory birds regularly visited the islands, and poultry had been introduced as well. What was lacking for the transmission of avian malaria, however, was an appropriate insect vector.

The necessary vector unfortunately was introduced in 1826 when the tropical-subtropical form of the night-flying mosquito (*Culex pipiens*) escaped from the water kegs of a ship anchored at Maui. Thereafter, the mosquitoes spread rapidly throughout the lowland areas of Hawaii, breeding in brackish water along the coast and in more typical surface-water habitats.

However, mosquito populations are largely unsuccessful above elevations of 600 m. Furthermore, birdpox virus ("bumblefoot") arrived with the domestic fowl of early European settlers, along with the introduction of another insect vector. The wake of these introductions brought havoc to the endemic birds of Hawaii. Today, the surviving species of honeycreepers are restricted to elevations where the insect vectors are absent.

An epizootic of rinderpest in Africa late in the last century represents the most infamous case of an introduced disease that produced calamitous results on native wildlife. The viral disease probably was introduced with oxen during the Italian military occupation of Ethiopia. Rinderpest killed vast numbers of wild ungulates as well as cattle, and also produced secondary effects. First, the deaths from rinderpest eliminated the reservoir for a deadly parasite carried by tsetse flies (*Glossina spp.*). The setting served as an example that led to large-scale slaughters of wildlife elsewhere in Africa.

Staggering numbers of wildlife were shot in futile attempts to mimic the devastation of rinderpest (i.e., remove the reservoir herds). Second, changes wrought by rinderpest produced anomalies in the distributional patterns of wildlife that still persist.

Even casual relocations of animals may lead to epizootics. In the 1930*s*, a sturgeon (*Acipenser stellatus*) from the Caspian Sea was released in the Aral Sea. Gill parasites carried by this single fish depleted stocks of native sturgeon (*A. nudiventris*) for more than two decades afterward.

What appeared to be a new viral disease among whitetailed deer was confirmed in 1955. The severity and pathological signs of the malady prompted the name epizootic hemorrhagic disease. Except for states in the extreme northeast and southwest, occurrence of the disease largely parallels the distribution of white-tailed deer in the United States and Canada.

Other species, including pronghorns and mule deer, sometimes are infected, but epizootic hemorrhagic disease is most evident in white-tailed deer. Based on carcass counts after epizootics, deaths among white-tailed deer outnumber those of mule deer at a ratio of about 23:1, with losses of whitetails reaching 60 percent of a single herd.

Mortality rates of infected animals approach 90 percent, and thousands of deer may succumb during outbreaks. Few organs are immune from the hemorrhages, but the heart, liver, kidneys, lungs, gastrointestinal tract, and spleen commonly exhibit lesions of varying sizes. Karstad et al. determined that the hemorrhaging results from malfunction of the blood's clotting mechanism, and from degenerative changes in the walls of blood vessels.

External symptoms include loss of appetite, weakness, salivation, fever, hemorrhages in the oral cavity, and, sometimes, the occurrence of blood in the feces and urine. Coma and death follow within 3-36 hours after these symptoms develop. The disease is sudden in its onset, often breaking out among large numbers of deer in single nonrecurring epizootics.

Known outbreaks of epizootic hemorrhagic disease have occurred in August, September, and October; the epizootics terminated abruptly with the first frost. In North Dakota and South Dakota, long periods of excessively hot, dry weather precede epizootics, but initial outbreaks of the disease occur when there are abrupt changes in temperature and barometric pressure accompanied by high humidity.

Arthropod vectors had long been suspected in the transmission of epizootic hemorrhagic disease, but it was not until the 1970*s* that midges of the genus *Culicoides* finally were associated with the disease's epizootiology. Effective control or treatment are unknown at present. Trainer and Karstad speculated that oral vaccines someday might be administered to deer in foods supplied during winter or droughts.

DISEASES AND BIOLOGICAL CONTROLS

The native Australian fauna has been supplemented by a host of exotic species, but none have proved more troublesome than the European rabbit (*Oryctolagus cuniculus*). After some earlier and unsuccessful attempts to establish rabbits, a successful transplant was achieved on the southeastern coast near Geelong, Victoria, in 1859.

They spread rapidly, reaching the west coast of Australia 16 years later, and ultimately occupying more than half of the Australian continent. The explosion of rabbits quickly led to severe overgrazing and to widespread wind and water erosion of the soil. Conflicts with the sheep industry were inevitable as the rabbits consumed forage otherwise allocated to livestock.

The networks of rabbit warrens also were pervasive disturbances in the rangeland system. Despite widespread efforts to control the rabbits with fences and poisons, little population regulation was effected. The exotic rabbits continued registering their impacts on the landscape well into the current century.

Then, in 1950, after long experimentation, the mammalian disease myxomatosis was introduced into the rabbit population. Whereas myxomatosis is a pox-virus whose pathogenic effects are self-limiting in its natural hosts (*Sylvilagus spp.*), this disease is especially destructive in European rabbits.

Marsupials and a variety of other native and domestic species virtually are unaffected, so that myxomatosis remained a virulent, host-specific control agent for an unwanted exotic species within the modern Australian fauna. Myxomatosis is spread by a variety of arthropods, particularly by mosquitoes; transmission occurs when the infected skin tissues (not blood) are carried from rabbit to rabbit on the mouthparts of the vectors.

Nodular tumors develop on the body, followed by internal hemorrhagic necrosis of the intestine, liver, and other organs. Fenner and Ratcliffe presented a full account of the disease's epidemiology, but suffice it to note here that no more than 10 to 20 percent of the rabbit population survived the initial impact of myxomatosis.

Other control measures remain in effect, however, because some rabbits developed resistance and the virus itself undergoes changes in its virulence. But because of myxomatosis, the rabbit population in Australia remains at only a fraction of its former level.

A novel experiment concerns attempts to immunize desert bighorn sheep against the viral disease known as bluetongue, or "soremuzzle," using natural vectors. Blue tongue infects both wild and domestic ruminants, including white-tailed deer, pronghorns, elk (*Cervus elaphus canadensis*), and domestic sheep and goats.

The disease inflames the mucous membranes of the gastrointestinal tract, especially affecting those of the mouth and nose. The animal's tongue swells, becomes discoloured and blue, and typically hangs loosely from the side of the mouth 24 hours before death occurs. A variety of clinical and pathological symptoms occur that may forecast death 7-8 days after exposure.

Because much of the original range of desert bighorns subsequently was grazed by domestic sheep, the suggestion arises that bluetongue carried by these flocks likely contributed to reductions in bighorn populations. Thus, reintroductions of desert bighorns may require large blocks of land where domestic livestock are excluded, a requirement that is obviously expensive—financially and politically-to implement. Alternatively, ways to rid bighorn ranges of the disease-carrying vectors would be needed—a virtual impossibility.

However, Robinson et al. presented experimental evidence that a common arthropod vector might be used to immunize desert bighorns. Gnats (*Culicoides varipennis*) are the natural vector of the bluetongue virus, and when given a blood meal that includes bluetongue vaccine, they become "mobile syringes" seeking out and vaccinating animals that cannot otherwise be approached by humans.

Results of experiments on captive bighorns were similar, whether the animals received injections by needle or if they received the vaccine from the treated gnats. Robinson et al. concluded that "where bluetongue is a proven problem in bighorn sheep, vaccination is indeed possible, even mandatory in the management of this species." Such imaginative methods as this undoubtedly will be required to restore desert bighorns in much of their former range.

LEAD POISONING: A MAN-MADE DISEASE

Besides introducing livestock and their associated diseases, humans have fostered other situations where new diseases bear on wildlife populations. In recent years, lead poisoning of waterfowl has become one of the more controversial issues attracting attention from a cross section of the sporting public.

The issue also has stimulated a large number of research projects, some of which have contradicted one another. Thus, lead poisoning has become a much-disputed and complex topic in the field of wildlife management.

Lead poisoning results from the huge amounts of lead shot-estimated at 3000 tons per year-deposited in the wetlands of North America by duck hunters. Waterfowl pick up shot while feeding and retain the lead in their gizzards; lead thereafter is absorbed slowly into the birds blood.

Some 2 to 3 percent, or as many as 2 million ducks and geese, of the North American waterfowl population succumb to lead poisoning each fall. This represents a loss equal to about 20 percent of the hunting bag each year. Severity of lead poisoning varies locally, depending on such conditions as shooting pressure, bottom firmness, water depth, and the feeding habits of the birds.

Other waterbirds, too, may experience lead poisoning. Up to 12 percent of the sora rails (*Porzana carolina*) in the coastal marshes of Maryland had ingested lead shot. Recent evidence also suggests that secondary poisoning occurs in bald eagles (*Haliaeetus leucocephalus*) feeding on duck carcasses that are contaminated, in part, with ingested lead shot.

Internally, symptoms of lead poisoning include atrophy of striated muscle tissues, distended gall bladder, anemia, fluid accumulation in the pericardial sac, erosion of the gizzard's grinding surfaces, and atrophy of the liver and kidney. Externally, bile stains the cloacal opening, and palsy causes wings to droop and impairs flying and walking activities.

Feeding also is curtailed so that emaciation usually becomes obvious, and affected birds often seek isolation and cover. Lead poisoning is widespread. In a questionnaire sent to 47 states, the U.S. Fish and Wildlife Service determined that lead poisoning has occurred in 21 states.

The disease occurs in all of the flyways and presents serious problems in 15 states. Tests have shown that several nontoxic materials are suitable as substitutes for lead in shotgun pellets, but steel has been selected as the most feasible replacement and remains the only nontoxic shot available to hunters.

In 1976, the Secretary of the Interior ruled that duck hunters must use only steel shot in certain "hot spot" areas where lead poisoning has been particularly severe. Steel-shot zones are required where more than 5 percent of mallard (*Anas platyrhynchos*) or black duck gizzards contain lead shot. In particular, marshes along the Atlantic coastline and the Mississippi Valley have been hunted heavily for decades; the accumulation of lead in these wetlands is significant.

In the first years of the zoning program, ingestion of lead shot in mallards was reduced by as much as 34 percent in some areas. Overall, however, the zoning regulations did not appreciably change the potential for lead poisoning in the Mississippi Flyway.

Ammunition manufacturers and many waterfowl hunters disagreed with the steel-shot policy. The objections of these groups focused on three assertions:

1. *Crippling loss*. Steel shot, because of its lesser density, does not have the same killing power as lead. Thus, crippling losses-those birds knocked down but not retrieved-will be greater with steel shot, and perhaps will exceed the losses from lead poisoning.
2. *Gun damage*. Steel shot, because of its hardness, will ruin shotguns. Accelerated barrel wear and choke loss are specific concerns.
3. *Cost*. Shotgun shells loaded with steel shot cost more than those with lead shot.

Each of the points was addressed in a major overview of lead poisoning by Sanderson and Bellrose. First, crippling losses have diminished in the years since steel shot has been used. No claim is made that steel shot is the direct cause of these reduced crippling losses, because the long-term trend already was headed downward. Nonetheless, the data clearly indicate that steel shot has *not* increased crippling losses.

In fact, if a cause-and-effect relationship is assumed, then the inference emerges that steel shot indeed has helped to reduce crippling losses in recent years (when both steel and lead shot were in use). In point of fact, the highest crippling losses occurred in years when only lead shot was used. Much of the loss of knock-down power associated with steel shot can be compensated for by using larger-sized pellets.

Table 4.3: Crippling Losses Before, During, and After Implementation of Steel Shot for Waterfowl Hunting. Data Are Expressed as the Mean Number of Knocked Down but Unretrieved Waterfowl per 100 Birds Retrieved by Hunters.

	Implementation of Steel Shot		
Species	*Before (1971-75)*	*During (1976-78)*	*After (1979-84)*
Ducks	21.6	20.0	19.5
Geese	14.6	14.9	14.0
Coots	29.0	28.2	27.1
All species	21.4	19.9	19.1

Second, the notion of barrel damage in modern full-choke shotguns has been disproved by tests conducted by arms manufacturers and gun experts. No claims of barrel damage were reported after 18,000 rounds of steel shot had been fired. A plastic cup in the shotshell eliminates virtually all the barrel erosion caused by steel shot.

Only in some older, thin-walled shotguns might steel shot expand the choke, but magnum lead loads also can expand chokes in these and some other types of shotguns. In the final analysis, the threat of barrel damage in modern shotguns is not a valid reason for rejecting adoption of a steel-shot, policy for waterfowl hunting.

Finally, there is the matter of cost. At present, shotgun shells loaded with steel shot indeed are more expensive than are those loaded with lead shot. The differential, however, varies with the gauge of the shotgun and other ballistics (e.g., "*magnum*" loads).

For 12-gauge shotguns, the price of steel loads runs 7-25 percent higher than cost of approximately equivalent lead loads. Retailers often discount lead loads but seldom do so for steel loads. Therefore, the price differential is somewhat exaggerated.

Also, components are now available for reloading shotgun shells with steel shot, a method that offers an economical means for switching to steel shot. In reality, however, the cost of shotgun shells reflects only a small part of the cost of waterfowl hunting. Because the average duck hunter expends 36 shots per year, the increased cost per hunting season is only about $4.50 more for shells loaded with steel shot.

Moreover, prices should decline with the increased production of steel-loaded shells. As Sanderson and Bellrose concluded, "the slightly higher cost of steel loads should not be a deterrent to their use, particularly in view of the dwindling populations of ducks and the keen interest of waterfowlers in perpetuating their sport." Pressure continued for a total ban on the use of lead shot for waterfowl hunting as more areas were added to the list of "*hot spots.*"

Indeed, Nebraska required the statewide use of steel shot for all waterfowl hunting beginning with the 1985 season. In 1986, after widespread debate, the Secretary of the Interior announced that lead shot would become illegal for waterfowl hunting beginping with the 1991 season. Ironically, the decision was based more on the secondary poisoning of bald eagles than on the direct effect of lead on waterfowl.

Regardless, the ban on lead shot will end the long history of a highly destructive, man-made disease in the United States. In Mexico and other nations, however, similar protection has not yet been addressed, and waterfowl continue ingesting lead shot.

WILDLIFE DISEASES AND HUMANS

Wildlife populations serve as reservoirs or carriers for some diseases affecting humans. Should we tenuously include commensal rodents as wildlife, then foremost of these diseases was the devastating Black Death that gripped Europe in the fourteenth century. Scholars of medieval history estimate that fully one-third of the population in western Europe—about 20 million people-succumbed during an epizootic of bubonic plague.

In Paris, the death rate was 800 per day, and by the time the disease had run its course, the toll had reached 50,000-half the city's population. Fortunately, bubonic plague never again inflicted such widespread damage on human populations, although statistics collected by the World Health Organization in 1967 indicate that more than 5000 cases occurred under wartime conditions in Vietnam.

Conversely, sylvatic plague directly concerns species clearly falling within the realm of wildlife (e.g., bobcats, *Felis rufus*, badgers, *Taxidea taxus*). This form of plague is caused by the same pathogen as bubonic plague (i.e., *Yersinia pestis*), but transmission stems from wild rodents, not from commensal species; fleas are the principal vectors in either instance, however. More than 230 species or subspecies of wild rodents are associated with natural infections of sylvatic plague.

The epizootiology of sylvatic plague is complex and is associated with the pathogen's persistence (e.g., in burrows) and with, the structure and social systems of the reservoir population. Sylvatic plague also is localized and is discontinuously distributed, factors that strongly suggest that specific relationships between the reservoir species and their environment have much to do with the disease's occurrence.

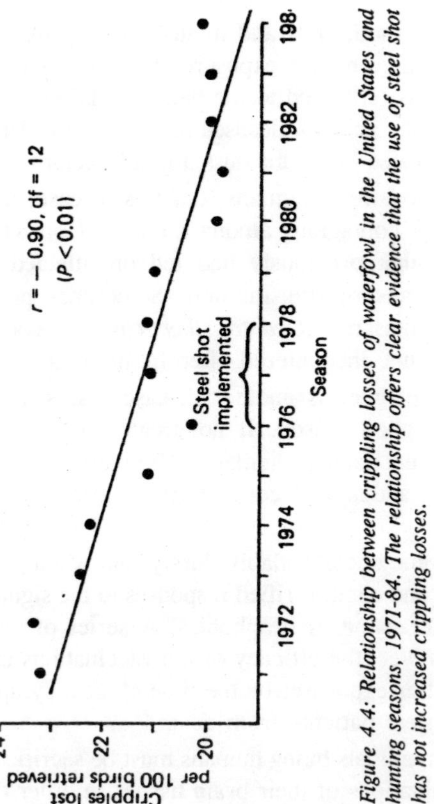

Figure 4.4: Relationship between crippling losses of waterfowl in the United States and hunting seasons, 1971-84. The relationship offers clear evidence that the use of steel shot has not increased crippling losses.

Four basic components seem involved, although not all may be of equal importance or in effect at one time. These are (1) fleas, (2) soil, (3) hiber-nating rodents, and (4) varying degrees of susceptibility among rodent populations to *Y. pestis*.

Cases of sylvatic plague may develop when humans visit prairie dog (*Cynomys spp.*) towns or other communities of wild rodents, but these are isolated exposures, not human epizootics. Nonetheless, mention of plague evokes strong currents of fear when cases are reported in the public media.

Such publicity sometimes leads to overreactions, as when prairie dog towns are sprayed aerially with massive amounts of pesticides. The intent of such treatments is to destroy fleas and other potential vectors, but too often the environment also is contaminated with persistent chemicals.

Barnes and Kartman (1960) described a more localized approach;

bait boxes, open at both ends and treated inside with insecticide, are placed in areas of high human exposure to rodents (e.g., campgrounds and parks). Rodents, attracted to the bait, are dusted as they enter the box. Not only are the animals cleansed of fleas, a populations remaining underground are treated When the dusted rodents return to their burrows.

Tularemia also infects humans, but this disease, although highly debilitating, is not contagious among humans. Contact with ticks or other arthropods that previously had fed on infected rabbits is the most common means of transmission. Sometimes persons skinning infected rabbits or muskrats (*Ondatra zibethicus*) may contract tularemia, but the disease is not encountered often by humans.

Rabies, like plague, is another disease that strikes fear among humans-and with good reason. If not treated immediately, rabies is virtually 100 percent fatal in humans. The pathogen, *a Rhabdovirus*, attacks the brain and spinal cord. Furthermore, the symptoms are horrifying.

Victims become uncontrollably thirsty, but when given water they begin convulsing and elicit terrified responses to the sight of water (thus the disease's other name, hydrophobia). A series of vaccinations can cure rabies. However, the efficacy of the vaccinations is dependent on treatment soon after exposure; by the time clinical symptoms develop, it is too late to save patients from death.

Accordingly, animals biting humans must be sacrificed immediately for critical examinations of their brain tissues in order to confirm, the presence of rabies. Otherwise, bite victims must undergo the series of vaccinations without benefit of any diagnosis (other than the bite itself). Because it often is impossible to examine the biting animal, persons may undergo treatment when they actually are not infected.

Rabies virus persists in the salivary glands of carnivorous animals; from there it spreads when an infected animal bites another animal or human. A few cases of rabies also have developed when humans breathed dust in bat caves. In some parts of the world, particularly India and the Philippines, as many as 15,000 people die of rabies each year, but only one or two deaths per year occur in the United States.

A vaccination program has eliminated rabies from humans in Great Britain, although a recent epizootic on the European mainland has renewed concern about pets reintroducing rabies. Rabies likewise is nearly always fatal in nonhuman animals, although some species of bats seem uniquely unaffected. The disease manifests itself in two strikingly different forms of behaviour: *furious* and *paralytic* (or "dumb") rabies.

In the furious form, the typical "mad-dog" symptoms are expressed, with the victim frantically running about, biting and snapping at other animals or, even at sticks and other inanimate objects.

Hooved animals bite and lash out with their legs, and infected birds attack with their beaks. In the less-common paralytic form, animals become semiparalyzed; they drop their jaws, and cannot bite or produce sounds. Many species of wildlife are implicated in the spread of rabies. In India, jackals (*Canis aureus*) are important carriers; red foxes (*Vulpes vulpes*) and badgers (*Metes meles*) are frequent carriers in Europe.

In the United States, the Centers for Disease Control (1980) reported the following cases of rabies for 1979: bats 756, foxes 140, raccoons 543, skunks 3031, and another 17 cases in other species. Woodchucks (*Marmota monax*) also have been identified as a new reservoir of rabies in the mid-Atlantic states, perhaps resulting from competition with raccoons for dens in areas of high rabies activity.

An epizootic recently spreading along the mid-Atlantic coast perhaps originated from raccoons imported into the area from Florida by a hunting club in 1977. Whatever the origin may be, rabies in raccoons has increased dramatically in the mid-Atlantic region, including metropolitan Washington, D.C..

The epizootic in raccoons eventually spilled into the dog and cat population, posing a clear threat to humans. See Bacon (1985) for a full review of the dynamics of rabies in wildlife populations. Rabies is particularly dangerous in urban settings. Raccoons (*Procyon lotor*) head the list of carriers in cities, because these animals adapt well to urban areas. Other species of urban wildlife, such as striped skunks (*Mephitis mephitis*), also are potential carriers of rabies but are less likely to be tolerated by humans.

Moreover, raccoons pose a greater threat of transmitting rabies to dogs, and therefore to people. Inoculation of pet cats and dogs clearly remains the best means of preventing rabies among humans, because pets often are the link between humans and wildlife. The number of human cases of rabies corresponds almost directly with the number of cases in dogs and, in turn, with the extent with which the dog population has been immunized.

Dogs used for hunting should always be inoculated. Fully 75 percent of 427 raccoons Hubbard (1985) tested for rabies in a rural area of Virginia were infected. A shortage of rainfall seemed linked with the epizootic in Virginia. The drought reduced the habitat, with the result that raccoons crowded into a still-suitable watershed where intraspecific

Table 4.4: Documented Cases of Rabies Occurring in Raccoons in the Mid-Atlantic Region of the United States, 1977-86. The Epizootic Eventually Included Cats and Dogs, Thereby Increasing the Threat of Rabies Infections in Humans.

	1977	1978	1979	1980	1981	1982	1983	1984	1985	1986
West Virginia	1		8	14	22	43	89	27	15	30
Virginia		3	4	7	102	645	545	158	102	139
Maryland					7	118	735	964	672	588
Pennsylvania						26	81	281	285	409
Washington, D.C.						5	158	12	4	29
Totals	1	3	12	21	131	837	1608	1442	1078	1195

competition probably induced physiological stress and lowered resistance to rabies infections. Rabies also occurs in wildlife associated with rangelands.

It seems important to distinguish between rabies carriers and reservoirs. Nearly all warm-blooded animals can be carriers; after contracting the disease, they may spread it by biting another animal. Carriers are themselves victims of rabies, as exemplified by species of the family Canidae.

In the case of true reservoirs, however, rabies still may be transmitted, but the reservoir species itself is not a victim. At least 25 species of insectivorous bats apparently are true reservoirs of rabies in the United States. In recent years, a few humans and several millions of livestock have died in Latin America from rabies transmitted by vampire bats (*Desmodus rotundus*).

Transmission of rabies by bloodsucking arthropods has not been demonstrated. Because of an understandable desire to control rabies, extreme measures occasionally are advocated to eradicate wildlife carriers. An epizootic of rabies in central Europe is characterized by a high incidence in red foxes; 70 percent of the more than 16,800 cases reported in Europe in 1979 occurred in foxes.

In Europe, foxes are slaughtered with guns, poison, and gas, but only in Denmark have such means been successful. A fox-free zone is maintained along the German-Danish border, but only with considerable expense and unrelenting effort; vacant territories are quickly colonized by immigrating foxes. After examining a population model for foxes, Anderson et al. concluded that culling methods will achieve little results except where foxes live in poor habitat.

Nonetheless, culling programs have been tried locally in the United States where, interestingly, the species of carriers may differ by region. Foxes are responsible for rabies epizootics in the Appalachian Mountains. Skunks are the primary carriers in the midwest, even though foxes are present in dense populations.

In, the southeast, rabies carried by raccoons is troublesome in Florida, Georgia, Alabama, and South Carolina, but the disease seems almost absent in the fox and skunk populations in these states. Foxes thus were the target of rabies control in Kentucky, whereas skunks were controlled in Ohio. Strychnine-treated baits were used in these efforts but, in Kentucky, 135 dogs, 25 cats, 202 birds and rodents, and 129 other animals accepted the poisoned baits in addition to 65 foxes.

Overall, the cost of control measures reached $208 per fox. At this rate, further reduction of costs would be required before continuation of the program could be justified economically.

Lloyd (1977), upon considering widespread fox control, concluded as follows:

> *The expense of depressing fox numbers nationally would be enormous and the results could not be guaranteed. In addition to the unwarranted economic, ecological, and social effects of such a measure, there is no justification for the slaughter of a wild animal on such a scale as a precautionary measure, against an event which is only remotely and locally probable. There is a better case for reducing the numbers of ownerless stray cats and dogs, and for imposing some restraint to the wanderings of dogs let out for the day while their owners are at work.*

Vaccination thus seems a better method than culling, although as the density of foxes increases, a higher proportion of the fox population must be vaccinated. An effective delivery system remains the major obstacle for vaccinating wildlife against rabies. Recently, however, biologists experimented with a technique that may help stem the rabies epizootic sweeping across the mid-Atlantic states.

The test was designed to determine if raccoons would accept vaccine-treated baits scattered over a wide area of Pennsylvania. However, an effective live vaccine sometimes can *cause* rabies; thus, with genetic engineering, the biologists inserted a gene from the rabies virus into the genetic material of another virus.

The product is a vaccine powerful enough to immunize raccoons but different enough from the rabies virus that it will not produce the disease. The vaccine still is not approved for use, however, but the delivery system was perfected in the interim. The baits were no more than a small sponge inside a plastic sandwich bag. The bags were perforated so that a coating of shellfish oil and other scents on the inside would attract raccoons.

The sponge, spiked with the vaccine, would be ingested after the raccoons tore open the sandwich bags. To test the delivery system, however, tetracycline was used in place of the vaccine. Tetracycline stains teeth and glows under the illumination of ultraviolet light. Hence, with the cooperation of trappers and hunters, a large number of raccoons were examined. The study revealed that nearly 70 percent of the animals had chewed open the test baits. Thus, pending approval of the recombinant vaccine, biologists may have a means of immunizing large numbers of raccoons against rabies.

5

Influence of Man and Nature

We shall define a park as an area that is designated primarily for the purpose of human recreation. This definition requires qualification in some national parks, as we shall see; and it excludes such areas as national and state forests and wildlife refuges where, although recreation also occurs, the primary management goal is something other than human recreation.

Parks are administered under various political jurisdictions, including governments of villages, cities, counties, states or provinces, and nations. This chapter deals with the ecology and management of animals in large nonurban parks. These areas are generally under jurisdiction of state, provincial, or federal governments. Wildlife in urban parks is considered in other Chapter of this book.

Textbooks on park management and outdoor recreation devote considerable attention to such topics as management of vehicular traffic, campground design, swimming facilities, location of concessions, trash collection, and sewage disposal.

However, the management of wild animals in parks receives only passing mention. Most considerations of wildlife in parks deal only with conflicts between humans and wild animals. Whereas problems with such animals as bears (*Ursus spp.*) are an important part of wildlife management in parks, other species and the natural communities to which they belong also deserve the attention of park managers and biologists.

Large herbivores, for example, frequently overpopulate parks where hunting and natural predators have been eliminated. The natural dynamics of ecological succession also foil attempts for preserving natural communities in parks; and the movements of animals in and out of parks illustrate that ecosystems in parks interact with human-modified environments outside.

This chapter reviews some special problems of managing wildlife in parks, including interactions between wild animals and park visitors, overpopulations of protected animals, natural succession, and interactions between animals in parks and surrounding lands.

ENJOYMENT OF WILDLIFE BY PARK VISITORS

Although it seems intuitively clear that wildlife enhances recreational values for park visitors, there is little quantitative information to support that assumption. Such data would be useful for describing the value of wildlife and for comparing wildlife values with other values associated with outdoor experiences (e.g., quality of camping facilities and pleasant scenery).

Kellert noted that an understanding of the satisfactions associated with people-wildlife interactions would aid intelligent park planning and management. Additionally, safe and relatively natural opportunities for human interactions with wildlife offer the public an educational means for gaining a better understanding of animals and ecological relationships. The sort of information needed, Kellert noted, concerns the types of visitors and their preferences for contact with various animals, links between types of habitats and wildlife-related opportunities, and species-specific tolerances of wildlife to humans.

Using interviews and questionnaires, Brown et al. (1980) assessed the recreational experience enjoyed by 312 back-country hikers in Colorado. The study quantified the various factors or segments contributing to the overall satisfaction of a hike through wild country. Hikers placed the highest psychological value on achieving a relationship with nature; this aspect scored +3.2 of a possible 4.0 points. Following that, among the psychological attributes of hiking were the escape from pressure (+2.9) and the benefit of exercise (+2.6).

The same hikers also scored wildlife values using another set of questions. The value of seeing large animals, such as bighorn sheep (*Ovis canadensis*), mountain goats (*Oreamnos americanus*), and deer (*Odocoileus spp.*), scored +2.7, as did the value of seeing ptarmigans (*Lagopus leucurus*), beavers (*Castor canadensis*) and smaller animals.

Table 5.1: Some Values Obtained by Cluster Analysis of Perceived Contributions to Recreational Experience of Back-Country Hikers in the Weminuche Area of Colorado.

	Value
Psychological Attributes:	
Relationship with nature	3.2
Escape physical pressure	2.9
Exercise	2.6
Freedom	1.9
Achievement	1.6
Reflection on personal values	1.3
Wildlife Values:	
Large wildlife (bighorn sheep, deer, mountain goats)	2.7
Small wildlife (beaver, ptarmigan, and other birds)	2.7
Good fishing	2.4
Naturally reproducing fish	2.4

The interest-in-wildlife values thus compared favourably with those of exercise (+2.6) and outranked such values as the personal achievement of hiking (+1.6) and the opportunity to reflect on personal values (+1.3).

Evaluations of this sort may be different for families using campgrounds, for hunters, or for birdwatchers, but the appreciation of wildlife by these or other types of park-users remains unstudied. Nonetheless, the study of hikers supports, in quantitative terms, the premise that wildlife plays a significant role in the recreational value associated with parks and other wild areas.

The popularity of shows featuring trained killer whales (*Orcinus orca*) and dolphins (*Tursiops spp.*) illustrates the high level of public interest in animals. Such shows inform thousands of people about the behaviour and intelligence of these animals, but the public learns little about the ecology of marine mammals and their natural environment.

Unlike marine aquaria, many parks have the resources to combine recreational experiences with education, thereby stressing the overall ecological setting in which animals live in the wild. To perform these functions, viewing facilities should be designed in ways that ensure minimum disruption of the animals' normal activities. In addition, an ecological understanding of what visitors see should be enhanced by the availability of self-guided tours, educational materials, and informed naturalists.

Many national parks in the United States and Canada have visitors' centers with informative displays and daily lecture programs emphasizing the ecological relationships of wildlife. Agreeing that wildlife in parks should be managed for human benefits and public education, Shaw and Cooper (1980) described how park managers can enhance the ways visitors appreciate animals.

The method is based on a system of guidelines that develop appropriate opportunities for viewing wildlife in parks. Some species have little or no tolerance for humans, however, and species such as mountain lions (*Felis concolour*) and wolves (*Canis lupus*) cannot be viewed easily.

Nonetheless, an extremely popular program at Algonquin Park, Ontario, treats visitors to nightly "*wolf howls*" in which wolves answer the calls of park guides. Other species have seasonal needs for seclusion, whereas at other times people may approach the same animals rather readily. Some endangered species at times may be tolerant of human intrusions.

For example, boat tours and a well-placed tower produce good views of whooping cranes (*Grus americana*) on their wintering grounds in Texas. However, similar arrangements on the nesting grounds of whooping cranes probably would be disruptive.

Because of their unique features, certain animals are more aesthetically appealing than other animals. In general, large mammals and birds are more popular than smaller species, and colourful animals attract more attention than drab forms. Interactions between parents and their young also are of great public interest, and predators have special appeal to most people.

Whatever the species may be, however, they should be viewed in settings that are as natural as possible. Kellert (1980a) thus did not recommend such practices as those carried out in Yellowstone National Park in the early 1900s when bison (*Bison bison*) were rounded up daily in locations where people could conveniently watch the animals feed.

The presence of natural habitat remains the essential difference between viewing animals in wild areas and in zoos; thus habitat management may be necessary in parks where viewing wildlife is a major objective.

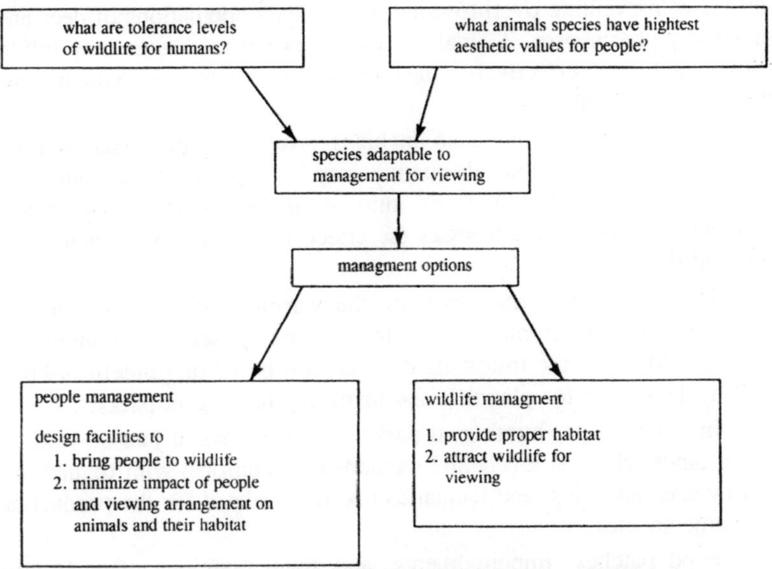

Figure 5.1: Management guidelines for developing wildlife viewing opportunities in parks.

Various designs are available for managing people who are viewing wildlife. These range from such simple things as roadside turnouts and picnic tables near water, to observation towers and specially designed buses. Some visitor centers are built underwater with windows offering a fish's eye view of aquatic life.

The U.S. Army Corps of Engineers has such an arrangement at Bonneville Dam, on the Columbia River in Oregon, where visitors can watch the ascent of salmon, trout, and other species in the fishway. Providing opportunities for viewing wildlife in natural settings presents park supervisors and wildlife managers with a major difficulty: attaining a proper balance between human-wildlife interactions without impairing the environment and disrupting the behaviour of the animals.

Thus, educating large numbers of people about wildlife while avoiding the disturbance of natural processes remains a paradox of park management.

Hunting in Parks

Recreational hunting may be appropriate in parks offering adequate areas of undeveloped land or water. Hunting currently is permitted on 41 areas under jurisdiction of the U.S. National Park Service. In parks where natural predators are absent, hunting may offer a desirable means of preventing overbrowsing by abundant populations of deer and other large herbivores. A small number of expert marksmen may fulfill-manageably and effectively—the immediate objective of reducing the number of animals.

But if the objective also includes providing additional outdoor recreation, a reasonable alternative may be a public hunt controlled by permits (provided that the animals are not excessively tame). Another consideration addresses the effect of hunting on the behaviour of wildlife.

That is, hunting may increase the wariness of animals, thereby reducing the opportunities for park visitors to see and photograph wildlife. Much of the following discussion is based on guidelines Fogg (1975) developed for planning and managing hunting in parks.

In many ways, hunting in parks can be managed just as it is on other lands. Harvest levels and methods may conform with regulations set by state agencies, and habitat can be manipulated for the production of game species.

Food patches, impoundments, and small openings often benefit nongame as well as game animals, and add to the enjoyment of park visitors during the spring and summer months. Such manipulations, however, should conform to the general purpose and plan of the park.

Because of potentially serious conflicts between hunting and other recreational uses of parks, however, the management of hunting requires special attention. A minimum of 160 ha of open land or water area should be available for hunting. For safety reasons, restrictions may be necessary regarding the density of hunters and the types of weapons they are permitted to use.

Rifles might be restricted to large parks, and shotguns and archery equipment may be allowed in smaller parks. Hunting seasons should coincide with times of low use by nonhunters, and boundaries of hunting areas should be defined clearly. Adequate buffer zones are needed between hunting zones and picnic areas, campgrounds, and ski trails.

Fogg (1975) concluded that hunting in parks remains a controversial issue, especially in densely populated parts of the world. It is a topic that requires thorough discussion, including public participation, before management recommendations are adopted.

National Parks

National parks are usually of grand scale. These areas encompass scenic and environmental features of national or international significance rather than those limited to local or regional importance. Yellowstone was the world's first national park, established by the United States Government in 1872. Since then, the National Park system has grown to include nearly 300,000 km^2 (including 178,000 km^2 recently added in Alaska).

The system consists of more than 40 parks, as well as more than 25 national monuments, historic sites, recreational areas, near-wilderness areas, seashores, and lakeshores. The concept of national parks has been so successful in the United States that more than 100 other countries now have adopted the idea.

In 1916, the U.S. Congress formalized the purpose of national parks in the United States with three mandates:

First, that the national parks be maintained in absolutely unimpaired form for the use of future generations;

Second, that they are set apart for the use, observation, health, and pleasure of the people; and

Third, that the national interest must dictate all decisions affecting public or private enterprise in the parks.

The National Park Service has experienced difficulty in reconciling the first objective of *preservation* with the second of *recreation*. As Fuller (1969) pointed out regarding a similar quandary for parks in Canada, "It seems never to have been spelled out whether pleasure was to come from the natural magnificence of the area or from artificial embellishments. The problem is still with us."

Preservation generally prevails as the motive for managing wildlife in national parks, but the traditional meaning of preservation was revised by a commitee reviewing the management of U.S. National Parks. After a year of study, the committee proposed a specific goal for managing national parks, as follows: "To preserve, or where necessary recreate, the ecologic scene as viewed by the first European visitors. . . . Protection alone is not adequate to achieve this goal. Habitat manipulation is helpful and often essential to restore or maintain animal numbers. . . . A greatly expanded research program oriented toward management needs to be developed."

That report set the stage for a new perspective on preservation-preservation of representative ecosystems and preservation by active management. It also admitted that the goal of preserving natural communities would require more scientific research. Thus, national parks in the United States have become sites for widely acclaimed research on wildlife.

The degree of manipulation that should be carried out, however, remains a delicate subject, and it varies from nation to nation and from park to park. Large herbivores, for example, are commonly cropped or culled for human consumption on the national parks in Uganda.

In Kenya, Olindo reported that surplus elephants (*Loxodonta africana*) are shot as a means of curtailing tree damage and the destruction of habitat for small animals. The park system in India, on the other hand, includes 8 areas where inner sanctuaries of at least 300 km^2 remain undisturbed for Bengal tigers (*Pantbera tigris tigris*). Game cropping in such areas is left to the tigers.

Lamprey (1974) noted that any philosophy of park management is flawed if it considers national parks only as animal sanctuaries and "attaches more value to animal life than to plant life." Unfortunately, natural and mancaused changes in natural communities are not always easy to distinguish.

Ecological succession was not understood when the original concept of preservation was established for national parks in the United States. Thus, the question of whether natural succession is desirable actually is a matter of defining the objectives of each park.

Lamprey (1974) cited an example in which the character of temperate and tropical woodlands is influenced by the frequency and intensity of grass fires. Fire has been a natural part of those environments for centuries. In the absence of fire, the woodlands become denser and thicker, and therefore unsuitable as habitat for some kinds of birds and mammals.

As a management practice, fire suppression clearly influences both the flora and fauna in these woodland communities. Conversely, an intensive fire may eliminate the woodland, again changing-but in greatly different ways-the character of the community for many years afterward. Park managers thus should address the question of what the community structure will be with or without fires, and thereafter decide whether natural fires should be suppressed.

A policy of fire suppression in a park established for the preservation of savanna species likely will eliminate the very species the park intended to preserve. In Africa, elephant populations in parks pose a difficult management situation. Elephant populations have been compressed into limited areas on several national parks because of habitat destruction in the surrounding areas.

As happens with overabundant populations of other herbivores, elephants overeat their normal food supply and thereafter decline in numbers. In this case, however, there is a time lag of several years during which elephants uproot trees for food on the upper branches and, in so doing, severely damage the park environment, even to the point of turning woodlands into grasslands.

The "*elephant problem*" has been dealt with in a variety of ways. Authorities shot elephants in several parks. In another park, management was intentionally passive: no controls were applied and the elephants damaged the environment, then died by the thousands. In the process, the elephants and a coincident drought created a grassland, which resulted in an increase in grazing ungulates.

In other areas, fire suppression slowly regenerated the woodlands and thereby offset the more dramatic and sudden damage caused by elephants. Park managers do not yet know what the "right" way is— or if there is a "right" way at all—for handling large numbers of elephants. Research remains the only means for answering such questions about wildlife management in national parks.

In 1962, at the First World Conference on National Parks, an international committee chaired by F. Bouliere of France prepared a seven-point statement on management of national parks. Highlights are as follows:

1. Management is any activity directed toward achieving conditions consistent with the plan of the park. It may involve manipulation of flora and fauna or protection from modification.
2. Few national parks are isolated from influences of surrounding areas. Interactions of parks with their surroundings include immigration and emigration of animals, the spread of fire, and the flow of water and air, including pollutants.
3. Climax communities such as rain forests and tundra need no modification.
4. Successional communities, such as grasslands, must be managed. Fire, for example, is an essential tool for maintaining open savanna and prairies.
5. Where some animal populations, because of loss of predators, immigration, or compression of habitat, threaten a desired environment, population control should be practiced.
6. Management should be based upon scientific research, and both research and management should be undertaken only by qualified persons.
7. Management based upon scientific research is desirable and essential to maintain some biotic communities in accordance with the objectives of a national park.

OVERPOPULATIONS OF ANIMALS IN PARKS

Elimination of both natural predation and hunting has created overpopulations of some animals in many parks. A consistent management policy has not been developed for handling overabundant herds of deer or elk (Cervus elaphus canadensis) in parks. As with elephants, the animals first denude the vegetation, then starve to death.

The elk herd at Grand Teton National Park migrates seasonally in and out of the protection offered by the park. After years of controversy, Congress finally authorized a measure for controlling the Grand Teton elk herd. Public Law 787 stated that "qualified and experienced hunters licensed by the state of Wyoming and deputized as park rangers by the Secretary of the Interior" could shoot elk in the park. Between 1951 and 1961, 5866 deputized hunters removed 1610 elk.

Artificial feeding of elk wintering on the National Elk Refuge in the Yellowstone-Grand Teton area of Wyoming has been a common practice. Park employees also periodically reduced the bison herd at Yellowstone National Park. Up to 400 animals per year were removed at times between 1936 and 1966.

Such "*herd reductions*" kept the bison population at a size consistent with the available range conditions. Public outcries usually ensued, no matter what controls were applied to animal populations in Yellowstone and other parks in North America. Shooting raised the ire of persons with moralistic and humanistic views of animals.

On the other hand, those with utilitarian attitudes were incensed if nothing was done and animals starved in parks. Deer are overcrowded on Angel Island, a 260-ha state park in San Francisco Bay. Angel Island became a state park after the site was abandoned by the military in the 1950s. Each year, hundreds of thousands of city dwellers from the Bay Area hike, bicycle, sunbathe, and picnic at the park.

Black-tailed deer (*Odocoileus hemionus columbianus*) offer an added attraction for visitors. By 1966, a growing population of more than 100 deer had overeaten the vegetation on Angel Island, and only unpalatable plants remained within the reach of the hungry animals. Deer begging tidbits from picnickers soon became commonplace. In November 1966, park rangers shot 50 deer as a means of averting starvation, but public opposition prevented further reduction of the herd and a widespread die-off followed.

The few survivors of 1966 gradually increased and brought the deer population back to the boom phase of the cycle. By 1975, 227 deer were counted on Angel Island, but in the following year the carcasses of 56 dead deer provided ample evidence of renewed starvation. The San Francisco Society for Prevention of Cruelty to Animals (SPCA) began feeding the deer, with permission from the California Department of Parks and Recreation.

Supplemental feeding began in the fall of 1976 and continued into 1977. The success of the feeding program was not evaluated, but the presence of 60-80 deer carcasses suggested that the effort did not totally prevent starvation, and the deer population apparently declined further.

A browse line appeared again in 1980, when the population was estimated conservatively at 150 deer. At that time, Dr. Dale McCullough of the University of California at Berkeley suggested that coyotes (*Canis latrans*) might be introduced as an experimental means of controlling the deer population on Angel Island.

It was hoped that a natural predator-prey system might gain public acceptance, but sentiments expressed to the California Department of Fish and Game (DFG) indicated otherwise, and the coyote plan was scrapped. Shooting once more was proposed as a means of thinning the herd, but the idea was rejected when the SPCA in San Francisco filed a lawsuit against the DFG.

Negotiations between the DFG and SPCA then produced a plan for removing deer from Angel Island: deer would be live-trapped and released on the mainland into a low-density population of the same subspecies. In August and September of 1981, with $20,000 from the SPCA, the DFG trapped and relocated 214 deer on a recently burned location on the California mainland.

Radio-telemetry studies showed that 85 percent of the translocated deer died in their new environment within a year, more than half within the first 3 months. Causes of death included malnutrition, poaching, and predation by coyotes and domestic dogs.

The researchers, led by McCullough, believed that the poor nutritional condition of the deer and their inexperience outside the controlled environment at Angel Island were responsible for the poor survival rate.

About 40 deer remained on Angel Island after the removal program. (The estimate of a total of 150 deer made in 1980 indeed was conservative.) The California DFG and Department of Parks and Recreation are working on a management plan to prevent renewed overpopulation of deer on Angel Island.

In view of past experience, however, it seems unlikely that any plan will satisfy all segments of the public. The Angel Island experience is not unique, and if a successful management plan is developed for Angel Island, it could serve as a model for controlling herbivores in other parks.

Several questions remain about the fate of animal populations in parks. Should we consider die-offs of elephants in Africa and elk in Wyoming as natural phenomena that have occurred throughout the ages? Or, have die-offs resulted from human interference with natural processes? Shooting presents numerous difficulties: determining the necessity for shooting; deciding how many animals should be shot, and when and where to shoot; who should do the shooting; what should be done with the meat and hides (and ivory, in the case of elephants); and dealing with opposition from the public.

Arrangements should be made for collecting scientific data from animals killed when populations are thinned in parks (e.g., for analyses of stomach contents, parasite loads, body condition, and reproductive status). Only long-term research will help determine the ways of managing parks for what we now regard as excess numbers of animals.

BEARS

In the evening of August 13, 1967, two young women in Glacier National Park were killed by grizzly bears (*Ursus arctos horribilis*) in separate unprovoked attacks. The sensational publicity surrounding that tragedy attracted world-wide attention. Management policies for bears in national parks thus came under criticism from several sources.

One critic proposed that grizzlies should be eliminated from national parks so that visitors would not be subjected to the potential threat of attacks. Before such extreme measures are adopted, however, the history of grizzly bears and their interactions with humans in parks should be examined.

Grizzlies killed a total of 5 park visitors during the first 97 years that national parks existed in Canada and the United States, and only 25 people had been injured before 1960. In the 1960s, injury rates increased from about 1 per 3 years to about 5 per year.

The increase in bear attacks was correlated with increased numbers of visitors, but the probability of a person being attacked nonetheless remained quite low: 1 injury per 1.5 million visitors in parks where grizzlies occur.

In the 1950s and 1960s, sows with cubs were involved with 37 (82 percent) of the 45 attacks where the sex and age of the bears could be identified. Of all known attacks, 56 percent occurred in campgrounds and 31 percent happened to hikers in back country. The frequent attacks in campgrounds apparently stemmed from an association with humans that developed when the bears fed at garbage dumps and when visitors deliberately offered bears handouts.

McArthur (1980) reviewed the changing patterns of bear attacks in recent decades. In Glacier National Park, concerted management efforts in the 1960s diminished the access of bears to human foods, and the rate of attacks thereafter fell from 1.7 per million visitors to 0.2 per million. But after 3 years (1969-71) without grizzly attacks, 6 injuries occurred in 1972-75 (1.04 per million visitors) and 5 in 1976-78 (1.02 per million visitors).

Of the 11 injuries in Glacier Park in the 1972-78 period, only 2 resulted from females with young, 6 from single adult bears, and 3 from subadults. The number of attacks increased in circumstances not related to food-namely in encounters with bears in remote areas-a pattern verified by Martinka (1982). According to McArthur (1980), the increased aggression of adult and subadult bears cannot yet be explained; nor have the events been identified that elicit bear charges toward humans.

In other words, grizzlies are unpredictable. It is debatable whether the potential for bear attacks has diminished with the removal of human-generated food sources. Bear attacks still occur and, given the nature of grizzlies, future attacks can be eliminated only if bears are exterminated from parks or if people are completely removed from grizzly habitat.

The question of whether bears should be eliminated was examined in a newspaper poll conducted about a year after the fatal attacks in Glacier Park. Of 3420 responses, only 104 (3 percent) favoured exterminating grizzlies in national parks. Accepting the danger of bears is probably the price visitors must pay for enjoying a truly natural environment.

Indeed, in the early 1980s two more persons died from grizzly attacks in Yellowstone Park. The injury rate of 1 per 800,000 to 1,000,000 visitors per year certainly compares favourably with a rate of 1 automobile injury per 100 people. Herrero (1970) concluded that humans must enter the domain of grizzly bears as cautious and alert visitors, thereby relinquishing the human role as the tamer and reducer of wilderness.

In such a setting, humans may not be the dominant species, and people become more truly a part of nature. Providing such a quintessential experience is the highest purpose that national parks can serve.

Since 1968, grizzly bear management in the Greater Yellowstone Park Ecosystem has been marked by conflicts between various researchers and the National Park Service (NPS). At the heart of the controversy are three issues: NPS decisions for eliminating garbage dumps where bears obtained much of their food; the NPS policy of removing bears from places where they may threaten humans; and declining grizzly populations.

The controversy includes those who want to protect grizzly bears as well as the voices of those who oppose the preservation of bears or who rank bears with low priority in park management. Suggestions include retaining wilderness for grizzly habitat by reducing road access and timber harvests in the areas surrounding Yellowstone Park.

Conversely, an employee of a forest products corporation said, "From my point of view, people are more important than grizzly bears". In 1983, the final Environmental Impact Statement was approved for managing grizzlies in Yellowstone. The management objectives were to preserve and maintain natural populations of bears as part of the park's native fauna and to provide for the safety of park visitors.

Major recommendations included:

(1) eliminating access to all human garbage;

(2) educating visitors with literature and warnings from rangers;

(3) closing some areas of high grizzly density to visitors;

(4) live-trapping and removing bears that persist in human activity areas;

(5) killing only those bears deemed dangerous by the Park Superintendent;

(6) monitoring bear numbers and distribution;

(7) providing supplemental food (carcasses of large herbivores) when natural foods are not widely available; and

(8) coordinating bear management with the U.S. Forest Service and state agencies.

In 1986, after several years of work by a federalstate committee, the Interagency Grizzly Bear Guidelines were published, covering lands managed by the National Park Service, Forest Service, Fish and Wildlife Service, Bureau of Land Management, and various state wildlife agencies.

The Guidelines describe procedures for dealing with grizzlies in five different management situations, ranging from places where grizzlies do not occur to bear "population centers" where grizzlies are abundant. The management activities are wide ranging, and include using bear-proof garbage containers, closing logging or mining roads to public use, and conducting logging in some areas during winter when the bears are hibernating.

The Wildlife Society (1986) approved a position statement on management and conservation of brown bears, including the grizzly and the Alaska brown bear (*Ursus arctos middendorfi*). The statement recognizes increasing conflicts between bears and human activities and the diminishing range and numbers of bears.

The Wildlife Society recommends several measures, including:

(1) encouraging coordinated efforts among state, federal, and provincial agencies to include bears in management plans;
(2) reducing human use of areas frequented by brown bears;
(3) eliminating domestic sheep grazing on public lands in the Greater Yellowstone Ecosystem;
(4) prohibiting the sale of all bear parts (e.g., claw jewelry);
(5) enforcing strict management of hunting;
(6) developing an accurate means of measuring population trends, including recruitment and mortality;
(7) reducing vehicle access into bear habitat;
(8) reintroducing bears into suitable but currently unoccupied habitat, especially in wilderness areas and national parks; and
(9) disseminating accurate information to the public on bear conservation and management.

One overriding difficulty is that grizzly bears are a K-selected species (i.e., long-lived species with low birth rates), and there are not enough bears to permit experiments with various management measures. The margin for error thus is small, and serious and long-lasting consequences might result from a failed management effort.

Grizzlies are not the only dangerous creatures occurring in parks, but they receive the most publicity. Bison and mule deer (*Odocoileus bemionus*) have killed park visitors, and black bears can be dangerous clowns. A popular cartoon describes the adventures of a lovable bear begging from tourists in "Jellystone Park," but all black bears are not as good-natured as this comic-strip counterpart.

In Great Smoky Mountains National Park in 1977-78, black bears injured 24 of the 17.7 million visitors. Thus, the injury rate in this case-1 per 700,000 visitors-is slightly greater than the injury rate caused by grizzlies in western parks. Tate (1980) studied the attack behaviour of black bears that were panhandling along roadsides in the Great Smokies Park.

She found that a bear was more likely to attack humans as a feeding session grew longer and as the number of different feedings increased. Older bears were more likely to attack than young ones, and males were more aggressive than females.

Hot weather and rain also increased the likelihood of bear attacks on tourists. These observations provide some basis for predicting behaviour of black bears in particular settings, but the management implications are unclear. As with grizzlies, the lure of food undoubtedly overcomes a bear's tendency to avoid humans, and each handout encourages more begging behaviour.

The concurrent roles of national parks-recreation and preservation-are highly strained when it comes to dealing with panhandling bears. Park rangers cannot easily stop tourists from tossing snacks to bears, but with vigorous enforcement of the "no-feeding" rule and intensive education of park visitors, black bears may regain their reputation as secretive and resourceful denizens of the forest.

Neither the image nor the reality of black bears as pitiful, subservient, and sometimes rebellious roadside beggars has any place in park management.

PRESERVATION, HUMAN POPULATIONS, AND PARK DEVELOPMENT

In North America, the arguments for and against resource preservation in parks, particularly in large national parks, are waged between two groups of relatively well-fed people. Such is not the case, however, in central and eastern Africa where hungry people look on parks as a source of food.

In Tanzania, Miller (1982) described the setting where thousands of wildebeest (*Connochaetes taurinus*) flourished in the protection of Serengeti Park, while outside the fence starving African families watched in hunger. In such a context, wildebeest may be considered a wasted and desperately needed source of human food, especially because many of the animals are killed and eaten by lions (*Panthera leo*) and other predators.

Hence, the question arises as to whether concerns for human welfare should override those for preserving natural systems. Must the concept of nature preserves such as the Serengeti Park be abandoned in favour of providing food for an ever-increasing human population?

Miller (1982) says the concept need not be abandoned, but perhaps national parks in developing countries should contribute tangible resources to local economies. He claims that arguments for "pure" preservation in parks are flawed because human influences already may have disrupted natural systems.

Fences prohibit the natural movements of animals; and roads, campgrounds, and concession areas in parks violate and displace natural environments. Hence, culling excess animals in parks for human food might be similarly justified on the grounds of serving the public interest. The existence of national parks in developing countries can be justified further when important watersheds are protected in ways that assure the availability of clean water for industrial and domestic consumption.

Parks also may serve as reservoirs for plant and animal species that can be propagated for use outside the park. Other parks in Africa are not under the same pressures as those so visible in the Serengeti. In Kruger National Park in South Africa, however, human intrusions have been a part of wildlife management. Material in this section is based on Smuts (1982), who described the interactions of humans, carnivores, and herbivores in African parks.

In the central district of Kruger Park, continued declines of zebra (*Equus burcbelli*) and wildebeest prompted a detailed search for causes. Grazers adapted to short grass, such as the zebra and wildebeest, seem more vulnerable to lion predation in wet years, when grass grows tall.

The general decline of these species halted temporarily during the dry years of the late 1960*s*, but resumed with the series of wet years between 1973 and 1977. The decline involved interactions among weather, food, and cover, and the respective sizes of the predator and prey populations. In some animal populations in Africa, the ratio of predators to prey animals was 1:1000; predation had little impact on the prey population in such cases.

In Kruger Park, however, the ratio is 1 lion per 110 prey animals. The lion population of 700 in 1975 required about 2500 wildebeest per year. The potential annual recruitment into the wildebeest population was only 3300 calves, leaving an excess of only 800 available for wild dogs (*Lycaon pictus*) and other predators. Predation obviously was accentuating the decline of wildebeest and zebra in Kruger National Park during the 1970*s*.

Park managers had two choices: let nature take its course or intervene and curb the declining numbers of zebra and wildebeest. In keeping with the current emphasis in national park management, laissez faire would seem the simplest choice, but the history of the central district of Kruger Park indicated that human influences may be responsible for the unfavourable predator-prey ratio.

Between 1933 and 1977, water developments in the park opened new grazing areas for native herbivores; 70 windmills and 23 dams were built during the period. As a result, wildebeest and zebra herds broke into smaller groups and reduced their migratory behaviour. Such changes, along with controlled burning and cropping of other species, initially increased the size of the zebra and wildebeest herds.

The same changes, however, also increased the vulnerability of the herds to predators. Proportionally more animals are on the fringes of small herds and thus more are exposed to predators, and newborn calves in smaller herds also are more noticeable to hyenas (*Crocuta crocuta*). The new water supplies also stimulated the growth of tall grasses, thereby offering lions better hiding cover and increased hunting efficiency.

Furthermore, humans cropped 3500 buffalo (*Syncerus caffer*) and 7500 impala (*Aepyceros melampus*) between 1968 and 1977, which reduced the buffering effect of these species. For a management goal, Smuts (1982) recommended that wildebeest and zebra herds once more should be formed into large mobile aggregations rather than remain dispersed and sedentary.

Water manipulation, prescribed burning, and reduced culling of elephants and buffalo in years of good rainfall were the prime means of encouraging formation of the larger herds. Because the predator:prey ratio seemed artificially high, the systematic removal of lions and hyenas also was part of the management plan.

However, immigration soon fills vacant territories, especially with lions, and defeats the purpose of the removal program. Thus, to minimize the replacement of lions by immigration or reproduction, the management plan recommended that the lion population should be cropped gradually, taking all from a single pride rather than a few individuals from several neighboring prides.

Predator control, however, also should include careful monitoring as protection against increases in other predators or increases in prey populations beyond the carrying capacity of the habitat. The management program in Kruger Park now is well entrenched and seems indispensable for the maintenance of confined plant and animal populations. Prescribed burning and the other practices focus, as much as possible, on providing adequate habitat conditions, and minimize the direct manipulation of animal numbers.

Parks in India have experienced pressures similar to those in Africa. The last stronghold of lions in Asia is a 1265 km^2 tract in India known as the Gir Forest. Besides lions, 25 species of mammals, 14 species of reptiles, and numerous rare birds occupy the Gir Forest. The "*forest*" actually consists of several habitat types, ranging from closed teak forest to thorny brush to open grasslands.

In 1963, the lion population numbered 266 animals, the descendants of about 12 lions saved when shooting was stopped in 1889. By 1968, however, the population was down to 177 lions. In recent years, the Gir has attracted growing numbers of tourists. The Gir Forest is not a declared nature preserve.

Instead, the site has been managed for teak production and for cattle grazing, of which the latter has posed the greater threat to wildlife. About 4800 Maldharis and 17,000 of their cattle occupy the Gir, and another 47,000 cattle move into the forest during the monsoon season. The Maldharis are impoverished pastoral people who barely subsist by selling ghee processed from milk.

Overgrazing and overcutting have marred the recent history of the Gir. In the 1960s, these abuses, along with export of cattle manure from the forest, reduced plant production to about 15-30 percent of former levels in areas occupied by the Maldharis. Estimates suggest that domestic livestock consumed 85 percent of available grass in the forest. Plant production on the Gir was almost nil.

Under these conditions, livestock comprise about 90 percent of the lion diet in the Gir. Large native herbivores, normally the prey of lions, were all but eliminated from the stripped forest. Desai (1974) noted, "It is a vicious and paradoxical position that lions feed upon cattle, and cattle in turn are gradually destroying the habitat of the lion."

In India, national parks are declared by the individual states, and a large part of the Gir Forest soon may become a national park in the State of Gujarat. Meanwhile, the government of Gujarat decided to "restore the ecological balance in the Gir and to ensure the survival of the lion and other wildlife in perpetuity" with the following steps:

1. To reduce overgrazing by closing the forest to cattle immigrating during the monsoon season.

2. To resettle the Maldharis and their livestock on "government wastelands" outside the forest, and prevent their reentry.
3. To construct and maintain a fence and patrol road around the forest.
4. To provide an alternate food supply for lions until such time as the native ungulate population increases and replaces cattle as the mainstay of the lion diet.

Costa Rica is a country with several new national parks. The most successful park, Santa Rosa, features a historical site where a battle for national sovereignty was waged. Surrounding the park are examples of dry tropical woodland, savanna, mangrove swamp, and gallery forest.

The public readily accepted designation of the battleground as a national rese ve, but an educational program was needed before the public was convinced of the ecological values of the surrounding areas. Another new park in Costa Rica is Poas Volcano, an extremely scenic location on an active volcano where a cloud forest is inhabited by spectacularly beautiful birds known as quetzals (*Pharomacrus mocino*).

Another park protects the nesting beaches of sea turtles (Cheloniidae), another a coral reef, and still other parks protect caverns, grasslands, lakes, and archeological sites. National parks were not established easily in Costa Rica. Opposition came from lumbering interests, hunters illegally taking rare wildlife, and apathetic government institutions.

Support came from local municipalities where tourism would flourish (but conflicts arose when the municipalities wanted to maximize tourist revenues without giving priorities to long-term park goals), from international groups (such as the International Union for Conservation of Nature and the Audubon Society), and local conservation groups.

When she was the nation's First Lady, Senora Karen de Figueres was a most influential ally of park development in Costa Rica. The initial strategy in Costa Rica was to manage a few parks in ways that would gain public acceptance. The first few parks included sites of distinct national interest, and once public support was assured, the park system was expanded to include areas of representative flora and fauna.

Costa Rican parks suffer from budget limitations, and international volunteers from the U.S. Peace Corps, the British Voluntary Service Organization, and the Caribbean Conservation Corporation assist with development and patrol duties.

In North America, some government lands are designated for timber production and grazing, whereas others are set aside for preservation and recreation. In most African countries, however, parks are the only designated use of government lands. Miller (1982) suggested that third-world nations promote "ecodevelopment" outside the parks.

These programs include establishing firewood plantations, creating extension programs with farmers, and promoting rural education. Without proper rural education and development, poor and starving people ultimately will invade the parks for food, fuel, and shelter. As the human population continues growing worldwide at a rate of 1.7 percent per year—thus doubling each 41 years-parks are becoming islands of nature surrounded by an increasingly man-modified environment.

The President's Commission on Americans Outdoors (1987) prepared a report containing elements of a vision for the future in the United States. The vision included a nationwide network of greenbelts of trails, rivers, and abandoned railroads linking urban and rural areas; protection of 2000 segments of rivers and their banks; and a populace with an ethic of respect for nature.

Foremost among the recommendations is a call for a national trust that would provide a minimum of $1 billion per year for land acquisition and park development. After reviewing the report, Pritchard (1987) noted, "These are difficult times for budgets. Yet we are foolish if we sell the backyard to pay off the mortgage.

We need to continue investing in our future." The executive summary of the report concludes, "We have to create ... opportunities by preserving and nurturing the natural world before we lose it forever. If we pay our debt to the great outdoors, we will be repaid many times over."

WILDLIFE AND RANGELANDS

Rangelands occupy about 47 percent of the world's land area. They characteristically are unsuited for cultivation but instead produce forage for livestock and wildlife. Rangelands also are associated with water, timber, and other natural resources.

In the United States, rangelands occupy about one-third of the country-much of it public land-mostly in the 17 states west of the Mississippi River, but also in the southeastern states. The potential for effective utilization of all range resources initiated the practice of range management, a discipline integrating biological, physical, and social sciences.

Range management is a biological science because it addresses interactions between vegetation and animals; physical because of the roles topography, climate, soil, and water play on rangeland utilization; and social because of the demands people place on the goods and services produced by rangelands. The practice of wildlife management is confronted by these same considerations, each requiring knowledgeable use of scientific principles tempered by sound judgment.

Of paramount importance to either discipline is that management of livestock, wildlife, and other natural resources conserves the integrity of the rangeland system without permanent damage. One generally envisions a range as a vast grassland somewhere "out West" grazed by roaming herds of cattle.

Whereas such a scenario is part of the picture, it is a restricted view of a much larger canvas of rangeland types. Arctic tundra, grazed by caribou (*Rangifer tarandus*), *is* no less a rangeland, nor are the hot desert-scrub grasslands and their bands of sheep. Grasslands in the Great Plains of North America are usually categorized by their height; tall, mid-, or short, although other categories are recognized in other regions.

Grazing also occurs in both deciduous and coniferous forests that are open enough to support herbaceous vegetation. These are found from the higher elevations of the Rocky Mountains to the coastal plains of the Gulf states. Savannas and coastal marshes also are valuable grazing resources.

In all, rangelands encompass a broad sweep of ecological settings, but each has in common with the others the utilization of forage by grazing animals.

Grasses

Grasses are by no means the only forages of interest to range managers. Shrubs, forbs, and even trees fall within the realm of grazing and livestock management. Nonetheless, the production of useful grasses remains a central theme, and some knowledge of grasses and their characteristics is essential for wildlife managers concerned with rangeland systems.

Agrostology is the study of grasses. Most agrostologists recognize Gramineae as the family of grasses, although some favour the designation Poaceae for the group. In all, more than 6000 species of grasses have been organized into 6 subfamilies and 26 tribes.

However, several other taxonomic systems have been proposed, but most systems for identifying grasses rely on the complex morphology of each species' inflorescence. The growth of grasses involves complex relationships, but a generalized overview will underscore how grasses respond to grazing. Further, we can compare how grazing may damage other kinds of plants. Plants produce new growth from specialized tissues known as meristems.

In shrubs and most other vegetation, new shoots grow from the tips of older stems. But in grasses, the location of the meristem producing new shoots remains at the base of the plant. Growth in grasses thus is initiated upward from the base. When upper leaves are grazed, grasses generate new herbage from the meristem remaining near ground level, replacing the consumed tissues.

In fact, modest grazing stimulates regrowth and, in doing so, produces repeated yields of forage each growing season. Without grazing, many grasses mature into rank, unpalatable vegetation no longer suitable as prime forage. The same capacity for regrowth results after fire or mowing removes the upper parts of most grasses.

Conversely, the meristem producing new shoots in most other kinds of plants remains at the exposed tip of their stems. For these, cropping of the terminal herbage usually impairs further regrowth of a grazed shoot. New growth must await activation of a dormant bud on another stem, which may not occur until the following spring.

This is why some woody plants appear "hedged" when their twigs are overbrowsed repeatedly. Many grasses also produce rhizomes, stolons, and tillers as a means of establishing new plants. In sum, major differences between grasses and other plants are the location and vulnerability of their growing points.

Additionally, the high ratio of vegetative to reproductive tissues enables grasses to withstand grazing. In general, a large area of grasses is devoted to photosynthetic activity, and thus to carbohydrate production. There is variation among species in this relationship, however. Grasses that decrease with heavy grazing generally have more reproductive shoots in proportion to the number of vegetative shoots.

Reproductive shoots are adapted for seed production rather than for their tolerance to repeated herbage cropping. Because most grasses grow rapidly, their leaves are able to transport carbohydrates produced by photosynthesis to other parts of the plant, either for continued growth or for storage. Young leaves thus import sugars from older, developed herbage, as does the root system.

Grasses vary in their rates of carbohydrate production and storage, with those species that do so quickly showing greater resistance to grazing pressure. Species that accumulate carbohydrates earlier in the growing season are better adapted for spring grazing, whereas those that are slower to produce mature leaves are less able to restore carbohydrates to their growing points.

Thus, a critical aspect of grassland management is the timing of grazing pressure. Grazing ideally is scheduled to coincide with the end of the active growth period so that new herbage production is stimulated by the removal of the older growth. However, old herbage may be deficient in its nutritional qualities, forcing a trade-off in the design of grazing schemes between maximum regrowth and forage quality.

Adaptations of grasses to growing seasons influence grazing management as well. Those species that produce most of their growth during fall, winter, or early spring are *cool-season grasses*, whereas those growing rapidly in the summer months are known as *warm-season grasses*. Ideally, grasslands subject to continuous grazing pressure should contain both warm- and cool-season species.

THE ANIMAL UNIT

The balance between the number of animals consuming range vegetation and the ability of the vegetation to withstand foraging is crucial to management. Ranchers can control the size of their herds, but this alone does not account for the foraging pressure of wildlife sharing the same rangeland. How then do we try to standardize measures for both livestock and wildlife?

The Animal Unit (AU) recognizes the various kinds of livestock-sheep, goats, and cattle-as well as the several kinds of wildlife dependent on range vegetation. One AU equals the live weight of a cow and a calf, or 454 kg, under the assumption that animals of this weight consume a constant amount of forage.

The average weights of all other grazing animals are converted to this standard. Thus, 9.6 pronghorns (*Antilocapra americana*), 5.8 mule deer (*Odocoileus hemionus*), 1.9 elk (*Cervus elaphus canadensis*) or 7.7 white-tailed deer (*Odocoileus virginianus*) equal 1 AU. Conversion to AUs not only permits assessments of foraging pressure, but also allows a common base for economic decisions.

For example, grazing fees on public lands are based on an AU allotment, giving ranchers opportunities to herd sheep (5/AU), goats (6/AU), or cattle, or some mixture of these. The AU allotment is based on the overall grazing capacity for each section of range, but it may be filled with different species or classes (e.g., steers, cows, and calves) of livestock allocated according to the AU equivalent for each.

Unfortunately, the AU does not consider different types of foraging pressure. That is, some species might require browse, whereas others subsist primarily on grasses. For example, about 10 pronghorns equal 1 AU, but, because cattle generally select grasses and pronghorns greatly favour forbs and browse, the AU equation fails to represent the potential carrying capacity of ranges where both animals forage.

Hoover et al. (1959) calculated that 105 pronghorns would actually consume the same amount of grass as one cow, concluding that "all the antelope in Colorado [then about 9000] would not eat enough grass to feed 100 head of mature cattle." Thus, the AU provides only an estimate of foraging pressure from all animals, irrespective of the specific requirements of each.

Management of Range Vegetation

The practice of range management is as diverse as the types of rangelands and the animals and plants growing upon them. In some instances, water development for livestock or wildlife may be the primary management consideration. In general, however, range management addresses the manipulation of vegetation with treatments such as spraying or by regulating grazing pressure.

No matter how intensively managed, range vegetation cannot maintain its integrity if it is abused by grazing animals. Range vegetation is managed to improve the quality and/or quantity of forage available for the production of livestock and, sometimes, for improving wildlife habitat.

Practices are used to promote certain classes of forage-usually grasses, but sometimes forbs or shrubs as well. Further, certain plants are desired because of species-specific differences in their nutritional values, palatability, or adaptability to local conditions. These often are seasonal in nature, so that some plants are favoured for spring or summer grazing, whereas others are desirable as winter forage.

To accomplish these goals, desirable species sometimes may be seeded but, more often, it is the removal of undesirable species that dominates the management regime (both practices may be undertaken in tandem, although sometimes the desirable plants flourish by themselves once the noxious vegetation is treated).

Where overgrazing has deteriorated a range, removal of the excess animals usually will initiate some recovery of the vegetation, but such recovery often takes long periods of time and may be economically unacceptable. Scifres and Polk (1974) recorded desirable changes after spraying a shrub-infested range that took place in about one-fifth of the time required for the same amount of natural recovery.

Thus, undesirable vegetation has become the target of mechanical, chemical, and biological methods of management. Invasions of woody species, particularly shrubby plants, have reduced the carrying capacities on many of the world's rangelands. The immensity of the problem is well illustrated in Texas, where woody plants infest some 36 million ha, or 82 percent, of the state's rangelands.

Woody plants on more than half of this area are so dense that little or no restoration of grass is possible without intensive management. Left untreated, mesquite (*Prosopis* spp.) and other shrubs continue to limit livestock production as their distribution and densities increase.

Diverse theories abound as to why shrub communities have expanded dramatically in the last century, but most of these implicate man's influences rather than precipitous changes in climate or other naturally occurring phenomena.

Overgrazing and suppression of wildfires figure prominently in most explanations of increasing shrub densities and invasions. In any case, shrubs (more commonly known as "brush") became the primary target of management practices on most rangelands. Today, however, brush management rather than brush eradication is the goal. Brush is a natural component of most rangeland and offers shade and browse for livestock.

Complete removal of brush is as unsound economically as it is ecologically. Land managers now are adopting a broader view of rangeland as an integrated system of plant communities. For wildlife, recognition of this concept coincidentally follows the long-standing principle of habitat interspersion and its creations of "edge."

A primary objective of range management on brushinfested ranges is to reduce the amount of woody biomass so that grasses and other herbaceous vegetation are favoured. Water-already a precious resource on most rangelands-also is conserved when the foliage of moisture-demanding brush is reduced, and more sunlight reaches the herbaceous understory.

Furthermore, dense brush physically interferes with many day-to-day ranching operations. Working cattle from horseback is almost impossible when brush impedes visibility, accessibility, and movement. Conversely, elimination of brush is unfavourable for many species of wildlife that now supplement the economic returns of many ranches.

A leasing system that permits daily or seasonal fee-hunting currently adds considerable income to private ranching operations, particularly in light of rising operational costs, periodic droughts, and changing livestock markets. In some regions of the West, hunting revenues may equal or exceed the income per hectare from livestock production, suggesting that the ranching industry will adopt new ways of managing land for both livestock and wildlife. Steuter and Wright (1980) defined the trade-off between brush cover and its relationship with deer densities against livestock production requiring other types of range vegetation.

This relationship indicated that deer numbers will diminish when and if managers remove brush on a large scale. However, if herbicides are applied in alternating strips instead of spraying large blocks, then as much as 80 percent of brush-infested rangelands may be treated.

Further, selective treatments of specific range sites within large pastures may overcome the negative impacts of herbicides on deer habitat while concurrently improving forage production for livestock. Box and Powell (1965) suggested that brush be managed as forage for both livestock and wildlife and not as woody weeds.

Mowing, for example, removes the physical barrier of dense brush, promotes water conservation, and generates regrowth of succulent, highly available browse. One year after mowing, brush regeneration also was suitable for bobwhite (*Colinus virginianus*) and turkey (*Meleagris gallopavo*) nesting, and as cover for deer fawns. Within 3-S years, adult deer and javelina (*Tayassu tajacu*) found the regrowth high enough for their cover requirements.

And, all the while, palatable forage was available to both cattle and wildlife. Wildlife potentially affected by range improvement techniques includes, among many others, pronghorns, quail, and deer. Of the several species of exotic grasses commonly used to revegetate ranges in Texas, only klein-grass (*Panicum colouratura*) appears to provide adequate forage for livestock *and* seed acceptable to bobwhites. A host of songbirds and other nongame species also depends on rangeland habitats, and techniques that alter the composition and structure of range vegetation influence these animals as well.

Recall that populations of "*lesser species*" often aιe keys in food webs and other ecological patterns, such as seed dispersal, of rangeland systems. For example, when forage-depleted ranges are seeded artificially with grasses and a monoculture subsequently develops, the numbers of rodents and lagomorphs in the new community often are reduced, presumably affecting the prey base available to raptor populations.

Mechanical Methods

Range management has at its command several ways to treat brush.

Each of these, however, must be assessed prior to use for the type of response desired. Individual differences in the tolerance and adaptation of woody plants and the soils on which they occur have much to do with the selection of treatments.

This seems particularly true where mechanical means are used. Shredding, roller chopping, root plowing, and chaining are among the more common mechanical treatments on brush-infested rangelands. Box found that 98 percent of the mesquite growing on fine sandy loam in south Texas was killed by root plowing, whereas on heavy clay soil, about 19 percent subjected to the same treatment died.

Conversely, other plants that were rather obscure in the pretreatment composition increased dramatically: two species of cacti increased 600 percent after root plowing the sandy-loam rangeland.

With such dramatic changes in vegetation, it is clear that equally profound changes likely will occur in the composition and density of animal populations on treated rangelands. The results include both the obvious cover and food requirements for native and domestic animals, as well as some less obvious results (e.g., nutritional and other changes, even in the same plants, between pre- and posttreatment vegetation).

For example, 5 of 6 species of brush showed increased crude protein content after mowing, a factor contributing to their increased preference values and forage ratings for deer and cattle following this treatment. However, mechanical treatments of this type usually enjoyed short-lived results as the succulent sprouts springing from the cut stems mature and steadily develop more woody growth.

At another extreme, woody plants such as big sagebrush (*Artemisia tridentata*) contain large amounts of essential oils that, while seemingly of nutritional benefit as a prime source of energy, may be indigestible and perhaps harmful in the rumens of mule deer. Such findings emphasize the subtle nature of nutrition in the management of woody vegetation as forage.

Mowing, instead of killing brush outright, effectively alters the growth form, or physiognomy, of the, plant community. Woody species such as mesquite or huisache (*Acacia farnesiana*) can develop into trees with sizable trunk diameters, whereas others such as agarito (*Berberis tri foliolata*) and catclaw (*Acacia greggii*) remain shrubby and seldom exceed 2-3 m in height at maturity.

Mowing reduces the canopies of shrubs and trees alike but, for sprouting species, the root system remains viable and generates new growth; sprouting occurs at the root crown lying below the cutting

Table 5.2: Preference and Forage Values for Selected Species of Brush Following Treatment with Mechanical Methods.

		Treatment Method					
	Soil Type	*None*	*Mowed*	*Roller Chop*	*K-G Blade*	*Root Plow*	*Root Plow and Rake*
Preference Value							
	Heavy clay	1,330	12,755	12,670	9,660	4,000	8,820
	Fine sandy loam	4,721	19,205	25,575	915	1,000	
Forage Value							
	Heavy clay	25	196	160	108	6	13
	Fine sandy loam	165	—	255	260	9	6

level of the mowing equipment. For mesquite, Wright and Stinson (1970) reported that about 25 percent of the removed top growth was replaced with new sprouts by the end of the first growing season.

Mowing also replaces armored stems or foliage, a common feature of many brushy plants, with regrowth that initially is less protected by spines and thorns. In sum, mowing reduces brush canopies and generally produces regrowth of the same species but, in doing so, succulent forage is regenerated at a height where it is accessible to browsing animals.

However, complete removal of the screening cover provided by brush may negate the benefit to deer of newly available forage resources. White-tailed deer otherwise commonly adapt to changes in food availability wrought by mechanical brush removal if adequate cover remains on the treated area.

Chaining also removes gross amounts of cover, often disrupting the behavioural patterns and distribution of deer. This was indicated when chaining reduced the canopy cover of bottomland deer habitat from 20 to 4 percent but otherwise did not alter the cover of forbs or grasses.

Previously, white-tailed deer numbers were four to five times greater in the bottomlands than in the surrounding uplands. After the bottomlands were chained, however, deer densities dropped to about half of their former numbers. Movements to and from the chained areas were limited to morning and evening and the animals attempted to use any clumped cover remaining in the chained area for concealment.

They otherwise retreated to unchained sites during the daytime, and when venturing into the chained areas, tended to remain near the edge of the cleared area. In Colorado, O'Meara et al. (1981) determined the aftermath of chaining on nongame populations. Whereas 10 species of breeding birds occurred on an unchained area, only 4 species were observed on similar sites chained 15 years earlier.

Further, the density of the bird population was reduced by half on the chained sites. Conversely, small mammals were more abundant on the chained areas but included fewer species compared to unchained habitats. Management procedures minimizing the adversity of chaining on nongame animals include (1) using lighter weight chains, and hence improving the survival of some shrubs and smaller trees, (2) selectively retaining trees with cavities, and (3) limiting the widths of cleared areas to 200 m.

Root-plowing, a method that also drastically reduces the cover of woody vegetation, seems equally inhibitory to deer movements and foraging behaviour. Deer in south Texas moved onto rootplowed areas at night in groups of 5-30 animals, but made little use of the forage available there, then returned to the cover of untreated brush during the day.

The stress of drought-induced shortages of forage was not enough to force deer into the open root-plowed sites where escape cover was absent. Further, not all deer left the brush cover even at night, and in the brush cover, they remained active during daytime. Drought was more devastating to the availability of forage on root-plowed areas than in stands of native brush.

On root-plowed sites, drought and overstocking of cattle produced severe shortages of forage, so that only the untreated brushlands could support either deer or livestock. After 25 or more years, root-plowed brush in south Texas showed long-term reductions in both the density and diversity of browse plants preferred by white-tailed deer, and increases in those of lesser preference. These results again strongly suggest that brush should be managed in small units or strips rather than in large blocks.

Herbicides

Aerial applications of herbicides are widely used to reduce undesirable plants on rangelands (for example, see Hylton et al. 1972 for sagebrush control with chemicals). Some are selective, or only partially effective on certain species, whereas other herbicides have a broader spectrum of effects.

The most widely used herbicides are those that attack broad-leaved plants without affecting grasses. Unfortunately, many herbicides also injure forbs as well as woody species. Such results are of mixed value for wildlife, depending on the importance of forbs as food.

Two months after spraying solid blocks of rangeland in south Texas, Beasom and Scifres (1977) determined that forb production was reduced from about 200 kg per ha to nearly 30 kg per ha; recovery took snore than two years. Species diversity also was affected; 15 months after spraying, only 13 of 30 forbs were present on the treated rangeland and others were reduced in density by as much as 75 percent.

Meanwhile, numbers of white-tailed deer were reduced by 60 percent on the sprayed site, in clear response to the loss of forbs. Other research has shown that white-tail diets contained as much as 68 percent forbs by volume, confirming the importance of forbs as a necessary

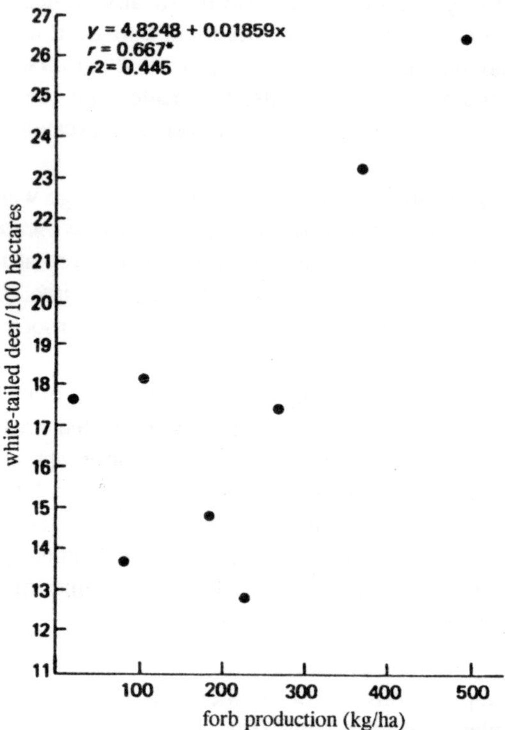

Figure 5.2: Relationship between dry weight of (orbs and deer densities after herbicides were sprayed on brush communities on south Texas rangelands.

component of rangelands managed for deer. Similarly, javelina populations were significantly reduced on sprayed areas because of the nearly complete elimination of prickly pear (*Opuntia* spp.), a food dominating 78 percent of their diet by volume with 100 percent frequency of occurrence. Turkeys were not affected in this instance, reflecting their more general diets and opportunistic feeding habits.

Based on the evidence at hand, efforts to reduce sagebrush with herbicides have severely restricted sage grouse (*Centrocercus urophasianus*) populations. In Montana, Wallestad reported that a 31 percent loss of sagebrush habitat near a strutting ground coincided with a 63 percent decrease in courting males, and Peterson (1970a) described a strutting ground with a long-term average of 54 courting males that diminished to only 3 birds within 2 years of spraying.

Nesting and brood habitats also were depleted by spraying. In Idaho, Klebenow (1970) found only one nest per 89 ha on sprayed sites, whereas nesting densities reached one nest per 26 ha on untreated rangeland. Spraying removed enough shrub cover to inhibit nesting, as shown by a comparison of cover at treated and untreated areas and nest sites.

Broods were more common on unsprayed sites where forbs generally remained more abundant. However, some individual species such as dandelions (*Taraxacum spp.*) occurred more frequently on the sprayed habitats and, as these plants are important food for juvenile sage grouse, some compensation for the loss of other foods was achieved. Nonetheless, a recovery time of about five years after spraying was judged necessary before nesting resumed and ten years before the original carrying capacity returned fully.

Martin (1970) found parallel results on sagebrush rangelands in Montana; herbicides killed 97 percent of the sagebrush, reduced forb coverage by half, and only 4 percent of all sage grouse observations occurred on the sprayed area. Man-made changes in vegetational composition clearly were responsible for the reduction of sage grouse in both Idaho and Montana.

In Wyoming, Johnson (1969) estimated that sagebrush requires 14 to 17 years to fully recover from herbicidal treatments, suggesting the spraying likely causes a similar impact on that state's grouse populations.

With planning, however, sagebrush may be treated with herbicides without wholesale damage to sage grouse habitat. Sage grouse favour nesting sites between 1650 and 1770 m elevation and begin concentrating their broods in June near swales, drainages, or other mesic locations as adjacent habitats dry.

Accordingly, Braun et al. (1977) proposed management recommendations that would minimize damage to sage grouse populations whenever ranges with sagebrush are treated. These include (1) no treatments

Table 5.3: Comparisons of Cover in Sagebrush Communities (Sprayed and Unsprayed) with Sage Grouse Nesting Cover.

	Shrub Cover (percent)				
Treatment or Location	***Sagebrush (Artemisia spp.)***	***Bitterbrush (Purshia tridentata)***	***Horsebrush (Tetradymia canescens)***	***Total***	***Basal Area of Forbs (percent)***
Unsprayed	13.5	0.1	0.4	15	3.2
Sprayed	5.8	1.9	0.6	7	2.4
Nest sites	16.4	0.9	0.7	18	3.0

within 3 km of strutting grounds, nesting habitat, or brood areas, (2) applying treatments in irregular patterns no more than 30 m wide, leaving untreated areas of at least the same width, (3) leaving 100-m strips of untreated sagebrush along the edges of meadows and drainages, and (4) overall, avoiding consideration of any treatment wherever sagebrush cover is less than 20 percent of the total range community.

Herbicides at times may produce selective results benefiting wildlife. In northern transition zones between prairie, deciduous, and coniferous forest types, spraying reduced low-quality deer foods and increased supplies of better browse species.

Deer were attracted to the sprayed plots for winter forage and for summer bedding, and fed four to five times more there than on adjacent unsprayed sites. Counts of pellet groups showed increased deer usage on the sprayed areas, especially in aspen (*Populus tremuloides*) areas, 8 years after treatment. Krefting et al. (1956) also stimulated productive regrowth of highly preferred deer browse when mature plants were treated with herbicides.

Spraying remains an efficient tool for managing many other types of habitat where dense, often monotypic communities preclude desirable amounts of diversity and interspersion of food and cover vegetation. For example, herbicides may improve habitat for lesser prairie chickens (*Tympanuchus pallidicinctus*) on ranges where shinnery oak (*Quercus havardii*) forms dense canopy cover. Prairie chicken numbers decreased as the cover of shinnery oak increased.

Hence, some reduction of the shrubby cover may result in larger numbers of prairie chickens, as suggested by experiments with a common herbicide, Tebuthiuron. Tebuthiuron applied at 0.4 kg per ha effectively controlled shinnery oak and increased grass production, yet did not reduce the availability and diversity of forbs required by lesser prairie chickens.

Fire

What maintains the integrity of grassland systems? Why have shrubs and trees not long ago replaced grasses in the course of plant succession? In part, the answer lies in soil characteristics and precipitation regimes, but as woody plants are scattered in grassland communities, other forces also must exert strong influences on grasslands.

Because ecologists have learned that fire favours grasses over woody plants, they attribute this force as much as any to the continued maintenance of many grasslands. This happens in at least three ways:

1. The growing points of most grasses are protected; they lie

near or below ground level so that fires do not often kill the meristematic tissues essential for regrowth. Conversely, the growing points of woody plants are exposed well above ground level where they are damaged easily by fire.

2. Grasses regrow rapidly after burning and most produce seed within the same growing season. Woody plants, by comparison, take several years to produce seed.
3. For grasses, fire removes only 1- or 2-year growth above ground, but for woody plants, burning causes a loss of fiber representing many years' accumulation.

Thus, the rate of development and maturity after burning greatly favours grasses.

Thus, one easily sees the implication for management of grassland communities and the grazing animals they support. If fires are repeatedly suppressed, woody vegetation indeed may develop and largely replace grasses. Coupled with overgrazing, long-term fire suppression enhances deterioration of productive grasslands into shrub-dominated ranges of diminished value.

Fire also increases the palatability of many grasses. That is, stands of old grasses may be rank and strawlike, and hence spurned by grazing animals. After burning, however, regrowth of the same grasses is tender, usually enriched with protein, and highly palatable.

For effective management, fires must be prescribed to fit local conditions. In California chaparral communities, for example, sprouting and nonsprouting species are abundant. If the interval between burns is too short-less than 15 years-fire will favour the sprouting species because nonsprouting plants have inadequate time to produce seed between fires. Conversely, long fire-free intervals favour nonsprouting species.

If only one noxious nonsprouting species is present in a community, such as one-seed juniper (*Juniperus monosperma*), two fires within 10 years will keep this species suppressed for 30 or 40 years. Frequent fires in communities dominated by sprouting species such as honey mesquite (*Prosopis glandulosa*) will reduce the cover of this and other shrubs but maintain a continuing occurrence of shrubs in the community. In all, prescribed burning requires considerable ecological knowledge.

GRAZING AND WILDLIFE

Grazing animals understandably influence the integrity of range vegetation. Bison (*Bison bison*) and pronghorn are the more obvious grazers coming to mind in considering once pristine rangelands, but jackrabbits (*Lepus* spp.), deer, prairie dogs (*Cynomys ludovicianus*), numerous other rodents, insects, and many birds also foraged on native rangelands. Although these animals certainly exerted some influence, rangeland vegetation coevolved with foraging wildlife into a dynamic equilibrium between consumers and producers.

With man's introduction of domestic livestock, however, a new force was exerted on rangeland vegetation, and the equilibrium of the past changed quickly. Livestock altered the composition of rangeland vegetation. Plants with high forage values became less abundant, creating a grazing disclimax whose development remains proportional to the stocking rate and its duration.

Livestock also alter the physiognomic aspects of rangeland vegetation. Tall grasses may be held at lesser heights and densities, so that ground cover and other physical features of the community are affected. For example, tall grasses used as bedding sites by pronghorn fawns also are desirable range forage for livestock.

If grazing reduces this cover to the point that fawns no longer have adequate concealment, fawn survival may be jeopardized by higher rates of predation. Influences of this kind also were illustrated by studies of Mearns quail (*Cyrtonyx montezumae mourns*) on ranges in Arizona.

Larger amounts of seeds and other quail foods were produced when more plants were grazed by livestock. Indeed, production of important quail foods more than doubled when grazing intensity increased from 50 to 91 percent of the range vegetation. But quail were uncommon or even absent in those pastures where plants were heavily grazed.

It became clear that the heavier grazing pressure, while producing more quail food, concurrently reduced escape cover below a critical threshold, and hence effectively eliminated quail from these ranges. The study demonstrated that no more than 50 percent, by weight, of the available forage could be utilized by grazing animals in order to maintain Mearns quail at optimum numbers.

Managers appraise the composition of rangeland vegetation to determine *range condition*. This appraisal is based on how much the current vegetation deviates from its potential at the range site. In other words, what percentage, if any, of the present community still represents climax vegetation? With few exceptions, climax grasses are preferred livestock forage and thus are known as *decreasers*.

Somewhat lower-quality plants are known as *increasers* because their percentage expands with grazing. A balance is sought between decreasers and increases so that, overall, range vegetation remains productive and useful forage. Range condition declines from excellent into classes of good, fair, or poor, as the percentage of climax species decreases, accompanied by a reverse pattern in the increasers.

With long periods of excessive grazing pressure, *invaders* become more prevalent in the community, reaching a point where the range's former carrying capacity for livestock and wildlife becomes severely reduced.

The welfare of livestock, of course, coincides with range condition, but so do many features of wildlife associated with rangelands. For example, range condition influences antler development of white-tailed deer. Larger percentages of yearling bucks with spike antlers-instead of multibranched antlers—were harvested from ranges in poor condition, whereas the percentage decreased when range conditions improved. In part, this may be explained by enhanced nutrition of deer on ranges in better condition.

Table 5.4: Sample Calculation of Range Condition Based on the Composition (Percent Cover) of the Climax Community Weighed Against Current Composition of Vegetation.

Species or Group	*Climax Vegetation (percent cover)*	*Current Vegetation (percent cover)*	*Current Proportion of Climax (percent cover)*
Sideoats grama (*Bouteloua curtipendula*)	100	10	10
Perennial threeawn (*Aristida spp.*)	5	10	5
Texas grama (*Bouteloua rigidiseta*)	5	5	5
Forb increasers	10	5	5
Woody increasers	5	20	5
Hairy tridens (*Erioneuron pilosum*	0	15	0
Annuals	0	35	0
		100	30

Table 5.5: Percentage of Yearling Bucks Harvested with Spike Antlers In Relation to Range Conditions in Two Ecological Regions of Texas.

	Percentage of Yearlings with Spikes	
Range Condition	*South Texas Plains*	*Edwards Plateau*
Good	34.5	26.7
Poor	58.4	59.7

The diets of white-tailed deer on ranges in excellent condition were 29 percent higher in crude protein and 27 percent higher in phosphorus than those feeding on poor ranges. Further, yearling deer maintained on experimental diets of low nutritional quality produced an average of 0.62 fawns, whereas those fed high-quality diets produced 1.63 fawns per doe.

Livestock and wildlife also may compete directly for food. Items in the diets of each may show strong competition for specific plants, but data are more often reported by forage classes: grasses, forbs, and browse.

Distinctions between these groups occasionally are unclear, primarily for some species of broad-leaved herbaceous plants having woody stems (known as *suffrutescents* or "half shrubs"); examples include Gardner's saltbrush (*Atriplex gardneri*) and winterfat (*Ceratoides lanata*). The wise manager also is aware that food habits may be seasonal.

Regional differences also occur in the diets of the same species. Furthermore, close study of interspecific foraging behaviour may show that parts of the same plants are consumed differentially. If so, competition is less than it might seem initially. And finally, a number of food-habits techniques are available, with each having some amount of inherent bias for determining diets accurately.

Stomach contents are commonly reported by volume and by frequency of occurrence, but, to be truly useful, these data should be accompanied by some measure of forage availability, yield, and nutritional value. Studies of competition among sheep, goats, cattle, and white-tailed deer indicated strong overlaps in diets, depending on season.

In winter, each of these ruminants competed for browse, with deer and goats showing the greatest degree of competition for browse and mast in all seasons. Sheep and deer each made heavy use of forbs, particularly in summer, when 65 percent and 68 percent of their respective diets were dominated by forbs.

However, Bryant et al. (1979) suggested that competition for forbs also occurred in winter and early spring. Cattle and goats did not compete strongly with deer for forbs. Grasses were used primarily by deer only in the spring when the plants were succulent, but if forbs and browse were absent at other seasons, grasses then were eaten in larger than usual amounts. Competition for grasses otherwise was greatest between cattle, sheep, and goats.

The inferences of these data become clear when the performances of deer herds are weighed against the accompanying stocking rates of domestic animals. In much of the Southwest, and especially in the thickly populated deer range in central Texas, summer is the critical season. Extensive losses of deer may occur when summer rains fail and forage is diminished.

If livestock already have depleted most of the forage, the few remaining food resources are subject to intense utilization. Deer first compete with goats for browse in winter, then are forced into a second competitive season in summer with sheep for forbs. Competition for grasses is largely between cattle and sheep, without major involvement of deer.

Continuous livestock grazing, when it includes sheep and goats, thus presents a highly competitive arena for deer. Warren and Krysl (1983) demonstrated that grazing and hunting pressure interacted with the food habits and nutritional status of white-tailed deer.

On an area with 20-25 percent harvest of deer, few exotic big game, and regulated grazing (cattle only), deer experienced better nutritional condition at a much earlier age than on another area where exotics were common, livestock of several kinds grazed continuously,

Table 5.6: Average Results from White-Tailed Deer Maintained Experimentally for 5 Years on Rangelands With and Without Livestock (Sheep, Goats, and Cattle).

		Deer Herd	
Livestock Stocking Rate	*Ha/Animal Unit*	*Adult Mortality (percent)*	*Change in Size (percent)*
Heavy	3.2	40	– 43
Moderate	6.5	14	9
Light	9.7	14	6
Deer only	—	5	32

and the harvest of deer was only 5-10 percent of the population. Comparisons of the diets of deer also reflected the better range conditions on the managed area.

Bobwhite apparently spread westward after livestock were establised on western rangelands, likely because of the physiognomic changes grazing wrought to the vegetation. The same alterations greatly expanded mule deer populations. Tall, dense grasses were replaced in part by annual forbs and woody species.

California quail (*Lophortyx californicus*) benefit from moderate grazing in humid regions that otherwise would support vegetation less suited for the birds. Moderate grazing also provided Attwater's prairie chickens (*Tympanuchus cupido attwateri*) with favourable nesting, escape, and winter cover, whereas ungrazed pastures were not used by the birds.

Ungrazed vegetation develops into thick mats of cover avoided by prairie chickens. In short, grazing can be a positive factor in the distribution and abundance of wildlife when the composition and physiognomy of range vegetation are appropriate. Undergrazed grasslands, as suggested above, once may have limited some wildlife populations, but in modern times overgrazing now seems far more critical.

When grazing replaced farming in northwestern Florida, the pressures of booming cattle prices and drought led to overgrazing that subsequently diminished the food and cover available to quail. Quail populations dropped when these changes in land use occurred despite attempts to manage quail with food plantings.

Likewise, Klimstra and Scott (1957) noted that overgrazing markedly reduced bobwhite nesting on pastures in Illinois. On southern pastures, Lay (1954) suggested that declines in bobwhite coincided with the increase in livestock and stated that "maximum numbers of quail and maximum numbers of livestock are incompatible."

Nonetheless, grazing can be manipulated for the betterment of both bobwhite and cattle. Bobwhite in Illinois usually nested in grazed pastures, likely reflecting the open ground cover that grazing produced. Furthermore, heavy grazing of selected "spots" of small size can create lower successional stages favourable for bobwhites; these should be grazed before the growing season begins so that the vegetation can respond during the same year.

A simple way to accomplish spot grazing is to move the winter feeding stations for cattle periodically, thus forming a limited patchwork of heavily grazed areas within a more uniform rangeland type.

Table 5.7: Returns and Production per 260 Ha for Three Levels of Grazing Pressure on Rangelands In Colorado.

	Grazing Pressure		
	Heavy	*Moderate*	*Light*
Number of livestock	53	47	27
Gain per head in 5 months (kg)	78	96	105
Gross return ($)	661	1027	724
Operating costs ($)	188	163	97
Net profit ($)	473	864	627
Profit/gross return ratio (%)	72	84	87

Overgrazing

Overgrazing represents not only eventual depletion of forage resources, but also may work against current income. Based on a 19-year study of grazing intensity in Colorado, moderate grazing yielded more profits than either heavy or light stocking rates.

As vegetation retrogresses with continued overgrazing, crucial soil and water relationships also fail, ultimately reducing the rangeland's carrying capacity for grazing animals, even after stocking rates are lessened. Rates of water infiltration on watersheds in South Dakota showed proportional relationships with grazing intensity.

That is, infiltration was lowest with heavy grazing and highest with light grazing. Heavily grazed watersheds also had the highest rates of runoff. Range deterioration is not without other measures of ill health. Taylor et al. (1935) recorded significant increases in insect numbers on overgrazed rangelands.

Typically, the number of species declines, but this loss in diversity is accompanied by a larger number of total insects. Ironically, forage-consuming insects such as grasshoppers show dramatic increases in numbers on overgrazed ranges. Grazing also may influence-one way or another-the abundance and diversity of lizard communities, birds, and small mammals.

Black-tailed prairie dogs and jackrabbits often are held responsible for depletion of range vegetation. Hansen and Gold (1977) found that the overall diets of prairie dogs and cattle overlapped by 64 percent, but many of the plants were grazed at different times of the year, thereby reducing the degree of direct competition.

Nonetheless, prairie dogs and jackrabbits are common targets of control programs on western rangelands. Jackrabbit "drives" often gain national attention in the news, as has the poisoning of prairie dogs, causing emotional responses in some sectors of the public. Human responses aside, the ecological issues may be complex, and directly or indirectly involve other wildlife.

In particular, endangered black-footed ferrets (*Mustela nigripes*) are intimately associated with prairie dogs, so that the fates of the two species remain linked. Large populations of jackrabbits and prairie dogs actually may be the result of overgrazing, not the cause of range depletion. These animals are associated with the early stages of succession in grassland ecosystems and thus are "weed species".

Bison herds apparently created favourable habitat for prairie dogs and jackrabbits in earlier times. Today, excessive numbers of cattle can produce the same or even more disturbances to grassland communities. Control of either prairie dog or jackrabbit populations may require no more than better management of livestock grazing.

Some ecologists claim this can be achieved simply with barbed wire, meaning that fences used to regulate grazing pressure will promote better range conditions, and hence fewer prairie dogs or jackrabbits.

In Arizona, Taylor et al. (1935) studied heavily grazed pastures separated only by barbed wire. The jackrabbits could forage freely on either side of the fence, according to their preferences. However, cattle continued grazing on one side. The result: jackrabbits were three to four times more abundant on the heavily grazed pastures.

When cattle were removed from a wildlife refuge in Oklahoma where prairie dogs were protected, the grass cover increased and the prairie dogs abandoned the site. In Kansas, prairie dogs never established colonies on a range revegetated with tall grasses even though five colonies were begun on overgrazed ranges nearby. Koford (1958) observed that prairie dogs rarely start new colonies where ranges are in good to excellent condition.

More recently, Uresk et al. (1982) compared the numbers of prairie dog burrows before and after fencing cattle from an active town site in South Dakota. The density of active burrows was twice as great where livestock continued grazing. These authors mentioned that the costs of controlling prairie dogs with poisons did not produce financial rewards, and instead recommended reducing livestock numbers as a means of natural control.

In Kansas, elimination of grazing during the growing season helped

Table 5.8: Insect Populations (1000s per 0.4 Ha) on Overgrazed and Properly Grazed Rangelands.

Range Condition	*Beetles (Coleoptera)*	*Flies (Diptera)*	*Bugs (Hemoptera)*	*Leafhoppers (Homoptera)*	*Bees, Ants (Hymenoptera)*	*Grasshoppers (Orthoptera)*	*Total*
Overgrazed	118	30	100	214	140	180	782
Properly grazed	50	28	8	52	28	20	186

reduce a 44.5-ha prairie dog colony to less than 5 ha after 4 years. Some of the interactions between livestock and prairie dogs undoubtedly are related to habitat. In shortgrass environments, prairie dogs may be the primary influence on range vegetation, whereas the intensity of cattle grazing seems the dominant regulator in tallgrass prairies.

Overgrazing, particularly during dry periods, was identified by Jackson and DeArment (1963) as an important factor influencing population levels of lesser prairie chickens. In a heavy grazing regime, highly palatable tall grasses are replaced by shorter species of lesser quality as habitat for prairie chickens.

Conversely, better grazing management-for example, grazing systems that periodically rest rangelands and use more moderate stocking rates-contributed to the increasing numbers of lesser prairie chickens in Colorado. On southwestern ranges, densities of grassland gamebirds probably depend on survival during the winter, and hence on the amount of residual vegetation available for food and cover.

If, after summer and fall grazing, too little residual vegetation is left, grassland birds will fare poorly during the winter and experience erratic changes in their abundance the following year.

Grazing and Trout

Unfortunately, relationships between grazing and fisheries have not always been integrated in resource management, with the result that streamside habitats and fish populations have been damaged. Riparian zones make up a small percentage of rangeland areas, yet because cattle and other livestock prefer the succulence and diversity of riparian vegetation, these zones receive disproportionate grazing pressure.

Besides damaging aquatic and streamside communities, this often means that forage available on nearby upland ranges remains unused. In Montana, Gunderson (1968) found that a section of ungrazed stream had 76 percent more cover for trout (Salmonidae) than did a grazed section of the same stream.

Undercut banks, overhanging vegetation, and other conditions desirable for trout were important in this evaluation. Furthermore, trout 15 cm or more in length were 27 percent more numerous and 44 percent heavier in the ungrazed section. Platts (1982) summarized 20 studies of grazing and its influence on fish populations and habitat; all but one concluded that grazing degraded streamside environments, and hence the local fishery.

The exception involved a grazing plan protecting streamsides on a well-managed sheep allotment. Sheep otherwise may severely degrade streamside habitats. A section of stream bordered by a heavily grazed meadow was about five times as wide and only one fifth as deep as a section where the meadow received light or no grazing. Recovery from heavy grazing may take up to 10 years and only then after most or all of the livestock are removed.

Bowers et al. (1979) reported that trout production increased by an average of 184 percent where grazing was light or eliminated, and suggested that production could be increased by about 200 percent if management decisions were made to optimize trout habitat.

They presented some management recommendations beneficial for trout production, including (1) implementing grazing systems that will create and/or maintain good trout habitat, particularly those that protect streamside areas until the fall months, (2) fencing easily damaged areas on the most important trout streams, and (3) using salt or water developments to attract livestock to other parts of the range.

Recently, however, Bryant (1982) found that neither salt nor alternate water sources appreciably reduced livestock utilization of riparian zones in Oregon, and cattle continued grazing streamside vegetation during the summer months unless these sites were fenced.

In sum, grazing systems and other management practices designed to meet the requirements of a livestock operation and maintenance of range vegetation also should consider their effects on riparian zones and the fisheries dependent on these environments. Too often, however, streamside studies of grazing and its influence on trout fisheries have not been rigorously conducted, and the results of these may not always be as instructive as supposed.

Grazing Systems

Several systems have been developed to supplement the traditional method of *continuous grazing*. These include *deferred-rotation sytems* of several types, but these always include one or more pastures in some stage of resting while others are grazed. The length of time each pasture in a deferred system is rested or grazed depends on the season, the kind of vegetation, and, of course, on the class and density of livestock.

Other grazing schemes are known as *short-duration systems*. These include high intensity-low frequency systems that exert heavy grazing pressure for short periods of time. Another, even more complex short-duration scheme is the Savory grazing method. In this case, the range is divided into pastures resembling spaces between the spokes of a

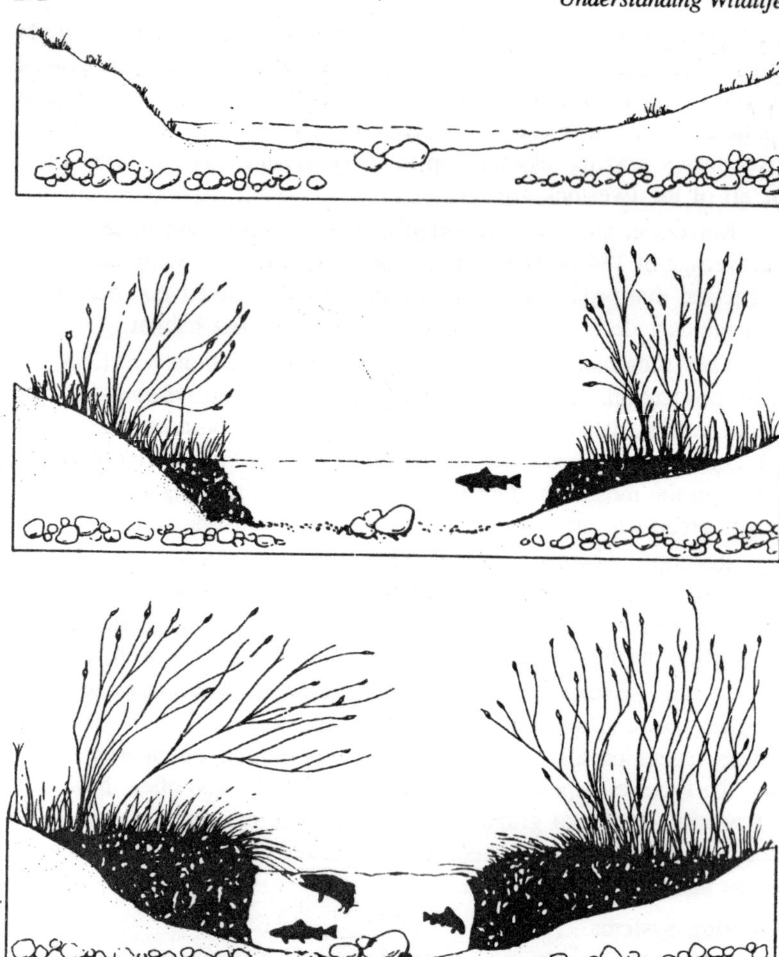

Figure 5.3: Schematic representation of stream conditions subject to heavy grazing (top). Banks are grazed and trampled, leading to increased stream width, shallow water, and poor habitat for trout. Shallow water may be warmed enough by direct sunlight to limit a trout fishery.

wagonwheel, with a common water source at the hub. The grazing period in each pasture is short, no more than a few days, before the livestock are moved to the next cell in the series. This and other grazing systems may permit large increases in stocking rates compared with continuous grazing.

The major differences between deferred and short duration grazing systems are the ratios of (1) area grazed to ungrazed at any one time and (2) the length of grazing and resting periods. With deferred rotation, at least one-half of the area is grazed and the grazing period at least equals the resting period. With short-duration systems, less than half the area is grazed at any one time and the grazing period is shorter than the resting period. Kothmann (1974) defined an array of terminology for grazing management, to which serious students should refer.

Anderson and Scherzinger (1975) described a grazing plan for cattle that improved the quality of winter forage for elk. Cattle grazed the vegetation in late spring and early summer, but they were removed before the end of the growing season.

This strategy allowed time for the plants to regrow and cure as forage of high nutritional quality. Without cattle, the ungrazed vegetation remained rank and of low quality. In sum, the cattle stimulated the regrowth of forage later used by elk. The winter elk population jumped from about 320 animals to 1190 in the 10 years after the grazing plan was implemented.

Furthermore, blue grouse (*Dendragapus obscurus*) numbers also increased under this grazing regime. Dual use of rangelands in Utah by mule deer and sheep produced similar results. In this case, sheep grazed in the late spring, reducing the amount of herbaceous plants, but subsequent regrowth of this same vegetation increased the proportion of green plants available to wintering deer.

Concurrently, the temporary removal of the herbaceous vegetation freed moisture and nutrients for bitterbrush (*Purshia tridentata*)—a major browse species-and increased its availability to the deer herd. Bitterbrush itself can be managed as forage for both sheep and big game if livestock grazing is terminated before the twigs begin growing rapidly.

After bitterbrush twigs have produced about one-third of their annual growth, even moderate use by sheep will curtail further growth, and hence the forage production of this important shrub. The density of white-tailed deer in Texas was highest in a seven-pasture, high-intensity, low-frequency grazing system when compared to either continuous or four-pasture, deferred-rotation systems.

Each of the pastures was grazed by a mixed herd of cattle, sheep, and goats. The seven-pasture system was grazed for 3 weeks, then rested for 18 weeks. Deer responded with a clear preference for the short-duration system, showing stronger preferences in proportion to the frequency of the rest periods. Further, the seven-pasture system also supported the highest stocking rate of livestock and produced high rates of hunter success and hunting revenues.

After careful study of the effects of grazing systems on habitat requirements of deer, as well as quail and turkey, Bryant et al. (1982) recommended a Merrill deferredrotation system in Texas for the optimum production of both livestock and wildlife. In contrast, they also suggested that continuous yearlong grazing was rarely of value to most wildlife.

Pastures in southeastern pinelands often degrade under continuous grazing. When these are managed with short periods of intensive grazing followed by long rests, vegetation important to deer and gamebirds increased while saw-palmetto (*Serenoa repens*) and other troublesome plants decreased.

These studies indicate that both livestock and big game can share rangelands profitably when an appropriate grazing regime is employed. Moreover, the effective stocking rate, measured by AUs, of livestock plus wildlife can be greater than with wildlife or livestock alone.

Some game birds also may respond favourably to grazing systems. Bobwhite densities were highest on a high intensity-low frequency system, followed by continuous grazing, then a four-pasture deferred-rotation system. The response seemed related to the increased amounts of forbs and bare soil, together with fewer grasses, produced by the "high-low" system.

These conditions favoured the movements and feeding activities of the quail. Kiel (1976) also suggested that thick stands of grasses produce few seeds suitable as quail food, impede the birds' movements, and reduce the production of winter forbs and insects. The needs of other game birds may be tied similarly to grazing systems. Merrill (1975) found that a four-pasture deferred-rotation system produced better nesting habitat for turkeys than did continuous grazing.

A rotation system also provided the flexibility needed to assure nesting and brood cover for waterfowl on western rangelands. When pastures in the system were rested or grazed only during the first part of the year, brood production increased the following spring. Conversely, late-season grazing reduced the amount of residual cover, and brood production the following spring decreased. On the average, the rotation system produced about four times as many broods as did season-long grazing.

Baker (1978) compared rates of nest predation between two grazing systems and continuous grazing using simulated turkey nests. Both grazing systems had higher rates of nest survival than continuous grazing. Nest survival was greater in pastures deferred for 41 days than in those deferred for 10 days.

At first glance, grazing systems might seem to reduce the success of ground-nesting birds, presumably because the temporarily concentrated livestock might trample more nests. However, trampling losses were similar between continuous grazing and a short-duration system tested with simulated ground nests.

Cattle seem to move more in the larger pastures required by continuous grazing than in the smaller cells of grazing systems, thereby offering at least as much opportunity for trampling nests as in a short-duration grazing system. Further, each pasture under continuous grazing is stocked all of the time, whereas those in the short-duration system were grazed only 6 percent of the time.

Hence, during a 40-day period-approximately the combined laying and incubation period for turkey, quail, and similar birds-only 87 percent of the total pasturage was grazed in the short-duration system, whereas all of the area remained utilized under continuous grazing. The rates of nest losses per week of grazing also were alike statistically in this experiment.

In sum, Koerth et al. suggested that short-duration grazing systems should not increase trampling losses of ground nests. As might be expected, each grazing system varies somewhat in its influence on wildlife. Each may increase or decrease the abundance and quality of food and cover for wildlife, or simply affect the social interactions between wildlife and livestock.

Elk preferred pastures managed with a deferred-rotational system in Oregon largely because this plan, rather than season-long grazing, reduced the disturbance of cattle even though there was no direct competition for forage. Holechek et al. summarized their review of grazing and wildlife relationships with the caution that the balance between defoliation and recovery must be assessed for any grazing system.

Excessive defoliation, even for relatively short periods of time, may not benefit either wildlife or livestock. Some vegetation may not recover from a period of heavy grazing with an equal period of rest. In fact, assessments of grazing pressure should emphasize the amount of residual vegetation, not the amount of forage removed by grazing animals.

Because plant production on western ranges varies with precipitation, the amount of forage utilized each year is not as important as the amount of vegetation left at the end of the grazing period. In droughts, even moderate grazing of the current year's production may leave too little residual vegetation to maintain the health of the range. Fortunately, it is far easier to measure the amount of residual vegetation than to measure the amount removed. By doing so, managers have a common point of reference for determining grazing pressure, and hence the welfare of the range ecosystem.

RANGE FIRES AND WILDLIFE

Wildfires exerted dynamic perturbations on vegetation and the organisms associated with plant communities long before mankind tamed fire for domestic use. Fires were surprisingly frequent in prehistory. Kilgore and Taylor reported the incidence of fires in the Sierra Nevada based on scarred tree rings of giant sequoias (*Sequoia sempervirens*) and ponderosa pine (*Pinus ponderosa*).

Giant sequoias were subject to fires every 10 to 20 years before 1875, with individual trees experiencing fires at intervals of 3 to 35 years. Fires coursed through ponderosa pine communities with even more frequency, averaging a fire every 6 to 9 years. Such frequencies are conservative estimates as they only include those fires severe enough to damage the cambium layer; lesser fires passed unrecorded over the centuries.

Fires in grasslands and other herbaceous communities cannot be estimated by the same technique, but one can safely assume that fire was a regular phenomenon in these types. Wright and Bailey (1982), after considering a variety of historical data, believed that prairie fires occurred at frequencies of 5 to 10 years. Where the topography of grasslands is more dissected, fires probably were limited to 10- to 30-year intervals.

As we have seen, grasslands indeed may owe their very existence to recurring fires. Other communities contain biological components dependent on fire (i.e., fire-adapted species) in ways that fulfill critical requirements in their life histories. Ecological history experienced dramatic changes when human beings began using fire: Uncontrolled, man-caused fires were more common.

In Alaska, for example, the intrusion of miners, trappers, and others who deeply penetrated a virgin land initiated more fires than would have occurred naturally, and about 80 percent of the evergreen forests there have burned since the turn of the last century.

Conversely, efforts were at least partially successful in suppressing wildfires. Advancing settlement brought with it organized efforts to prevent fires and to put out those that did occur. Roadways acted as fire breaks, as did lanes cleared expressly for that purpose. Fire protection is known to everyone familiar with "Smokey the Bear," smoke jumpers, and forest rangers. Finally, Chapman and Stoddard are credited, respectively, with initially determining the ecological role of fire in the management of southern pine forests and bobwhites.

Their work was a pioneering assessment of fire ecology (sometimes accompanied by cries of heresy), a forerunner of today's acceptance of practical fire management in many vegetational types. Now, prescribed burning has become an ecological tool for forest, range, and wildlife management.

We should emphasize that fires ordinarily do not kill significant numbers of wildlife. Most animals escape the ravages of fires and only occasionally are carcasses found afterwards; some of these may be of animals already dead or dying before the fire. Howard et al. (1959) concluded that there was little chance of wild vertebrates becoming entrapped in fires; virtually all mammals and birds they observed simply avoided a fire set in an annual grass-brush community in California.

Their experiments determined that rodents in simulated burrows 5-18 cm deep died only when temperatures there exceeded 59°C (surface temperatures reached 149°C), with these losses occurring primarily beneath fallen logs. Interestingly, some forms of wildlife may themselves deter fires. For example, California quail, rodents, and cottontails (*Sylvilagus floridanus*) maintain trails or remove enough herbaceous vegetation from the bases of brush clumps so that the cleared areas become effective fire breaks.

However, fires occurring during the nesting season may destroy nests, eggs, or fledglings, and prescribed burning clearly should be scheduled to avoid that possibility. The major result of fire remains its impact on habitat conditions. Left alone, wildfires may accrue either positive or negative outcomes. Fires create dramatic changes in the environment, benefiting some species of wildlife at the expense of others. In northern forests, this relationship is clear between the responses of moose (*Alces alces*) and caribou, respectively.

In grasslands, fire also influences wildlife populations. Among game birds, bobwhite show the most remarkable responses to fire management. The oft-cited standard that quail could not achieve greater densities than 2.5 birds per ha remained widely accepted until prescribed burning was practiced on lands otherwise managed for timber and grazing.

Stoddard established the role of fire in the management of bobwhites, and densities of 5 birds per ha eventually were attained with effective use of this tool. Winter burns on rangelands for brush control in southern Texas also initiated short-term increases in several measures of bobwhite abundance.

These were pronounced in the first year after the burning, but diminished as the vegetation recovered and the amount of bare ground decreased. Feeding, roosting, and travel were enhanced for quail on the newly burned ranges. Reid (1953) also recorded that 1- and 2-year-old burns produced greater amounts of quail food than older burns.

Prairie chickens also respond to fire management. Booming grounds (leks) may be abandoned when residual vegetation from the previous year is so dense or tall that the birds' courtship activities are inhibited; grasses and forbs on booming grounds should be maintained at heights of less than 15 cm.

Prairie chickens in Illinois preferred recently burned areas for their booming grounds and new sites were selected by the birds in response to late winter burnings; inactive booming grounds also were reoccupied after they were burned. Cannon and Knopf (1979) suggested that burning may encourage prairie chickens to move into new habitats or to recolonize their historic ranges.

Stimuli associated with newly burned sites may cause the birds to move into burned areas, offering an alternative to transplanting as a means of reestablishing prairie chickens within their former range. The additional habitat also may permit more males to take part in breeding activities.

Prescribed burning has proven equally valuable for management of prairie chicken nesting habitat. In Illinois, Westemeier (1972) found nest densities of 3.8 ha per nest versus 2.4 ha per nest between unburned and burned grasslands; these data were recorded 2-4 years after burning.

Because much of the native Illinois prairie has been replaced with cultivated, cool-season grasses, prescribed burns of these in August give better nesting results, whereas on warm-season prairie grasses, burning in March is best. Thus, prescribed burning must be tailored by season to account for differences between altered or natural habitats.

Similarly, Chamrad and Dodd (1972) found that the beneficial effects of prescribed burning on habitat managed for Attwater's prairie chickens varied with grazing. Fire enhanced the habitat only on ungrazed grasslands, presumably because either fire or grazing separately can maintain those physiognomic features of the vegetation attractive to the birds.

Accidental fires created new strutting grounds for sage grouse,

Table 5.9: Bobwhite Abundance Two Years After a Rangeland Bum (Winter) in Southern Texas.

Bobwhite Census Method	*Two-Year Index of Bobwhite Abundance Following Burning*				
	Area	*Spring*	*Fall*	*Spring*	*Fall*
Along transects	Burned	9.0	15.0	10.8	7.8
	Control	3.0	8.0	4.5	9.0
Trapping	Burned	0.5	3.3	1.3	0.3
	Control	0	0	0	0
Flushes with dog	Burned	7.0	5.0	0.8	0.1
	Control	4.0	4.0	0.2	1.8
Vocalizations	Burned	849	95	378	56
	Control	215	105	260	136

leading to the suggestion that prescribed burns of 0.4-4.0 ha might be useful in otherwise homogeneous sagebrush communities. However, because some brush cover also is critical (15-20 percent cover seems optimal), a burning program should be on a long rotation (up to 20 years).

On the birds' spring and summer ranges, staggered burning dates will create a mosaic of habitat with a full array of food and cover requirements. Forbs are particularly important as food for sage grouse broods, and these plants respond well to burning. Conversely, prescribed burning is not recommended on winter ranges as the birds then rely on mature sagebrush for their food and cover needs.

The image of a mourning dove (*Zenaida macroura*) nest brings to mind a flimsy platform of twigs rather insecurely placed in a tree. Thus, if fire were used to remove the woody vegetation, the apparent conclusion would seem that doves might fare poorly whenever rangelands were burned.

Evidence to the contrary suggested the adaptability of mourning doves nesting on burned-over rangelands; the birds instead nested on the ground even when some trees still were available. Nesting densities were greatest in the current year's burn and decreased each year thereafter, suggesting that the amount of ground cover was an important habitat characteristic.

A comparison of nest success between ground nests and those in trees showed nest success at 21 percent and 15 percent, respectively.

Wind damage caused the diminished success of tree nests. Predation rates were similar, and production from the ground nests largely offset any losses resulting from removal of the trees.

FENCING

Pronghorns, although often called "antelope," are actually a species indigenous to North America not closely related to the true antelopes (Bovidae) of the Old World. In his explorations of the American southwest, Francisco Vasquez de Coronado was likely the first Western man recording encounters with pronghorns.

Some three centuries later, the developing livestock industry entered the pronghorn's realm, and among the inevitable changes that ensued was the fencing of rangelands. Fencing controls livestock movement without need of herders, prevents intermixing of separately owned stock, and may promote the proper usage of forage when herds are manipulated between pastures.

Usually, barbed-wire fences posed little threat to pronghorns; the strands were widely spaced and often loose enough for safe passage of pronghorns through or under the fence, yet they still confined cattle. With sheep, however, woven-net fences were required and pronghorns no longer could move through these barriers for forage or winter cover. Although physi

cally able to do so, pronghorns by nature do not jump over confining obstacles, so that net fences became serious barriers for animals adapted to a free-roaming existence. Large numbers have died, particularly in severe weather when entire herds were cornered by sheep-proof fences.

In 1882, during the first winter after a 97-km drift fence was completed in the Texas Panhandle, a blizzard forced large numbers of pronghorns into a pocket along the fence where, unable to proceed further, some 1500 were killed by settlers.

In another instance, drought reduced a population by 40 percent, largely because net fences confined pronghorn herds to forage-depleted ranges shared with livestock where they were forced to consume low-quality or toxic vegetation. Other effects of fencing on pronghorns, including injury and starvation, are mentioned by Gross et al. (1983).

Spillett et al. (1967) studied 22 types of fencing arrangements that might confine sheep yet not hinder pronghorn movements. They recommended a net fence of 81-cm maximum height or a 66-cm net fence topped by a 10-cm gap and a single strand of barbed wire.

As these are shorter than the fences normally used by sheep ranchers, the considerable savings for posts and wire costs favour adoption of fencing that simultaneously meets livestock and wildlife needs. Mapston et al. (1970) designed a horizontal pass that relied on the broad-jumping abilities of pronghorns.

Livestock were confined by grillwork, similar to a cattle guard, overlying a shallow pit, whereas pronghorns easily jumped across the same barrier. A grill about 2 m^2 is sufficient. The grillwork should be elevated about 25 cm and installed with earthen ramps on each side.

Topography is important in locating pronghorn passes. Sites should be selected where livestock exposure is minimal and pronghorn exposure is highest, although no site or structure will be completely effective for confining all types or classes of livestock.

Fence corners and hilltops are good locations for pronghorn passes, whereas sites near salt licks, water sources, livestock trails, and roadways should be avoided.

Elsewhere, other fencing situations sometimes cause other conflicts between livestock and wildlife interests. When fencing on cattle ranches in Zambia was destroyed by roaming wildebeest (*Connochaetes taurinus*) and zebra (*Equus burchelli*), game officials were forced to shoot numbers of the offending animals. Between 1927 and 1958, nearly 32,000 elephants (*Loxodontaafricana*) were shot in Uganda to protect agricultural operat-ions, whereas only 8170 were killed by licensed hunters during the same period.

In Botswana, large numbers of wild animals are killed by fences, and the damage they cause is reported to exceed $100,000 annually, yet even more fencing was planned to isolate cattle from the potential reservoir of foot-and-mouth disease. Wholesale removal of elephants, giraffes (*Giraffa camelopardalis*), and other large browsing species to protect fencing subsequently increased the amounts of shrubby vegetation on African rangelands, so that the brush now must be controlled to encourage herbaceous forage for livestock.

In Kenya, barbed-wire fences on rangeland surrounding Nairobi Royal National Park block the traditional lines of movement for game crossing the sanctuary's boundaries, threatening the park's future value. Fences around small wetlands eliminate the trampling and foraging of cattle on shoreline vegetation important as food sources or nesting cover for waterfowl.

Kirsch (1969) found reductions in breeding pairs, nest densities, and nest success for waterfowl nesting on grazed pastures and concluded that shoreline grazing was harmful to waterfowl production. Grazing damage, including trampling, is somewhat selective by species and community; aquatic communities may not be affected, whereas some shoreline food plants such as smartweed (*Polygonum spp.*) may fail to recover from trampling even after cattle are removed. In all, the effects of grazing on wetlands are a function of site, animal pressure, plant zonation, and composition, with these factors varying locally and regionally.

However, the benefits of fencing may be short-lived if cattail (*Typha spp.*) later dominates littoral zones in dense, monotypic communities; food plants are crowded out and duck nests in these areas seem especially vulnerable to skunks (*Mephitis mephitis*) and other predators attracted to the dense cover.

Management potentials nonetheless exist for these situations. Mundinger (1976) described a rotational grazing system that increased brood production by 50 percent on grazed wetlands. Fences permanently protecting parts of wetlands should leave the deeper sites accessible to livestock so that water is available even during dry periods, whereas fencing the remaining shoreline maintains undisturbed zones that are potentially available for waterfowl and other wildlife.

High-speed thoroughfares necessarily are bordered by fences that keep livestock off roadways. Wildlife, particularly deer, pose the same problem for traffic safety but require fences that are higher and remain flush with the ground's surface.

Deer often seek the forage available on roadsides or medians, and as they sometimes successfully penetrate even "deer-proof" fences, they then are entrapped on the roadway by the same fence designed to prohibit their access. A recent survey indicated that deer-vehicle accidents represent an average cost of $648 per incident, including property damage, injury, and loss of life, thus giving highway engineers and wildlife managers an economic basis for judging the cost-effectiveness of safety devices and/or reducing deer herds.

Reed et al. (1974) found that one-way gates along a high (2.4 m) fence bordering an interstate highway in Colorado effectively allowed mule deer to leave the roadway. Fenced roadways that cross the migratory paths of large mammals pose still another problem. Mule deer migrations between summer and winter ranges are interrupted by deer-proof fences unless other means allow their safe passage across busy highways.

A special underpass located on a well-established migration route permitted about 61 percent of the local deer population to migrate safely beneath an interstate highway, but a somewhat larger and more open underpass likely would have even better effectiveness.

BURROS AND RANGELANDS

Spanish explorers of the sixteenth century introduced domestic burros (*Equus asinus*) into North America. Later, burros became the mainstay of prospectors and others requiring dependable, sturdy pack animals for the rugged terrain of the American West. Burros ere the domestic descendants of the African wild ass, a species of three races endemic to the arid zones between Algeria and Somalia.

Given this heritage, burros adjusted readily to range environments in the western United States when they escaped or were turned loose at the end of the mining era. Burros eventually established large feral populations in California, Nevada, and Arizona. The versatility of burros to cope successfully in various ecological settings is reflected in their diets.

In one area, burros consumed 4 percent grasses, 30 percent forbs, and 61 percent browse, whereas in another, the composition—almost reversed-was 61 percent grasses, 11 percent forbs, and 28 percent browse. Moreover, burros remain in good health, despite seasonal deficiencies in the quality of their forage, without suffering the nutritional consequences affecting native ruminants.

Burros, with their cecel digestive systems, enjoy an ecological advantage over ruminants in sparsely vegetated habitats . Bighorn sheep (*Ovis canadensis*), cattle, and other ruminants require foods whose particles are small enough to pass through the recticulo-omasal orifice. As cellulose and other fibers increase in the diet's content, the time required to reduce these to the appropriate size in the rumen is lengthened, depriving the ruminant animal of adequate nutritional benefits.

Conversely, burros are not similarly limited and can utilize a diet high in fiber. They and other equines can ingest more forage with a more rapid rate of passage (compared to ruminants) at the expense of reduced digestion of cellulose. Thus, when supplies of low-fiber foods-usually preferred forage-are exhausted, burros continue feeding on a diet of high-fiber foods, whereas ruminants cannot.

In short, a larger percentage of the total vegetational biomass (both high and low fiber species) is available to burros than to ruminants. Burro populations largely are free of natural regulation, and the only effective control fell to ranchers armed with rifles. In the ranchers' view, burros competed with livestock for forage, and shooting presented a direct measure for reducing their numbers.

Without control, burro populations can increase 20-25 percent within 18 months. In Death Valley, aerial censuses found that burro populations jumped from 1426 animals in 1978 to 2500 in 1981, indicating that even more rapid rates of expansion are possible.

Collectively, these observations give clear indication that burros experience few of the ecological restraints typical of most native or domestic animals in arid environments.

The damaging impacts of burros on public land in the United States have been assessed in detail. Overgrazing and trampling by burros altered both composition and densities of vegetation and small rodent communities, compared with a burro-free site in an otherwise similar setting.

Without burros, 28 species of vascular plants occupied 80 percent of the area; with burros, 19 species of plants covered only 20 percent of the plot. Species diversity of small rodents also was higher in the absence of burros, and the density of these mammals was about four times greater than where burros occurred.

As discussed further in Chapter 18, burros also have displaced bighorn sheep and, without removal of the burros, few bighorns will ever again occupy Death Valley National Monument and other public lands in the western United States.

Palo verde (*Cercidium* spp.) is a staple in the diets of burros; these trees are browsed throughout the year but especially in late summer and fall when grasses and other vegetation are less available. Palo verde provides a rich source of phosphorus and carotene at that time. The feeding behaviour of burros is particularly destructive to palo verde and other woody plants.

Burros break off large branches but consume just a small part, leaving the remainder untouched. Only the large end of the branch is chewed, along with some of the bark. In contrast, bighorn sheep forage at the tips of palo verde branches, consuming only the new growth produced annually.

Observations of burros feeding on palo verde revealed that the animals browse for about 30 minutes at a time, removing an average of 23 limbs per feeding period. Because of the movements and activities of burros, their influences on range vegetation vary largely in proportion to habitat preferences dictated by terrain and the proximity of water. Burros typically concentrate in dry washes where their heavy utilization of forage is pronounced; a comparison of washes with high and low utilization showed vegetational differences of 2.8 percent and 8.6 percent in canopy cover and density ratings of 252 and 721, respectively. These effects varied with distance from water, with the heaviest browse utilization occurring near permanent water and the lightest utilization at distances of more than 2.5 km from water. Riparian habitats, in particular, receive heavy browsing pressure during the summer months.

GAME RANCHING

Unfortunately, the term "game ranching" may have two very different meanings. First, game ranching sometimes refers to those pay-for-hunting enterprises where big game (usually exotic species) is harvested for sport. Large sums are involved, with trophy animals commanding fees exceeding $1000 per head.

Further mention of exotics and the economics of this form of game ranching is made in other chapters of this book. The second meaning of game ranching concerns the husbandry of native animals in *situ* for the production of meat and other products. In this case, game ranching is a variation of range management that otherwise concerns the husbandry of domestic livestock on rangelands.

The basic principle of game ranching is that native species are far better adapted to local conditions than are domestic livestock. In short, attempts to raise cattle, sheep, or goats on many rangelands would be better forgone in favour of direct management of the same ranges for native species.

The model best illustrating game ranching is the herding of reindeer (*Rangifer tarandus*) in northern Scandinavia by Lapps. Similar reliance on cattle in such a climatic and ecological realm would be uniformly disastrous for animals and people alike. Regrettably, however, the time-proven lesson of the Lapps has not been fully learned by other peoples; and ill-suited livestock are still "forced" into environments where they may be no more than marginally successful.

The concept of game ranching is developing in Africa but has not yet been widely adopted in the United States. Broader adoption of game ranching probably rests upon three criteria: (1) a pool of native species possessing large body sizes, behaviour, and other features associated with livestock production, (2) national demand and need for protein in human diets, and (3) the availability of rangelands for the conversion of forage into meat and other animal products.

Had North American grasslands remained open range, one could speculate that bison, and not beef, might have become the staple meat in the United States. Nonetheless, enterprising ranchers in the United States might develop domestic strains from their herds of exotic big game. Stocks of these, when returned to their native rangelands overseas, may well initiate profitable ranching operations and ready sources of red meat. Nilgai antelope (*Boselaphus tragocamelus*) are well established on rangelands in southern

Texas and, if selectively bred for their latent domestic values, this stock might become the nucleus of a ranching industry in parts of Asia. Eland (*Tragelaphus oryx*), the largest species in the antelope family, already is at least semidomesticated and seems likely to offer people of several African nations a new source of protein.

Cattle and the large pool of antelopes in Africa are related taxonomically in the family Bovidae, but comparisons between cattle and antelopes often show striking differences in their respective efficiencies and tolerances under African range conditions.

The history of cattle in Africa dates to well before the Christian era, but even this long period of adjustment has not adapted them fully to the stresses of heat, disease, and drought experienced in Africa. Zebu cattle (*Bos indicus*) have been the traditional breed of the Masai, but even with their tolerances for African conditions, calf crops seldom exceed 50 percent and annual mortality is about 15 percent.

By comparison, the most advanced management in Africa yields calf crops of 80 percent and losses of about 5 percent. Furthermore, zebu characteristically have slow growth rates and delayed maturity (i.e., mature cows weigh 272 kg and calve at intervals of 18-24 months). Water shortages during the African dry season interact strongly with the availability of forage for cattle.

During the dry season, the ranges nearest permanent water are severely overgrazed, and the cattle must be driven farther away for forage. At first, a full day's trip each way (covering some 16 km) is required and the cattle have water only every other day on a rotation between feeding and watering; as the forage becomes less available, an even longer cycle without water occurs.

Cattle experience considerable stress during the normal dry season, but in prolonged droughts, only minimal forage is obtained with ever-increasing walking distances, and cattle die in massive numbers. Three-quarters of 450,000 head likely died in a single district of Kenya in 1961. Even when new waterholes are constructed, the buildup of cattle may quickly destroy the range.

In Senegal, Riney (1967) reported the deterioration of previously ungrazed grasslands into desert four years after water was developed for cattle. In contrast, antelopes are particularly water-efficient, having adapted various ways of conserving the water they consume. They excrete smaller amounts of body wastes per unit of body weight and even these have less water content than those of cattle.

Sweating also is reduced compared with cattle, and species such as the eland, oryx (*Onyx gazella*), and Grant's gazelle (*Gazella granti*) raise their body temperatures during the day so that sweating is not initiated until an upper limit is reached. For example, the temperature of a 500-kg eland can rise from 39°C to 42°C during the daytime, thus conserving 5 liters of water.

The food habits of the native antelopes also favour efficient water intake; by feeding at night, when the relative humidity is at its highest, the animals' forage contains larger amounts of moisture than during the daytime. Some browse plants contain more than 50 percent water at night, even during droughts. An eland eating the leaves of *Acacia* can derive 5.3 liters of water per 100 kg of metabolic body weight, an amount corresponding to its needs for maintaining a constant body weight.

At the extreme, the large-bodied addax (*Addax nasomaculatus*) virtually never drink, but instead obtain all their moisture from the forage they consume; this species is adapted admirably for arid rangelands where cattle cannot exist. Cattle were excluded from nearly 40 percent of Africa by tsetse flies (*Glossina spp.*) and the lethal trypanosome parasites they carry.

This subject is mentioned later, but suffice it to note here that native wildlife are not susceptible to nagana (or n'gana), the animal form of the disease known in humans as sleeping sickness. Conversely, only with expensive methods can cattle remain free of nagana on many African rangelands.

Other diseases affecting cattle in Africa include those borne by ticks (e.g., East Coast fever, anaplasmosis, and redwater) that require weekly dipping or spraying to keep livestock disease-free; a large variety of still other diseases (e.g., anthrax, rinderpest, and contagious bovine pleuropneumonia) also require constant vigilance.

Perhaps the strongest argument for game ranching lies in the natural efficiency of native species to utilize diverse range forage. In short, they convert range vegetation into meat more efficiently than cattle. The foods and feeding habits of native animals are either diverse or adapted to ways that maximize utilization of the available forage.

Many species also produce higher weights of usable meat compared with cattle. Eland, for example, produce more than 75 kg of lean meat per 100 kg of carcass, whereas cattle yield only 55 kg, or 73 percent as much.

Maximum production of meat per area is achieved when large animals of several species share a common rangeland without competition or degradation of the vegetation. Several species of African big game show remarkable adaptations in this regard.

Some are grazers, whereas others forage on browse, so that nearly all forms of vegetation are consumed. Conversely, cattle thrive on a narrower selection of grasses and generally ingest these only when they are succulent or properly cured.

Furthermore, even when the same plant is utilized by two or more different species of native animals, either spatial (e.g., having stems high or low above the ground) or temporal (e.g., having different growth stages) separations occur. Giraffes obviously are able to forage well above the level of other animals, so that the browse on a single tree is used concurrently without interspecific competition. Ecological partitioning also is shown by four grazing species eating the same kind of grass.

Zebra select the upper stems of the grass, taking lignified material that antelopes are unable to digest readily. *Topi* (*Damaliscus lunatus*) then eat the lower stems, and wildebeest graze the leaves. With these materials removed, the grass produces new shoots from its base that are selected by Thomson's gazelles (*Gazella thomsoni*).

Thus, a naturally balanced system has evolved for the native species—both plants and animals-that cannot be matched by the much narrower feeding niche of cattle and other domestic livestock. In sum, these features strongly indicate that animal husbandry in Africa is better practiced by game ranching than by similar attempts with cattle, sheep, or goats.

Capital investment is minimal and many native species offer rapid financial returns because a larger percentage of their populations can be removed annually. Relatively rapid growth rates and the high stocking densities possible with native species clearly suggest the benefits of game ranching in Africa.

The underlying principle, however, may well be applied elsewhere, especially where transportation and marketing facilities already may be established. From the standpoint of wildlife management, game ranching need not exclude fee-hunting. Trophy animals might still be harvested under field conditions and in natural settings.

Further, the financial rewards from a well-managed game ranch should assure not only perpetuation of the stock but also maintenance of wildlife habitat.

An African Saga

Tsetse flies throughout history have shared much of Africa's native rangelands with vast herds of big game. Several species of flies are involved so that, collectively, they infest a broad continental belt south of the Sahara. Their stinging bites are annoying but, because they also are vectors of trypanosome parasites, tsetse flies are in fact deadly insects.

Some of the parasites kill people and nearly all are lethal to livestock. However, a natural immunity largely protects native wildlife from what is known as sleeping sickness in humans and nagana in animals. The net effect was that the flies and parasites they carry effectively prevented occupation of the African rangelands by domestic livestock-and without their herds, few pastoral peoples settled the lands.

Tsetse flies thus represented a biological barrier to human encroachment, leaving much of the African landscape essentially as a pristine

Table 5.10: Selected Comparisons of Growth Rates and Standing Crop Weights Between African Antelopes and Livestock

	Weight in kg		
Species/Herd	*Gain/Day*	*Adult Males*	*Approx. Standing Crop-kg/km²*
Eland (*Tragelaphus oryx*)	0.33	726	
Wildebeest (*Connochaetes taurinus*)	0.24	208	
Kongoni (*Alcelaphus buselaphus*)	0.23	150	
Topi0.20 (*Damaliscus lunatus*)	132		
Domestic cattle	0.14	454	
Domestic sheep	0.05	45	
Mixed herds of wild ungulates			12-17 thousand
Cattle only			3-5 thousand
Cattle, sheep, and goats			2-3 thousand
Sheep and goats			0.4-2 thousand

wildlife preserve. Parts of this setting yielded to the handiwork of modern man. Pressures to establish cattle on the rich grazing lands led to mass killings of wildlife so that the sources of trypanosome infections might be eliminated.

Entire herds of zebra, bushbuck (*Tragelaphus scriptus*), warthog (*Phacochoerus aethiopicus*), and other large animals—reservoirs for the parasites-were slaughtered. Even a partial recounting of the kill is staggering.

In Zululand during 1929-30, some 26,000 head were shot solely to maintain a disease-free buffer zone around a game reseve; in Tanzania, 8000 rhinos (*Diceros bicornis*), gazelles, giraffes, and lions (*Panthera leo*) were killed in one experimental unit; and in Uganda, more than 161,000 animals fell to rifles in the name of tsetse-fly control.

Next, the insecticide era began. Vast areas of the African range were sprayed to control tsetse flies. More recently, work on vaccines suggests that cattle, and possibly humans, might be immunized temporarily against the parasites, and efforts toward an effective biological control of the flies may be promising.

Thus, a disease of continental proportions may soon be eliminated, and with it the sufferings of a large human population. Few clear-thinking persons would argue against the control of a dreaded disease, but the ecological aftermath may not be as bright for African wildlife.

The heavily shot game populations have, or will, recover as other methods are employed to fight nagana, but the underlying conflict remains no less prominent than before: settlement and land use versus wildlife habitat. Dynamic changes seem sure to follow as extensive grazing lands are opened to cattle and their herders.

The problems are ecologically complex, and include the cultural values of the indigenous human population. Briefly outlined, these are as follows:

1. More cattle will be stocked, eventually leading to overgrazing. Sophisticated grazing systems are not yet widely adopted in Africa and the new ranges will surely deteriorate under continuous grazing pressure as others have in the past. The heaviest grazing pressure centers on the same waterholes where wildlife drink. Unfortunately, cattle are not efficient users of either grass or water in comparison to native wildlife, and overexploitation of these resources is almost certain, especially in periods of drought.
2. Cattle are a measure of status and wealth for many native

peoples, and grazing schemes that might otherwise sustain their forage may be countermanded by local cultures. Cattle, although providing products for human consumption, also are living bank accounts that increase with every calf.

Additionally, cattle have become part of the social life of many native people. In Zambia, for example, cattle are paid to a bride's father by the future son-in-law, slaughtered to commemorate a girl's eligibility for marriage or to mourn deaths, and given as recompense for hostile acts so that revenge is avoided. In such cultures, a premium is placed on the largest possible herds.

3. Native wildlife may be viewed as competitors with cattle for forage and water, and human tolerance for sharing the range with wildlife may diminish. For example, the Masai in Kenya attach fundamental and spiritual significance to their cattle, and they perhaps will abandon their traditional laissez-faire attitude toward native animals (grazers and predators) as disease-free rangelands are opened. Furthermore, direct measures to control wildlife often are carried out unwisely. When 1000 warthogs were shot in a single operation in Senegal, the meat was left to rot because the natives were Muslim, and no scientific use was made of the animals for research.

Index

E

F

G

H

I

S

T